Battered But Not Beaten...
Preventing Wife Battering in Canada

by Linda MacLeod

June 1987

Canadian Advisory Council on the Status of Women

Prepared for the
Canadian Advisory Council on the Status of Women
Box 1541, Station B, Ottawa, Ontario K1P 5R5

This document expresses the views of the author and does not
necessarily represent the official policy of the CACSW.

Available free of charge from the
Canadian Advisory Council on the Status of Women

Cette publication existe aussi en français.

Table of Contents

Acknowledgements i

Introduction: After the Laughter 1

Embracing the Complexities of Wife Battering 9

Shattered Hopes: The Meaning of Wife Battering
   for Victims and Survivors 11
What Do We Know About the Battered Women and the Batterers
   in Canada? 19
The Social Costs of Wife Battering 31
Through Women's Eyes: Our Growing Understanding of Wife Battering . . 37

A Realistic Model of Prevention:
Building a Network of Support 47

Sheltering 49
Programs for Children 69
Criminal Justice Initiatives: The Law as a Symbol of Change 78
Programs for Batterers 93
Community Support 102

Conclusion: Prevention Through Caring,
Continuity, and Support 111

Appendices 121

Notes 167

Bibliography 175

Acknowledgements

Although technically written by one person, this book is a synthesis of the thoughts, wisdom, and support of many people. First and foremost, women working in transition houses across the country gave hours of their scarce and valuable time to complete the written questionnaire. As well, some agreed to speak to me in person to clarify points and exchange ideas. Workers at all the provincial/territorial associations of transition houses were amazingly enthusiastic, responsive, and helpful. Special thanks to Connie Chapman in British Columbia; Jamie McKay, Ardis Beaudry, and Jackie Gaboury in Alberta; Sandra Flett, Sharon Swann, and especially Rhonda Johnson in Saskatchewan; Joey Brazeau in Manitoba; Trudy Don in Ontario; Norma Prophet in Nova Scotia; Cheryl Hebert in Newfoundland; and Joanne Ings in Prince Edward Island. Although I was not able to travel to New Brunswick or the Northwest Territories, Blanche Nowlan and Libby Thornton in New Brunswick and several members of the staff at the shelter in Yellowknife fielded my many questions and helped reassure me that New Brunswick and the Territories would be represented in the study. In Quebec, the staff of the Regroupement provincial des maisons d'hébergement et de transition pour femmes victimes de violence helped me to hire Jocelyne LeBlanc, my invaluable assistant in this study. Both Jocelyne and I extend our sincere thanks to all the staff members at the Regroupement, but particularly to Danièle Frechette and to Diane Prudhomme.

Four of the women mentioned above were also central in the creation of the mail-out questionnaire. I would like to again thank Trudy Don, Sharon Swann, Rhonda Johnson, and Connie Chapman for their help throughout the project.

Diane Wood of Status of Women Canada was particularly helpful in keeping me up-to-date on federal and provincial initiatives. Staff Sergeant Bob Holmes, at the national headquarters of the Royal Canadian Mounted Police, kept me abreast of the police perspective and the many difficulties and tortured decisions police face in dealing with wife battering. Susan Thomas-Gilman of the National Clearinghouse on Family Violence unselfishly made her knowledge, resources, and wisdom available to me on a moment's notice.

This book is also the product of the information and time so generously provided by Crown attorneys, provincial /territorial/ federal government employees, counsellors of men who batter, academics, and especially police officers.

There are also a few key people who provided inspiration and thus deserve special mention. Jocelyne LeBlanc acted as my French alter-ego in Quebec, conducting all personal interviews in that province as well as all follow-up calls with francophone transition-house workers. Her expertise and enthusiasm were essential components in ensuring the accuracy and completeness of this project. Maude Barlow, one of the most progressive thinkers concerning violence against women known to the author, provided support and inspiration. Lorraine Greaves, of the National Action Committee on the Status of Women, helped stretch my thinking. Thanks are also owed to the staff of the Canadian Advisory Council on the Status of Women who worked long and hard on the preparation and production of this study, and especially to Jim Young, English editor, whose thorough editing helped to clarify my thoughts on many of the complex issues examined in this book. Nicole Morgan, my eternal and brilliant muse, presented me with the creative spark which ultimately generated the book. And of course Neil, Lauren, and my mother, as always, reminded me that families can still be havens of encouragement, support, and hope.

Finally, and most importantly, this book is the result of the perceptiveness and sincerity of the battered women I spoke to or heard from through their letters. To these women, I offer my genuine thanks and hopes for a happier, non-violent future. You have given me the reason to write this report. You have changed and expanded my thinking immeasurably. I hope you can hear your wishes and wisdom in my words.

To all the above contributors, I thank you repeatedly for your time and generosity in sharing so many of the insights and details for this book.

L.M.

As part of the mandate of the Canadian Advisory Council on the Status of Women to inform and advise the federal government on issues of concern to women, the Council is proud to present this new book, entitled *Battered But Not Beaten: Preventing Wife Battering in Canada*.

The issue of wife battering was first raised by Council members in the late 1970s and led to the first national study of this problem. Following the 1980 publication of *Wife Battering in Canada: The Vicious Circle* by Linda MacLeod, the Council passed a number of recommendations dealing with this crime.

Council members were equally pleased when Linda agreed to review and assess the progress that has been made in the past seven years. We are confident that *Battered But Not Beaten* will be invaluable to the public, parliamentarians, those involved in helping battered women and their families, and battered women themselves, as we strive for a future free from family violence.

Sylvia Gold
CACSW President

Introduction:

After the Laughter

Just a few years ago, wife battering was still a laughing matter for some of Canada's political leaders. On May 12, 1982, when the problem of wife battering was raised in the House of Commons as a serious and widespread reality suffered by one out of ten Canadian women,[1] laughter echoed through the House.

Canadians took notice of this incident. An unthinking and public display of levity about such a grave problem generated a high level of public outrage, concern, and insistence among front-line workers and members of the general public, that policy-makers help translate this concern into action.

Government officials rallied in response to this public outcry. The results have been impressive. Canada became the first country to adopt a nationwide charging policy, encouraging police to lay charges in wife-battering cases.[2] Several provincial/territorial governments launched large-scale public education programs. National task forces were created. More money was allocated to services to help battered women and their children. The number of transition houses providing shelters for battered women more than tripled from 85 shelters in 1982,[3] to 264 shelters in 1987.[4] Counselling programs for batterers grew as well. Wife battering was identified as a priority concern in the two most recent Throne speeches (1984 and 1986) and Canada has participated in spreading awareness of wife battering in the international community.[5]

Beyond The Crisis

The result is that few Canadians today would laugh at the statement that wife battering is a serious problem. It is now generally recognized that too many women are hit, kicked, beaten, punched, and terrorized by their husbands or partners.[6] But ironically, the very seriousness with which Canadians now view wife battering may be limiting our understanding of the problem.

In fact, our continued progress in reducing the impact and incidence of wife battering may be threatened by the fact that we now take wife battering deadly seriously. Genuine and widespread fervour to prevent wife battering may be colouring the way we are approaching the problem, and influencing the success of our hoped-for solutions.

When wife battering became an official priority, the problem seemed horrific yet clear — women in Canada, like women around the world, were being physically brutalized by the men they lived with and often loved. A concern with incidence became central to our understanding of the problem with which we were dealing. Knowing how many women and what types of women were battered seemed crucial in identifying adequate and appropriate responses to the problem.

The focus for action also seemed clear: these women must be protected, supported, and helped to leave a dangerous situation. Everyone working in this field knew that the ultimate goal was to end wife battering in our society, but in the meantime there were women whose very lives were in danger. Because wife battering is a life-and-death problem, the action focus, by necessity, was on identifying all those women who were being battered so they could be protected from the violence.

Because the focus was on the crisis, the procedures needed for dealing with this problem seemed obvious as well. Give the woman a safe shelter, arrest the man, and insist through the courts that he keep the peace and his distance from his wife. Then, give the woman the information, referrals, and support she requires to forge a new life without violence and probably without the batterer.

This early clarity of vision was essential to allow the decisive action necessary to rally public and professional support around the problem. The early clarity of vision accomplished much. But at the same time it produced quandaries and inconsistencies: it failed the test of reality — the test of battered women's realities.

Battered women were not always prepared to support the simplistic "bad man-good woman" assumption at the basis of most crisis responses. Battered women did not always want to support a service and crisis response network which gave support to **her** as an individual but did not offer support to the batterer, to their children, or to the relationship. A surprising proportion of battered women kept returning to their husbands/partners, despite the brutality of the relationship. Battered women rarely blamed the batterer totally. Battered women wanted to talk of relationships. Battered women spoke of the illogic of relationships. Battered women wanted to talk about love.

And incidence did not necessarily help us define adequate responses because the same services were not considered appropriate by all battered women. At any rate, counting battered women was not always simple. Battered women did not want to be counted, did not always see themselves as "battered women", did not always accept the idea that they are somehow different from other women or even that their experiences are so far apart from those of other women. And then there were women who had never been physically struck or threatened but defined themselves as battered women on the basis of psychological battering.

These failed reality tests have raised questions and have challenged service-providers and policy-makers to re-think the assumptions on which programs and services are based. Today, we are at a crossroads in our understanding of and response to wife battering, and the emphasis is shifting from the crisis to prevention. Crisis responses must continue to be honed, it is widely acknowledged, but increasingly, service-providers and policy-makers believe that prevention and effective crisis responses are necessarily intertwined.

Today, optimism over the accomplishments of the past few years is mixed with a recognition that if we want to significantly reduce or even prevent wife battering we must **act** on the recognition that wife battering is a complex problem. It has long been **recognized** that wife battering is a problem involving emotional bonds and hopes for the future as well as physical and psychological pain, a problem with costs not only for the battered women, but for their children, their partners, their extended families, their friends, their communities, and for society as a whole.

But this complexity is difficult to translate into action. And so to take action we have simplified the problem — focussed on the **physically** violent act, provided support and protection to **individuals**. It became unpopular to even talk of relationships when dealing with wife battering. Wife battering was reduced to a series of acts — violent acts by a man against a woman for which the man must take responsibility. For the purpose of action, wife battering was individualized. It was individuals who suffered and individuals who battered. Criminal justice intervention which is based in individual responsibility was stressed. Individual counselling programs, particularly for the batterer, multiplied. Psychological theories of battering proliferated. A concern with incidence, with numbers of charges, with numbers of women needing shelter grew. The enormity of the problem became the justification for continued, concerted effort. Pressure was put on services to prove their importance through the number of battered women or batterers with whom they dealt.

But the concern with incidence and the emphasis on individuals and physically violent acts did not provide a foundation on which to build prevention programs. To fashion prevention programs, it is now increasingly realized that we must once again acknowledge the complexity and irrationality of the problem. More than this, we must dare to embrace this complexity. We must be willing to accept that battered women are not so different from other women, that battering relationships may not be so different from "normal" relationships. Perhaps battering is simply an extreme manifestation of characteristics of most sexual relationships. Perhaps battering is simply a caricature of our ideal of romantic love with its emphasis on intensity, isolation, and total mental and physical possession and obsession.

Further, we must be willing to acknowledge that there may not be any clear solutions to wife battering because all battered women do not have the same needs. We must also acknowledge that there is not even one solution for each battered woman: every woman may have many different needs and find different services appropriate and helpful as she changes, along with her relationship and the violence. Our responses to wife battering must reflect the ever-changing experiences and needs of women, children, and men caught in the battering cycle. We cannot look for a single panacea for wife battering. No single diagnosis or prescription is likely to be successful. Instead, we must respond to the needs of battered women, their children, their partners, their extended families, and their communities at different points in the changing process of battering, if we are to move decisively toward more effective crisis and follow-up programs and ultimately toward the prevention of wife battering in our society.

What This Study Does

The purpose of this report will be to grapple with the complexities of the problem and to promote this changing sensitivity to wife battering, already emerging in policy and service communities. The study has six goals:

- To reiterate that wife battering is a serious and widespread problem with far-reaching costs.
- To applaud the progress which has been made over the past few years in responses to wife battering, and to encourage continued, appropriate government efforts in this area.
- To speculate on the limits of a sensitive and appropriate government response, by exploring the ramifications for battered women, their children, the batterers, and for society of a continued increase in government intervention and of institutional rather than less formal family and community responses to wife battering.
- To help give battered women and front-line workers a voice in policy making so that the initiatives supported and developed by governments will reflect the varied and changing experiences of women who are battered.
- To expand on the need for acceptance of a multi-stage, multi-dimensional response to wife battering. There will rarely be a one-step solution in cases of wife battering. This characteristic of wife battering and the changing needs of battered women must be repeated because there is the risk that because no **one** solution is **the** solution, that existing and proposed programs will be labelled failures. We

must instead recognize that a constellation of inter-connected services to reduce the costs and prevalence of wife battering is needed.

- To begin to envision, with the help of the words and wisdom of battered women and their advocates, the next stage in our attempt to understand violence against women in the home and to expand our perspective to support a united vision of a future which does not include wife battering and which recognizes that to prevent violence in the family, we must stop doing violence to the family.

What This Study Does Not Do

This study does not provide a startling new exposé about wife battering. Its purpose is not to shock, but to build on good intentions and proud accomplishments. This study does not emphasize incidence, for an emphasis on incidence encourages us to simplify wife battering, to distance ourselves from it, to count it instead of understanding its complexities and the meaning of the violence for battered women, their children, and the men who batter them.

The one in ten figure referred to in the House of Commons in 1982 was taken from the 1980 report *Wife Battering in Canada: The Vicious Circle*, published by the Canadian Advisory Council on the Status of Women (CACSW). This book, written by the same author as the current study, was the first national attempt to estimate incidence and to collect information on wife battering in Canada. It shocked both policy-makers and the public with its documentation of the problem, the one in ten statistic, and its effect on women at all socio-economic levels of society. Awareness was raised and wife battering quickly became a priority on Canada's social policy agenda. This was crucial, because the will to change and improve the situation for battered women was vitally needed at that time.

Today, however, such an estimate would not have the same effect. Awareness is already raised. An estimate at this time could instead lead to an oversimplification of the problem, a continued blurring of the complexities so important to our future progress in this area. It is very tempting to define the seriousness of wife battering in terms of numbers. But there is always a danger implicit in defining the seriousness of any problem in this way. If the numbers go down, public and institutional support for the problem may also go down. However, if the numbers go up, critics can accuse the news-bearer of falsely inflating the figures, or can conclude that ongoing programs are ineffective and should be cancelled.

This study rejects an emphasis on incidence as the ultimate measure of the seriousness of the problem. Nonetheless, a thumbnail summary of the incidence findings will be provided to allow us to move to another level of dialogue.

A Thumbnail Summary Of Incidence

Briefly, the study found that, in 1985, in the 110 houses which were able to provide statistics on the number of battered women who stayed in their houses, 20,291 women were accommodated. Of that number, 15,730 were admitted explicitly because they were physically, psychologically, or sexually abused by their husbands or partners. The majority of the remaining women were admitted because they said they were homeless (either transient or in a housing crisis). However, it should be noted that house workers report that some women initially use housing as an excuse for requesting shelter because they are too embarrassed to reveal that they have been battered. Extrapolating from these figures, it is likely, if we had similar statistics for all 230 shelters which existed in Canada at the time of writing,[7] that about 42,000 women were accommodated in crisis shelters across Canada, almost 33,000 explicitly because they were battered by their husbands or partners.

In addition, even though most houses are very reluctant to turn away any battered woman who needs shelter, almost all are forced to turn a large number of women away. Only ten houses reported that they had not refused any woman accommodation in 1985. Excluding these ten, on average each shelter was forced to turn down one request for shelter out of every two, because of lack of space. In some houses, this ratio is much higher. For example, one house in Toronto reported that they turned away ten women for every one they sheltered. Based on the average number of women turned away, this means that at least another 42,000 women needed accommodation. Therefore, from these calculations, in 1985, a total of almost 85,000 women stayed in crisis shelters or requested such shelter. At least 65,000 of these were women who requested shelter explicitly because they were battered by their partners or ex-partners.[8]

As staggering as this figure is, it is far from representative of the total number of battered women in Canada. This is because by no means all battered women seek shelter in transition houses. Although there has been no national study which answers the question of how many women are battered but do not seek shelter in a transition house, one study done in London, Ontario, where a comprehensive and coordinated range of services exists for battered women, estimated that 89% of the battered women who sought help in their community in 1985, did not seek or require emergency shelter, but instead needed such non-residential services as referral, counselling, information and/or accompaniment to court.[9]

Applying this estimate to the totals means that almost 600,000 battered women across Canada may have sought some sort of outside help, and of these, about 532,000 may have sought help but did not require emergency shelter. This estimate of course tells us nothing about those women who are battered but report their battering to no official agency or front-line service. Even if we "guesstimate" that two out of three women report their battering to some official agency — a very conservative estimate according to front-line workers interviewed — this would mean that almost one million women in Canada may be battered each year.

How The Study Was Done

This study grapples with the complexities of wife battering and offers a new understanding which is forged by the hopes of battered women and those who work most closely with battered women, their children, and their husbands or partners. It will become clear through this report that battered women and front-line workers must have a voice in policy making if the resulting programs offered to them are truly to recognize the often changing nature of their needs and are to respond to these needs.

Accordingly, this study, like Wife Battering in Canada: The Vicious Circle, is based primarily on statistics and interviews provided by transition-house workers, and on personal interviews with battered women. A lengthy questionnaire (see Appendix B) was sent to known transition houses, associated safe-house networks, provincial/territorial associations of transition houses, and second-stage shelters. As well, the author and her assistant conducted face-to-face interviews with many transition-house workers and representatives of the provincial/territorial associations of transition houses, with selected police officers, Crown attorneys, court workers, provincial government officials, workers in second-stage houses, and with counsellors of men who batter. (For a complete discussion of this study's methodology, see Appendix C.)

Through The Eyes Of Women

Through the eyes of women, this study will point to the richness of exploring an understanding of wife battering beyond an understanding based on incidence. Their words will suggest that it is essential to go beyond incidence in our estimation of the seriousness of wife battering.

Throughout this study, it will be stressed that wife battering is a serious problem because it is a type of violence which potentially affects all families as well as all women in intimate relationships outside a family context. No family is entirely immune since, according to our current knowledge, wife battering is learned behaviour which is reinforced by our social institutions. Wife battering is also a serious problem because any prolonged suffering and injustice is a problem which deserves attention whether endured by one hundred or one million. Wife battering is a serious problem because it has far-reaching implications for all of us. Wife battering is a serious problem because it alerts us to the fact that despite some improvements in women's status and options, many women are still not given the options and benefits they warrant and need.

Finally, and on a more hopeful note, wife battering as a social issue has significance because the building societal reaction against it reveals the growing intolerance of all people to violence, and particularly to systematic violence directed against one group of people. Wife battering is an horrific problem, but the social response to this problem is a harbinger of change. Our concern with wife battering is a sign that we are working together as a society to build more options and a less violent world, not only for women but for all people in Canada. Accordingly it is the quality of our response and the depth of our understanding of wife battering, not the number of women who are battered in Canada, which will guide the exploration of wife battering that follows.

Through this current book the CACSW once again hopes to challenge the perceptions of Canadians concerning wife battering, to advise policy-makers and officials about the quality of progress which has taken place, and to increase government and public awareness of the need for further initiatives and services.

This report will chronicle the vast strides Canadians have made in the field of wife battering since 1980. It will also provide a vehicle to address the complexities and contradictions which could impede further progress. In addition to reviewing the progress to date, it will synthesize the broader definitions of wife battering emerging among service-providers and policy-makers, profile battered women who come to transition homes, explore the social costs of wife battering, and look at advances in program development and service delivery in terms of their impact on battered women and their children. Finally, the report will explore various options and proposals for action to more closely mirror the meaning of battering and intervention for battered women and to move us closer to a future which does not include wife battering.

Embracing the Complexities

of Wife Battering

Shattered Hopes:
The Meaning Of Wife Battering
For Victims And Survivors

More Than Physical Violence

I was hit plenty by my husband over the years. I had a couple of concussions, broken ribs, and I'm still deaf in one ear from him always hitting on that side of my head. But you can't understand what I went through if you only talk about the beatings. Hitting, punching, kicking — these things hurt your body, and they leave some scars, but mostly your body heals. What hurts me even more now is that with my husband I never had a chance to do anything with my life. I haven't been able to make plans for years. And now I feel like I gave so much love to him but I never even really had love back.

(comment of one battered woman on
what wife battering meant for her)

As this description so graphically portrays, wife battering is more than physical violence. It is self-evident that the brutality characteristic of many cases of wife battering is still the most life-threatening, the most dramatic, and the most obviously repugnant aspect of violence against women in the home. It is also undeniable that battered women will always need effective help to escape and prevent this physical violence. But despite the continued emphasis which must be placed through crisis services on physical violence, it is essential to recognize that wife battering, from the women's points of view, cannot be understood and truly responsive services cannot be provided, until the emotional and psychological environment in which violence occurs is understood.

The battered women interviewed for this study told stories of horrific incidents of violence, and spoke of their need for protection during and after these incidents. But these same women rarely emphasized the physical violence when they talked about what hurt them the most. They talked about degradation, the theft of control over their lives, of emptiness, the loss of hope, and of their misplaced futures.

One woman wrote of her lost hopes:

You know what hurts me most? We used to be so happy, so much in love. I want those days back. I want to dream again, to make plans, to see a future for us and our kids. I just ache to feel loved again. It's been so long since anyone's said a kind word to me, been gentle with me, made me feel special. Bruises and bones heal, but this ache never goes away.

Another spoke of the power of wife battering to degrade women:

The thing that's most hurting for me is the way he makes me feel so dirty, so filthy. He treats me like a dog, worse even. He tells me I'm ugly and worthless. He spits on me. It's not enough to hit me and kick me. He spits on me. Sometimes I think the hitting is better than being made to feel so low.

Yet another elaborates on her fears for the future and for her children:

I hurt most about my kids. About their future. They'll never feel proud to bring their boyfriends and girlfriends home to meet their parents. They're just little now and they never bring their friends over here. I worry when they see me crying. I worry when I can't play with them because I'm too sore. I worry that one day soon they won't even have a mother. I worry about that a lot — about what will happen to them, about whether they'll end up like me or end up in jail.

These heartfelt statements emphasize the importance of psychological battering and the ramifications of the battering for all family members. Many women also spoke of the strong bond many battered women have with their husbands. The strength of this bond is reflected in one woman's words:

I really love him and I think he still loves me. How can someone who loves you treat you so bad? Someday I'm going to have to leave because my nerves will break down or I'll be hurt too bad. But in my heart I don't think I'll ever want to leave him really. I'll always miss him and I'll always feel sorry for him. I worry about him even now. Why doesn't anyone see that he's sick? It's hard for him too, and it's very hard for the kids.

These first-hand "definitions" of battering reinforce the complexities and contradictions inherent in the experience — complexities which must be faced if society is to respond meaningfully to the needs, hopes, and experiences of the battered women in Canada.

These complexities — the emotions, bonds, and needs of those who live with violence — are not static. Battered women see the battering differently and feel differently about the batterer at various times in the relationship. Accordingly, they need a variety of social responses and services to correspond with these changing feelings and experiences. As one woman explains:

Right now, I'm really angry at everything he's done to me and the kids. I'm so glad I finally had the guts to phone the police. It took me so long to phone the police — years and years of hell.

Looking back on it, I feel so silly, but the first few times he hit me I was just shocked, and then he'd be so nice, so loving for a while afterwards, that I'd blame myself and feel sorry for him. The women at the shelter say that just about everyone goes through that. Then I just started to feel numb. Maybe I had a nervous breakdown or something. I just about never went out of the house unless I needed groceries or had to take the kids to the doctor. I didn't want to face anybody asking how things are with Bill and me. For those years I kept going with stupid dreams. I kept hoping that things would change. What else could I do? I couldn't see any other way out.

Another woman reveals how different women can experience wife battering and define appropriate solutions so differently depending on their circumstances and the length and severity of the battering relationship. She describes why she couldn't empathize with the other women staying at a shelter for battered women:

I'm not like them. I really love Tim. I can't wait to get back to him. He's got a problem and I can't go back until he promises to get some help for his problem. It's not just for me, but I've got to keep the kids safe. Most of the other women here seem so hard. They're always talking about 'that bastard did this, that bastard did that'. I hope I never feel like that.

A shelter worker adds to these illuminating descriptions:

The reason I think transition houses are so important is that they can be many things for different women. For one woman they can be a way to physically survive, for another they provide shoulders to cry on, for another they introduce her to things she can do to make it on her own. You can't lump battered women and their needs together. You need just about as many different solutions as there are battered women. No one answer is right for everyone.

Through these statements, the women quoted above stress that wife battering is not only physically and psychologically brutal, it involves an ever-changing experience and it is like running an emotional marathon. Battered women run the emotional gamut from fear, shock, despair, love, anxiety, guilt, anger, forgiveness, and hope. Many run this marathon over and over again at different times in their lives. For many battered women, the psychological brutality and the emotional treadmill are far more devastating than the physical violence.

The importance of psychological battering and the emotional turmoil battered women experience are well recognized in the literature. Deborah Sinclair, a social worker and front-line advocate, describes these emotional changes along a continuum from victim to victor. As she states:

Briefly described, an assaulted woman starts in the victim position. Feelings associated with this position include fear, minimization, isolation, depression, helplessness and internalized blame. . . . She moves through many stages, including anger, ambivalence and mourning before she develops a sense of self-worth, an ability to be assertive and a renewed sense of trust in her judgement.[1]

Ms. Sinclair goes on to counsel her readers that "resolution of ambivalence requires practice"[2] and a kind of testing of alternatives. She emphasizes that women must make their own decisions, at their own pace.

Unfortunately, interviews conducted for this study with transition-house workers, counsellors, and battered women reveal that the emotional changes women experience are too often interpreted by service-providers as an indication that battered women "don't know what they want" and therefore that service-providers should decide what is best for them. This attitude is used to explain away the battered woman's needs at any particular time and to dismiss the woman's ability to make decisions for her future, thus perpetuating her entrapment in ambivalence. This attitude leads to program and policy planning which does not adequately consider differences among battered women nor the different stages that individual battered women experience. This attitude that professionals know better than battered women what is best for them has also hindered the development of operational definitions of wife battering to more closely mirror the meaning of battering for battered women.

Of course, people hoping to help battered women have long recognized, from the women's descriptions of the violence, that wife battering is a multi-dimensional phenomenon involving various types of physical and psychological violence. And over the past seven years, realization of the scope of the violence and the consequences of psychological violence, as well as the recognition that it is necessary to address a wider definition of wife battering through appropriate programs, have expanded considerably.

In 1980, when the Canadian Advisory Council on the Status of Women published its first report on wife battering in Canada, it was defined as follows:

*Wife battering **is** violence, physical and/or psychological, expressed by a husband or a male or lesbian live-in lover, toward his wife or his/her live-in lover, to which the `wife' does not consent, and which is directly or indirectly condoned by the traditions, laws and attitudes prevalent in the society in which it occurs.*[3]

In that report, wife battering was presented in terms of three types of violence: physical violence; psychological violence directly initiated by the husband or partner in the form of constant denigrations, taunts, purposeful inconsistencies and/or threats; and the psychological violence which the woman experiences when she tries to get help outside the family only to find that help is too often just not there. In this early definition, the Council did make an attempt to define wife battering broadly and to express the sentiments of many battered women that psychological violence is at least as painful as physical violence. However, the central emphasis in this early work was placed on the physical violence in battering to clearly emphasize that wife battering can be a life-threatening problem and that immediate and decisive intervention was essential.

Many major policy-oriented documents followed this report in the next few years. While they generally acknowledged the importance of psychological violence, the authors tended to put it aside as something too broad and amorphous to deal with at that time. For example, the Standing Committee on Health, Welfare and Social Affairs of the House of Commons, in its 1982 report on wife battering, did not provide a formal definition, but revealed:

> We have found that wife battering is not a matter of slaps and flying crockery. Battered women are choked, kicked, bitten, punched, subjected to sexual assault, threatened and assailed with weapons.[4]

The emphasis on physical violence, sometimes to the exclusion of psychological violence, was not generally a sign of insensitivity, but rather a conscious decision to deal with the physical dimension because it could be life-threatening and because it was through the physical battering that battered women could be most readily identified and helped. It was recognized that many thousands of women in Canada were experiencing potentially life-threatening crises, and that these crises would have to be dealt with if deaths and serious injuries were to be prevented.

In addition, it was feared that an emphasis on psychological violence would lead to the conclusion among members of the Canadian public that wife battering is no more serious than a typical verbal family argument, and that this conclusion would mean a diminishing of public support for action against wife battering.

Since the early 1980s, however, the focus has been changing. While the devastation and seriousness of physical violence is still rightfully recognized and stressed, there is almost universal concern that wife battering be understood in a much more multifaceted way. It is now clear and well known that the psychological violence experienced by battered women is very different from a ''typical'' argument. Psychological violence in a battering relationship generally consists of overt or veiled threats of violence, and the systematic erosion of the woman's control in the relationship and often in all aspects of her life. The words of battered women help clarify this understanding.

> It's probably hard to imagine, but I used to pray that my husband would hit me, or do whatever he was going to do to me. I figured the pain couldn't be worse than living in constant fear. No, he never hit me, but I was a nervous wreck just the same. He'd threaten, laughing, that some day, sometime when I was least expecting it, I'd meet my maker, that he was planning the perfect crime and would never be caught. He'd read all the books he could get his hands on about husbands killing their wives, and leave them around I think so I'd read them and feel even more frightened. If I ever tried to talk to him about what he was doing to me, and I used to try early on, he'd just pretend it was all a joke and say I had no sense of humour, or was crazy or something.

Another woman expressed the same feelings.

> It was almost worse before he started beating on me. For two years he just used to threaten me, you know the way you do with a dog — just raise his hands or pretend to slap me but never touch me — but he'd do it with the most wicked look on his face.

Yet another woman describes some of the other dimensions that psychological wife battering can take.

> People have said to me, you didn't have it so bad — my husband broke my arm, or pulled out all my hair, or whatever — all yours ever did was yell at you. Maybe they're right, but I can't imagine that physical violence could be any worse. I even have trouble telling you some of the things he did to me. It started with him refusing to have sex with me. But it wasn't just like he didn't want to — it seemed like he'd do everything in his power to make me think he was interested. Once he even brought home a sexy nightgown and asked me to try it on. Then if I showed any interest he'd just humiliate me and tell me that's all I ever thought about and what a slut I was. After a while it was more than just that. He knew I was scared to death of heights and he'd find any excuse, you know if we were driving or something, to stop high up and he'd hold me tight by the arm or around my neck right up close to the edge. He'd also force me to stand right at the edge of the platform in the subway even though I'd just about be sick to my stomach with the fear. Finally, when I just couldn't take it any more he made me burn my favourite dress, because he said it was too tight and made me look even more like a tramp than I already did. Oh, once he also made me cut up all the pictures I had of a good friend because he said she was a bad influence on me.

Psychological violence, as these descriptions illustrate, can involve several dimensions. Deborah Sinclair has identified five different forms: making threats against the victim, her loved ones, her pets or her property, or even threatening suicide; forcing her to do degrading things, like washing her mouth out with soap or licking dishes clean; doing things that will terrorize her; verbally attacking her personality, attitudes, or beliefs; and controlling her activities.[5]

Increased awareness of the many facets of psychological violence in battering relationships has reinforced the recognition that violence is rooted in an unequal power relationship between the batterer and his victim, and in the often almost total psychological and sometimes physical control of the batterer over the battered woman.

> Wife assault involves the intent by the husband to intimidate, either by threat or by use of physical force on the wife's person or property. The purpose of the assault is to control her behaviour by the inducement of fear. Underlying all abuse is a power imbalance between the victim and the offender.[6]

The current definitions of wife battering being adopted by policy-makers, researchers, and service-providers across Canada acknowledge the importance of control and of psychological violence in battering and so mirror much more closely the definitions implicit in the descriptions of battering provided by battered women.

The Alberta government in its 1985 publication, *Breaking the Pattern: How Alberta Communities Can Help Assaulted Women and Their Families*, acknowledged that assaultive behaviour can take many forms, including but not limited to: physical abuse, emotional and psychological abuse, sexual abuse, and economic abuse.[7]

The Quebec government in its 1985 report, *Policy Respecting Assistance for Abused Women*, declared:

> Violence toward women takes several forms: blows, burns, rape, sexual assault, threats, verbal and psychological abuse and so on.[8]

Similarly, the resolution on wife battering adopted by the Seventh United Nations Congress on the Prevention of Crime and the Treatment of Offenders, held in Milan, Italy, in September 1985, stressed "that the problem of domestic violence is a multifaceted one. . . ."[9]

Transition-house workers across Canada are also currently grappling with the most appropriate and illuminating term to describe violence against women in the home. Many no longer believe that the term "wife battering" accurately portrays the multifaceted nature of wife battering or conveys the importance of psychological battering in these violent relationships. On the written questionnaire prepared for this study, workers were asked if they felt that the term "wife battering" appropriately describes the violence experienced by women in the home. Eighty per cent said they would prefer a term that would emphasize the multifaceted nature of the violence. All of these workers wanted less emphasis placed on the physical assault aspect of the violence and more on the emotional, verbal, economic, and sexual violence experienced by women. Forty-one per cent of the workers suggested that "violence against women in the home" would be more appropriate. Eighteen per cent preferred "wife abuse". Two innovative workers suggested introducing the term "domestic terrorism".

The remaining 20% wanted to go even farther in expanding the definition to emphasize the link between wife battering and all violence against women and to remove the stipulation that the violence must occur in the home. These workers tended to stress the societal roots and approval or reinforcement of the violence and the secondary victimization that so many women who are battered experience at the hands of institutions they approach for help. Of these workers, 10% suggested using the term "woman abuse", 4% preferred "women in crisis or distress", 5% preferred just "abuse", and 1% suggested "women robbed of dignity".

It is also important to note that even among those workers who still preferred the term "wife battering", the majority wanted it retained only because of its familiarity to the Canadian public. However, they insisted that it be defined in an expanded way to encompass psychological, sexual, physical, verbal, and economic violence. Because of the lack of unanimity expressed by shelter workers with respect to a change in terminology, the latter stance will be the one adopted in this report. Accordingly, the term "wife battering" will be used throughout, but it will be used in accordance with a new definition.

The following definition of wife battering was developed by the author to better reflect the multifaceted nature of battering emphasized by shelter workers and battered women, and to incorporate the current state of our knowledge of the scope of wife battering.

> *Wife battering is the loss of dignity, control, and safety as well as the feeling of powerlessness and entrapment experienced by women who are the direct victims of* **ongoing or repeated** *physical, psychological, economic, sexual and/or verbal violence or who are subjected to* **persistent** *threats or the witnessing of such violence against their children, other relatives, friends, pets and/or cherished possessions, by their boyfriends, husbands, live-in lovers, ex-husbands or ex-lovers, whether male or female. The term "wife battering" will also be understood to encompass the ramifications of the violence for the woman, her children, her friends and relatives, and for society as a whole.*

This new definition reflects society's growing awareness of psychological violence as a central element of wife battering. It is also emphasized in this definition, and will be repeatedly stressed throughout this book, that it is the **persistence** of the violence that establishes violence as battering. It is this persistence, the horror of living with the constant threat of violence, whether psychological, physical, sexual, verbal, or economic, which most debilitates the women who experience battering and which transforms so many Canadian households into prisons. This is not to say that one single brutal assault by a man against his wife should not be taken seriously, and should not be dealt with expeditiously as a criminal assault. However, until the violence is repeated, or until the woman is subjected to other forms of abuse by her husband or partner, this single incident will remain an assault — according to the definition just presented and used in this study — and not an example of battering. It bears noting, however, that episodes of physical violence are almost always preceded by a period of escalating psychological, verbal, or economic violence. Therefore, it is probable that such totally isolated events are rare.

Some of the new stipulations in this definition of wife battering require further explanation. For example, it may appear incongruous that "ex-husbands" and "ex-lovers" are included in this definition. This inclusion reflects the growing realization that many women do not escape their batterers through separation or divorce. In fact, the violence sometimes becomes more brutal after the woman leaves. These findings will be elaborated on in later sections of the report.

In addition, economic violence was included because shelter workers and battered women increasingly recognize that many batterers allow their wives no access to money at all or very limited access based on the batterers' whims and arbitrary rules. This control occurs even in some families where the woman works for pay. Denying the woman any control over money is a means by which the batterer can restrict and monitor the woman's actions, can increase her dependence on him, and can establish or reinforce her status within the family as an inferior and untrustworthy person.

Economic battering can be the sum of consciously cruel acts of withholding money and can have serious ramifications for the safety and health of women and children. One woman describes the problem:

> I used to think that his total control over the money was just a quirk, wasn't worth worrying about. After all, I was at home with the kids all day and I usually had $2 or $3 that he'd leave me. I didn't really need any more. Then one day he went away on a business trip for a week. He bought us some groceries before he went and left me with $10 for the whole week, to feed me and three kids, saying with a smirk that I'd better make it last, because it's all I would get. Well, we ran out of food after three days and we nearly starved trying to feed me and three kids on $10 for four days. But the worst was that my middle boy got hit in the mouth with a stick and should have gotten stitches, but I didn't even have bus fare to take him to the hospital and I was scared of what my husband would do if I asked a neighbour for money.

Why Aren't Violent Women Included In This Definition?

Most service providers and academics involved in the area of wife battering now recognize that, while the numbers of men as victims and women as batterers are small, there are, in fact, some men who are battered by their wives. Murray Straus and Richard Gelles, who have conducted two household surveys (1975 and 1985) on wife battering in the United States, have found clear evidence of women using violence against their husbands in both surveys. In addition, a few battered women interviewed for this study spoke of their violence as equal in frequency to their husbands' violence. However, as Straus and Gelles state:

> The meaning and consequences of that violence is not easily understood. For one thing, as pointed out elsewhere . . . the greater average size and strength of men and their greater aggressiveness . . . means that the same act (for example, a punch), is likely to be very different in the amount of pain or injury inflicted. . . . Even more important, a great deal of violence by women against their husbands is retaliation or self-defense. . . .

One of the most fundamental reasons why women are violent within the family but not outside the family is that their own home is where there is the greatest risk of assault for a typical . . . woman.[10]

On the basis of these considerations, therefore, how should violence by women against men in the home be dealt with? Battering, whether perpetrated by women or by men, is always a serious matter. However, husband battering is not sufficiently similar to wife battering to warrant its inclusion in a more general definition of "spousal battering". To clarify, while it is recognized that cases of violence against men by their wives do exist, and they should be taken very seriously and dealt with promptly and effectively on an individual basis, the battering of men does not generally have the same physical consequences as the battering of women. Even more importantly, the battering of men is not reinforced by the current structuring of inequality in Canadian society which exaggerates the battering of women. As a result, the options open to men who are battered are, at least in theory, more numerous.

A few female batterers were encountered during the course of this research. They had identified themselves as batterers, usually on the basis of a public awareness campaign in their provinces which detailed the characteristics of batterers and their victims, as well as the stages in the cycle of violence. These women were all very articulate and expressed the belief that they assumed the traditionally dominant male role in their relationships. These women supported the contention, therefore, that battering is rooted in socially created male and female roles, and that battering is not so much biologically sex-based as socially gender-based. This contention is shared by the author and is supported in other research studies.[11]

However, without discounting the experiences of these women, it must be remembered that the question of the battering of men has been used repeatedly to discredit the validity, importance, and magnitude of the problem of wife battering. It is discouraging that the suffering of one group should be in competition with the suffering of another group for public acceptance, attention, and resources. The battering of all people, whether female, male, young, or old, should be taken seriously. However, to ensure the best apportioning of social and economic resources, those Canadians who are battered and who have the greatest needs deserve and require the most attention. Since men tend to have greater financial security, better jobs, less responsibility for children, and greater credibility in society, they generally are less in need of support than women who are battered. For these reasons, then, women who are battered will continue to be the focus of this report. Nonetheless, because of the public interest in "the other side of the coin", because of the danger of competition between advocates for male and female victims of violence resulting in the demise of services for Canadians who need help to deal with or escape violence, and, most importantly, because many battered women state that they believe the violence is sometimes shared and experience great guilt about their violence, the battering of men will not be left out of this report, but will be dealt with whenever it is appropriate and information is available.

It is the hope of the author that, by facing this problem squarely and by more conscientiously listening to the women's reports of their own violence, we can illuminate the reality of violence against men and reduce the amount of competition which exists between those who are advocates for women and those who feel a false reality is being created through an emphasis only on the women. The author also hopes that, by introducing this element of complexity, productive research will be stimulated to explore the values attached to control and the use of control and violence by men and women caught up in battering relationships.

What Do We Know About The Battered Women And The Batterers In Canada?

What Are The Socio-Economic Characteristics Of Battered Women Who Stay In Transition Houses?

Statistics unique to this study are based on data provided by transition houses. Therefore, they focus on the characteristics of battered women who have stayed at shelters. However, when combined with information gathered through personal interviews with battered women and shelter workers, the following data attest to the broad range of women who are battered in this country. It is important to note that women who stay in shelters tend to have few financial options and so are unable to find alternative shelter on their own. As a result, they tend to be the poorer and younger battered women of Canada.

The statistics that follow, therefore, will tell us much about the characteristics of battered women who stay in shelters for battered women. They will also tell us much about the hopelessness and the imprisonment of poverty. They will remind us that poverty is a women's issue and that many women who are battered have few choices, because they are poor, other than to return to their husbands. However, our increased knowledge of wife battering tells us that poverty does not explain the battering. Nor does it explain why so many women continue to live with wife battering.

It is clear, however, that poverty can create a psychology of defeat. Poverty limits choice and eventually limits the individual's ability to make decisions and to plan for the future. The poverty of women is an issue which must be addressed when considering the problem of wife battering. It is unlikely that women will attain the dignity and be able to make decisions and take actions which will free them from violence while they live with the indignity and hopelessness of poverty.

Not all transition houses which responded to the written questionnaire for this study collected information on the socio-economic characteristics of the women who stayed with them. Accordingly, the statistics which follow are based on data provided by the 98 houses which both responded to this questionnaire and kept detailed statistics on the characteristics of the women they served.

The majority of women who stayed in transition houses in 1985 were young — 14% were under 21 and 56% were between 21 and 34 years of age. Nonetheless, a great variety of women were sheltered in transition houses. Twenty-four per cent of the women were between 35 and 49 years of age and 6% were 50 years old or older. Transition-house workers also reported informally that more and more teenagers who have been battered by their boyfriends, older women in their sixties and seventies, and pregnant women are coming to them for shelter.

Given the young age of the majority of women who stay in shelters, it is not surprising that 70% of the women came with children. Of the women with children, 39% had only pre-school children, and 22% had one or more pre-school children as well as one or more children between five and 11 years old. Another 26% of the women had children who were all between five and 11 years of age. This means that 87% of the women with children who came to the shelter had young children who all required constant supervision. The average number of children per woman was two.

The majority of the women had been living with their partners before they came to the shelter. Fifty per cent of the women were legally married and 28% were living common-law. Only 10% were single, 7% were separated, and 5% were divorced. It is noteworthy that 22% of the women in the sample were single, separated, or divorced, compared to only 13% in the 1980 study *Wife Battering in Canada: The Vicious Circle*.[1] There is increasing evidence in this study, as well as in other recent studies, that separation and even divorce do not protect women from violence. Jean Giles-Sims reports: "Of those who never returned to the man after they left the shelter, 44% reported at least one violent incident with the man. . . . Physical distance, separate residences, and legal restraining orders did little to prevent violence."[2] Similarly, Desmond Ellis has found that women who are separated and/or divorced are more likely than women who are married or living in a common-law relationship to be victims of violence at the hands of their ex-husbands or at the hands of other men.[3]

Of the women who were married or living common-law, few were newlyweds. Only 8% of the women had lived with their spouses less than one year, 34% had lived with their partners between one and five years, 33% between six and ten years, and 23% more than ten years.

In the majority of the cases, violence was not a new occurrence. Fifty-nine per cent of the women had previously left their partners because of violence. Seventy-six per cent of these women had left because they were physically or emotionally battered, 5% because they were sexually assaulted by their husbands, 4% because of financial abuse, 11% because of the physical or emotional abuse of their children, and 3% because of the sexual abuse of their children.

Despite the violence, and in addition to caring for their children, 20% of the women were working outside the home for pay. Of these women, 8% worked in professional occupations (such as law, teaching, or nursing), 25% in white-collar jobs (clerical, secretarial), 21% held skilled blue-collar positions such as machine operator or cook, and 38% worked in unskilled blue-collar jobs such as waitressing. The occupations of the remaining 8% were simply designated as "other".

Of the women who worked outside the home for pay, 41% earned less than $7,000 a year, 27% earned between $7,000 and $10,000, 27% earned between $10,000 and $20,000 a year, 3% earned between $20,000 and $34,000, and 1% earned more than $34,000 a year. Statistics Canada estimates that, in 1985, a family of three in a large urban centre (500,000 population or more) with an income of less than $18,060 was living in poverty. In a small town (30,000 to 99,000), a family of three would require $15,995 to avoid poverty, and $13,243 would be needed in a rural community. This means that, of the women in this study's sample who were working for pay, at least 68%, and possibly as high a proportion as 95% (the total percentage who earned under $20,000), would be living below the poverty line if they left their husbands and tried to support themselves and their children with their own earnings.[4]

However, most of the women who came to transition houses in 1985 were already living in poverty when living with their husbands. Forty-three per cent had a family income of less than $10,000 a year, and 32% had a family income between $10,000 and $20,000 a year. Thus, according to Statistics Canada's definition of poverty, approximately 75% of the women and children who stayed at transition houses in 1985 were living in poverty.[5]

The family income of most women who stayed in shelters in 1985 was not only low, it was probably unstable. Only 38% of the partners of these women worked regularly, 33% were unemployed, and the remaining 29% worked irregularly or seasonally.

If the women in the sample decided to leave their husbands, more than two-thirds could be hindered in a job search by low education. Seventy per cent of the sample had not completed high school. Twenty-two per cent had a high school diploma. Only 6% had been to college or technical school as well as high school and 2% had a university degree.

These statistics add a practical dimension to the emotional bonds women feel for their husbands and their concern for their children's futures which keep so many battered women with their partners. Most of the women who stayed in transition houses in 1985 had little education and small children. It is possible that many had never worked for pay. Certainly, the majority were not working for pay when they came to the shelter. Thirty-four per cent of the women who stayed in shelters were from out of town, and 3% were from out of the province. For these women, leaving their partner also meant leaving their home community, having to change their children's school, being cut off from friends, relatives, and familiar places. For most of these women, therefore, leaving means a very uncertain future. Even if their lives with their husbands are also uncertain and brutal, being on their own with small children undoubtedly and **realistically** looks equally terrifying for many of the women in the sample. The difficulty of leaving is evident in the finding that 67% of the women in the sample had already stayed at the transition house they were currently living in — 48% once before, 12% twice, 6% three to five times, and 1% more than five times. This statistic does not take into account other transition houses these women may have stayed in.

What Do We Know About Wife Battering In Middle- And Upper-Class Homes?

It should be reiterated that this picture of poverty does not represent the whole picture of wife battering. While the numbers are relatively small in the present sample because primarily poorer women come to transition houses, it is interesting to note that, in terms of the scope of wife battering, 2% of the women who came to transition houses in 1985 had a family income of more than $45,000 a year. In addition, transition-house workers reported that many of the women who called for information, advice, or telephone counselling, but not shelter, were middle-class and upper-middle-class women, many of them women working outside the home. This information is reinforced by recent statistics collected by the Battered Women's Advocacy Clinic in London, Ontario. Their figures reveal that the women who come to the Clinic for advice, information and/or counselling, but not for shelter, tend to be slightly older, better educated, and with a high level of employment skills and experience.[6] Stacey and Shupe, in a U.S. research study, also speak of middle- and upper-class women who do not leave their husbands and who do not go to shelters, but do make use of crisis lines. They even suggest that:

> . . . the abuse they [middle-class women] suffered was often more severe than that of the shelter residents (although not quite as frequent). What is more, sex abuse was more often reported by Help Center clients [who were mainly middle-class women] though it is of course possible they were simply able to recognize it.[7]

What Do We Know About Battered Women Who Suffer Double Isolation?

The problems and obstacles facing battered women who seek shelter in transition houses are overwhelming, as the statistics above begin to suggest. However, some sub-groups of battered women face even greater hurdles in trying to deal with the violence. To appreciate the true scope of wife battering, both in terms of incidence and human suffering, the particular problems of these largely invisible groups of battered women must be recognized. While it is not known exactly how many women do not report being battered, this study's research gives some information on groups of women who are particularly prone to suffering in silence. These women are, in fact, doubly isolated, not only by being battered, but by geographic, linguistic, cultural, racial, physical, or mental barriers.

Women Living In Rural Or Isolated Areas

To be a battered woman is, by definition, to be isolated — to have few friends, often limited access to money, and to be trapped in a cocoon of secrecy. Although battered women in urban areas have seemingly insurmountable barriers to over-come in order to reduce their isolation, the obstacles are multiplied greatly for women in rural areas. Statistical data on battered women in rural areas are extremely limited because of the cost of undertaking these studies among a widely scattered population.

However, there is evidence from past studies that family violence may be even more prevalent in rural and isolated areas than in urban areas.[8] In addition, alcohol abuse, which is frequently linked to wife battering, has been presented in the research as an even more important factor behind most forms of victimization in rural and isolated communities.[9] Research also shows that personal factors, family ties, and long-term friendships play an important role in the way battering and crimes generally are reacted to and dealt with in rural environments.[10] Close personal ties between the battered woman or the batterer and people who are potential sources of help may inhibit the reporting of wife battering. In fact, research suggests that victims of crime generally are less likely to report crimes in rural locations, especially in small, homogeneous communities, because of the strong value the community places on maintaining relationships.[11]

The isolation created by the often secret and hidden nature of wife battering is also increased by the geographic isolation typical of rural and isolated areas. This isolation is particularly pronounced in northern communities. Research on the needs of all victims of crime in the north, and in rural areas in the south, stresses that this isolation contributes to an urgent need for information services by battered women in rural and isolated areas.[12]

For example, one province-wide study carried out in Manitoba which compared the needs of urban and rural battered women, found that 55% of the rural calls included a request for information along with a request for referral and/or counselling, compared to 44% of the urban calls. It is also striking that the average time spent dealing with a call for information and referral from an urban resident was about 9 minutes, compared to over 31 minutes for a rural resident.[13] These findings suggest that battered women who live in rural areas need more basic information on wife battering and their options than do battered women living in urban centres. These findings may also suggest that the information and referral needs of women in rural and isolated areas are more complex because there are fewer services available to them and because the difficulty of gaining access to existing services is greater.

In rural and isolated areas, research indicates that accessibility to information about legal and other service options, probably through a toll-free hotline, is a primary need. The second most frequently described need reported in one study is for counselling, including alcohol counselling.[14]

However, in rural and isolated areas, lack of information about services available and the barriers to service which can be created by close personal ties throughout the community are not the only problems. As mentioned above, access to criminal justice, health, and social services is often more difficult because the services simply don't exist or because transportation is not available. Public transportation is generally non-existent and distances to services can be prohibitive, even if the services are available. In northern Canada, for example, victims do not have ready access to the court system. The isolation of northern communities has necessitated the use of a circuit court system to bring the justice system to these centres — a kind of "drop-in", travelling court which allots only certain court days each month to a community. The back-log in cases which often results from limited service and the resulting delay in having cases resolved can contribute to the decision by victims to "simply not bother with the courts". Thus, limited access to often inadequate services tends to reduce the willingness of rural women and men to seek out official services.

The research done for this study expands on the picture of the isolation suffered by rural women. The mail-out questionnaire used to collect data did not explicitly ask how many women who came to each house were from rural areas. However, transition-house workers reported that, overall, 34% of the women were from out of town. We can assume that a proportion of these women were from rural communities. Given that only 24% of women in Canada who are married, living common-law, separated, or divorced live in rural areas,[15] this would suggest that a surprisingly large proportion of battered women were from rural communities. In personal interviews, rural women spoke of the years they endured the violence simply because they couldn't manage the logistics of leaving.

> Farm work isn't like city work. My husband wasn't gone from eight in the morning till five at night. He could pop in at any time. He kept a close guard on the pick-up and on my comings and goings. I'd have to ask him for the keys. There was just never a safe time to leave. Once I tried keeping the kids home from school when I knew he was busy with haying. And you know he just stuck around that day even though the haying had to be done. How could I get away?

Another woman commented:

> He has a lot of friends around where we live and I come from another village, so they're not so close with me. He gets his friends to keep an eye on me. Oh, he makes it like a joke, but for me it's like being in jail.

Other rural women spoke of the major leap of leaving their community to go to a nearby town or city:

> All my friends, relatives, my whole life is at my home. It had to get so damn bad before I could decide to leave all that behind. I don't like the city. I don't know anybody. Now I can't go back. Where would I live? There aren't apartments and welfare housing on the farm. If I go back home, it has to be to him and more beatings. I don't know where to turn.

Transition-house workers frequently spoke of the non-existence of public transportation and the prohibitive distances faced by women who live in rural areas. Shelter workers also felt that women in rural areas experience a bigger problem with the attitudes of police and doctors.

> The police and doctors in our area are not aware of the provincial charging policies, and the doctors especially find it hard to side with the women against the men, because they might have delivered the husband, or grown up with him.

Some workers said that when rural women try to get away and want to lay charges in a nearby town or city, police often tell them they have to return to their communities to lay charges.

The closeness of the community also means that rural women often need extra reassurance that any contact with a transition house, with a counsellor, or with the police will be discreet and legitimate. However, secrecy is pretty hard to guarantee when the woman's phone is on a party-line system.

While these links can create problems, the importance of community can also create special advantages in the search for solutions in rural areas. One police inspector commented that, if police serving rural areas can be convinced that charging is appropriate, charging policies could be a particularly effective deterrent in rural areas simply **because** the batterer knows the police officer:

> If someone you've had to your house socially and who you really respect tells you it's wrong to hit your wife, that message will mean a whole lot more than if a stranger tells you the same thing.

In addition, in rural communities where public awareness is high, informal reports emphasize that networks among different service agents are far more effective because it's not just a job, but a friendship, that is at stake. Reducing or eliminating wife battering can quickly become a matter of community pride. As one house worker phrased it: "For the most part, rurals stand very united . . . they stand very tight".

Aboriginal Women

Fifteen per cent of the women in this study's sample were Indian — 10% treaty Indian and 5% non-treaty.

Many aboriginal women live in rural or isolated areas and so share the types of isolation described in the previous section. However, aboriginal women are also isolated from sources of help by discrimination and by linguistic and cultural barriers.

A large proportion of aboriginal women feel alienated from the "services" offered to other battered women. They are distrustful of the criminal justice system and fearful that any contact with the criminal justice system or social service agencies could result in their children being taken away from them. Overall, aboriginal women and men are more culturally attuned to mediation, reconciliation, and communal responses.[16] They therefore tend to reject services based on an adversarial or divisive model.

Further, more aboriginal women than non-aboriginal women defend their husbands or partners as victims of society and explain the battering in terms of the displacement of aboriginal peoples, and particularly of aboriginal men, from their traditions and chosen lives. They describe their husbands or partners frequently as doomed to unemployment or low-paying jobs and poverty. Therefore they are reluctant to cooperate with any service which they feel will make things even harder for him. They want the violence to stop, but they see the society and its influences as more responsible for the battering than the batterer himself. This shared anger, felt by some aboriginal women and men against the white community, reinforces strong community pressures to rely on one's own kind, to keep the family cohesive, and so to stay in relationships despite the violence.

The aboriginal women who are probably most isolated are those who live on reserves. Reserves have their own policing systems and are usually under the jurisdiction of a regional council which is responsible for social welfare. As a result, reserve women rarely have access to outside social and health services. Many of the men on reserves are particularly concerned about maintaining the status quo and keeping outsiders out. Social change and an increased population on many reserves have brought with them a culture of poverty, unemployment, alcohol abuse, and social dissolution which encourages violence and which has resulted in an escalation of violence in the family, sexual assaults, incest, and attacks against the elderly.[17]

Alcohol has featured prominently as a major cause or factor in most violence in aboriginal communities. The vulnerability of some aboriginal women who are battered is increased by the common belief that alcohol is "something that 'takes over' so that the victim may not feel victimized by the person [who committed the crime] but by the alcohol."[18] This perception of alcohol as an uncontrollable force behind the violence discourages a constructive solution and tends to absolve the offender from responsibility for his actions.

To compound the vulnerability of many aboriginal victims of wife battering, a high value is attached to familial privacy, the cohesion of tightly knit extended families, and the authority of men within these families.[19] The result is that violence becomes accepted as a private and an inevitable part of life, and the woman does not see "outside" services as realistic options for dealing with being battered.

In a 1979 study of aboriginal people, 81.3% of those interviewed suggested that the relationship between aboriginal people generally and the police needed to improve.[20] In the same study, more aboriginal people were critical of the police and saw them as part of the "other" side. Since that time, relations between aboriginal people and the criminal justice system do appear to have improved somewhat, largely as the result of the growing trend toward the use of aboriginal police on northern and southern reserves,[21] but many aboriginal people are still distrustful of the dominant culture's criminal justice system.

These factors in the compound isolation of aboriginal women can be augmented — for those aboriginal women who do seek outside help — by discrimination against aboriginal women in some communities. Many transition houses reported no such discrimination. They employed aboriginal staff members and had experienced apparently good integration between aboriginal and white residents. Other house workers spoke of very real barriers in their search for help, created by discrimination. One worker in a western province said that, in her community, some non-aboriginal women seeking shelter had actually asked if there would be aboriginal women staying at the house, and many declined to come because there were aboriginal residents and workers. In houses situated in communities where discrimination is this extreme, house coordinators and workers reported that it is very difficult to find aboriginal workers because they are treated with such disdain and hostility by non-aboriginal residents.

In most of the houses which served some aboriginal women, the problem was not this overt, but, nonetheless, the aboriginal women tended to feel isolated from non-aboriginal women in the house. Referring to aboriginal women, one shelter worker reported: "They do their best not to be in the house and will often leave the room if people are talking". Another worker provided the following illuminating comment:

> The native women don't feel at home here. They come to us because there's nowhere else to go, but they don't really trust us. . . . They are constantly worried that we'll call Child Welfare. There's a growing split between native women who want to integrate and those who want to separate, but most native women would really like their own services.

Finally, a transition-house worker in British Columbia reminds us: "We've worked very hard to overcome the myths of women who are battered by their partners. Let us work just as hard to overcome the myths about native women".[22]

Immigrant Women

As with aboriginal battered women, it is misleading to look at all immigrant women as members of a homogeneous group. Nonetheless, there are certain general experiences and perceptions which tend to shape the needs and responses of battered immigrant women when attempts are made to provide help. The numbers of immigrant women who stayed in transition houses in 1985 were far fewer than the numbers of native or rural women. Only 6% of the women were legal immigrants sponsored by a relative (usually their husbands) or an employer. An additional 2% were either staying in Canada illegally without the knowledge of the Department of Immigration or they were temporary visitors from another country. As well, nine "mail-order brides" stayed in a transition house in 1985. Of the sponsored immigrants, it was known that, for 23% of the women, their husbands had been their sponsors and the sponsorship had broken down either because the woman left or because one of the partners had filed for separation or divorce.

While the numbers we are dealing with are **relatively** small — only about 3,400 immigrant women across Canada stayed in transition houses in 1985 — the numbers of immigrant women who are battered but do not report their violence are likely to be much higher for several reasons. In addition, the problems of these women are particularly poignant because of the many kinds of isolation they experience.

Linguistic isolation is one major form. While linguistic isolation need not be experienced only by immigrants, of course, given the multicultural nature of Canada, and the fact that there are two official languages, many immigrants, particularly those from the far east, do not speak either of Canada's official languages.

Transition-house workers reported that language barriers between residents and staff posed a problem in 47% of the houses. However, only 7% of the houses ever had to turn down a request for accommodation because they were not able to communicate with a woman in her language. In the majority of cases where this occurred, the woman spoke only Japanese, or a Chinese or East Indian language or dialect. (Despite the language problem, women manage to locate or be directed to transition houses. In the majority of cases, these women are referred by the police, hospitals, welfare workers, or immigrant community groups.) In 58% of the transition houses in Canada, services were available, to some extent, in both official languages. No cases were reported where a woman who spoke either French or English had to be turned away. Most houses, even if they did not have staff who spoke the non-dominant official language in their region, were able to find someone to act as a translator. This was also generally true for women who spoke other European languages.

Language barriers are not the only form of isolation these women experience. Many immigrant women have a very negative image of the police because they come from police states. It is therefore very difficult for them to see the police as potential sources of help. In addition, many immigrants are afraid of being deported and are therefore very hesitant to involve any official agency in their problems.

The fear of deportation is not unrealistic. As a sponsored immigrant, usually sponsored by her husband, the battered woman is often dependent on the man who beats her, both for her economic support and also for her right to stay in Canada. Further, as recently as May 16, 1986, the case of Mrs. Helga Muselmann of Hawkesbury, Ontario, was raised in the House of Commons. Mrs. Muselmann had received a letter dated April 30, 1986, from Employment and Immigration Canada:

> . . . stating that she had one month to leave the country because she and her husband
> were in breach of a ministerial permit. The breach in question is that the husband has

been convicted of a crime. The crime he committed was that he beat up his wife, a crime which the victim rightfully reported to the police. The conclusion is that this woman is now being asked to leave the country because she reported a battering husband.[23]

Linguistic and cultural isolation as well as fear frequently keep immigrant women trapped in their more familiar ethnic communities and in menial low-paying jobs.

The cultural mores of many immigrant groups still condone wife battering as a way of keeping women in their place. They define wife battering as a strictly personal matter which should not be discussed. To make such a private matter public is considered a source of shame for the whole family and sometimes also for the whole ethnic community. "As in many cultures, the use of physical force to keep wives in line was long condoned in Korean society", a woman columnist for a Toronto Korean newspaper stated. "But once you let it out, it's shame for the whole family".

Further, this study points out that immigrant women may feel they should "repay" the shelter for housing them and so do more than their share of housework. They may thereby create resentment or ridicule among the other women. In addition, the fact that some shelters will not accept adolescent boys poses a particular problem for some immigrant women because of their double isolation and because they have no one with whom they can leave their boys. Five per cent of the Canadian shelters surveyed would not accept boys over 12, 10% wouldn't accept boys over 14, 50% turned away boys over 16, 13% over 17, and 25% over 18 years of age. Many immigrant women, like non-immigrant women, will not leave a violent situation unless they can take all their children with them, or can in some way guarantee their safety. Because few immigrant women have friends outside their small community with whom they could safely leave their older children, their only option is to bring them to the shelter. Therefore leaving is simply not an option for them if the transition house nearest to them will not accept older boys.

No matter how supportive shelters for battered women may be, the long-term prospect of leaving her husband to face what she fears will be an often harsh, uncaring future of rules, regulations, high expectations, and few opportunities to house and support herself and her children is terrifying enough for any battered woman. For the immigrant woman, this fear is frequently paralyzing. Even more central, for a woman who does not speak either one of Canada's official languages, who does not understand the society, its rules or customs, it is virtually impossible for her to discover if help is available and where to find it. Immigrant women, like aboriginal women and rural women, desperately need outreach programs to provide information about wife battering and about the assistance available to them.

Teenaged Women

An unexpected group of women who also suffer double isolation are the growing numbers of teenaged women who are battered by their boyfriends. While houses are not yet keeping statistics on this phenomenon, many transition-house workers spoke of their dismay and feelings of helplessness at the rising number of battered teenaged girls who are seeking help from the shelters. Shelters cannot officially house women until they reach the age of majority in their province or territory (which varies between 14 and 18), or until they reach an age defined as "adult" under the Canada Assistance Plan or social services regulations for the province/territory. Workers feel helpless as well when faced with these young women because most of them are still living with their parents, have no children, are still going to school, and therefore, according to our "practical" notion of factors which should make escape possible, should be able to make rational choices such as choosing to end the battering relationship. As one worker commented:

> *The rising incidence of date-battering and date rape reminds us how much of the woman's inability to stop the battering is wrapped up with her self-image and her desperate belief that she needs a man.*

Workers also linked the rise in teenaged battering to the increase in sexually intimate relationships among teenaged couples.

> *The strength of emotions these young girls feel in the throes of a passionate relationship is often overwhelming. It clouds their reasoning. It clouds their self-respect. It even clouds their instinct for survival. But strong passion is hard to abandon. They just can't let go, and they almost all feel they can't go to their parents with their problems.*

The practical and legal problems faced by these young women are often different from those faced by the majority of women who stay in transition houses. Most workers felt that existing transition houses would probably not provide an ideal environment for these women. Instead, workers generally agreed that teenaged battered women need special programs to raise their self-esteem and to help them move out of their relationships so that they don't become battered wives.

Disabled Women

There is no reason to assume that women disabled from birth or before marriage will be less prone to violence than non-disabled women. In addition, many battered women suffer from permanent disabilities as a result of being battered. Yet this group of women is virtually invisible, and services for battered women do not respond sensitively or adequately to their needs. More and more large government buildings are wheelchair-accessible and have facilities to accommodate the hearing- or sight-impaired. However, the needs of community services for battered women to have these capabilities as well is not generally recognized by funding agencies. As a result, only 29% of the existing transition houses reported that they were wheelchair-accessible, and only 12% reported having a staff member who is proficient in sign language. Further, because they were unable to provide the special care and assistance these women need, according to the assessment of transition-house workers, 4% of the houses have a policy of refusing women with severe visual impairment and 1% refuse women with severe hearing impairment.

Women with mental handicaps, psychiatric problems, or addictions have even fewer alternatives. Sixty-four per cent of the houses had a policy of refusing women determined on intake or through the referring agency to have psychiatric problems, 42% refused women with suicidal tendencies, 68% refused women with active drug dependencies, and 66% refused women with active alcohol dependencies. Transition houses refused these women because they simply had neither the specially trained staff nor the facilities to deal with them appropriately. Further, many workers expressed the belief that, for the sake of the other women and children in the house, given the close quarters of most houses, it would be extremely disruptive to integrate routinely any of these groups of women in the houses. Nonetheless, these same workers were profoundly compassionate toward these women and disturbed at the lack of services available for them. One woman summarized the problem as follows:

> *In many ways, these women with so many problems are the most needy of all and yet they have nowhere to go. Our society has tried to deinstitutionalize the whole area of mental health, but they have not replaced big institutions with community facilities. Women are coming to transition houses begging house workers to fill the gaps left by the attempt of the wider society to forget that these problems exist. We can't do it all. We are put in the terrible position of having to gear our service to the majority of our clients and simply turning these other women away. What happens to them when they have nowhere to go for help?*

Women On Military Bases

The military community is a closed and self-sufficient constellation of people and services. Military bases have separate legal, social, and medical services and some residential facilities, all organized under a unified command structure. This situation offers a unique opportunity to create an integrated and cohesive set of services to deal with wife battering. At the same time, however, the closed nature of military communities and the special characteristics of military life can increase the isolation and suffering of battered women on military bases.

At the time of writing, no substantive Canadian research on the special problems of battered military wives or battered enlisted women could be located. Therefore, the information which follows is based primarily on conversations with transition-house workers and military wives familiar with the special problems of this doubly isolated group of battered women.

Military families suffer an undue number of stresses caused by the nature of military life. Low-ranked personnel frequently experience chronic financial problems because of the low rates of pay offered at these levels. Frequent separation between spouses to take courses and to fulfil special assignments is common. There is also a greater percentage of intercultural marriages in the military community than in the general population, a factor which can place additional strain on a family experiencing other stresses. Alcohol use is a dominant part of the military culture. Further, the military community is based on a rigid hierarchy of power and the ethos that "might is right", an ethos which rewards and encourages violence.

The military life can also exaggerate the isolation of battered women. Frequent moves characterize military life; women married to military men are often separated from friends and family. On-base housing is limited in many locations and, as a result, military families may be forced to locate a great distance from the base in order to find affordable accommodation, thus increasing the separation of the women from a potential support group of other military wives. Women on military bases are also expected to use military health, social, and legal services. They are thus isolated from the wider civilian service community. One woman said that when she went to an outside, non-military psychologist for help because she was afraid to report her battering to anyone on the base, the psychologist called the chaplain on the base to alert him to her visit.

Military wives also fear that they will lose whatever security they have by exposing the violence. They may be concerned that reporting the violence to base officials could jeopardize their husband's chances for promotion and diminish any chances they both might have for a more secure financial future. In addition, within the military community, the woman's status is defined through her husband. If her husband leaves her and she is living on the base, she is given 30 days to find new accommodation. Further, the rigid hierarchical structure of the military can reduce her chances of receiving effective intervention, particularly if her husband is a high-ranking officer. If she calls for help, but the person sent to intervene in the incident is of lower rank than her husband, the batterer may refuse to take orders from the intervenor and may use his rank to threaten or intimidate the woman's potential helper. The risks of reporting are therefore very high, and the promise of help uncertain.

The military community in Canada is taking steps to deal sensitively and effectively with wife battering on its bases. A number of individual bases have developed programs to assist battered women. In Kingston, Ontario, there are safe homes on the base and a social worker who helps counsel and support battered women. The base in Halifax, Nova Scotia, is in the process of developing a resource centre and crisis line for battered women. And on the Penhold, Alberta base, the women's resource centre maintains ongoing liaison with community services potentially helpful to battered women.

Unfortunately, to date, all initiatives taken have been individual and local. Despite the efforts of the Organizational Society of Spouses of Military Members, there is still no commitment within the military to develop a nation-wide program network.

What Do We Know About The Batterers Of Women Who Stay In Shelters For Battered Women?

Many women stay with their husbands or partners because they feel sorry for them, because they believe the men "would have nothing without them", or because they assess the men to be "sick". While these beliefs have been interpreted by some service-providers, policy-makers, reporters, and members of the general public as empty rationalizations for staying, this study's statistics show that, in terms of life chances, the partners of the women in the sample may, in fact, have pretty dismal futures. Only 38% of the men worked for pay on a regular basis. Of the men who were working for pay, only 4% worked in professional occupations, 10% in white-collar jobs, and 27% in skilled blue-collar jobs. Fifty-nine per cent worked in unskilled blue-collar or "miscellaneous" jobs.

Sixty-one per cent of the men had **not** completed high school (a percentage just slightly lower than the proportion of women who had not completed high school). Twenty-one per cent had completed high school but had no specialized training, 11% had some college or technical school, 3% had a college or technical school diploma, 3% had an undergraduate university degree, and only 1% had a graduate degree.

Many of the men had other strikes against them as well. Twenty-five per cent of the men had criminal records. Of these, it was reported that 13% had been convicted of assault against their wives, 23% of assault against someone else, and 41% of other charges. The previous criminal charge was unknown for the remaining 23%. Fourteen per cent of the men were on probation. Twenty-four per cent of the women reported that their partners had a history of drug abuse and 52% reported that their partners had a history of alcohol abuse.

Although it is not possible to create psychological profiles of batterers from the data collected in this study, since batterers were not interviewed directly, other research studies paint a surprisingly consistent picture of the psychological make-up and related behaviour of batterers. These profiles also reinforce the women's perceptions that these men do have very little without them. Batterers are portrayed as men with very low self-esteem who are isolated and emotionally dependent on their partners.[24] These comments are not intended to whitewash the actions of batterers, nor are they intended to create excessive sympathy for these men. The same psychological profiles also indicate that batterers have a strong need to be in control and to see their lives as externally directed. As a result, they rarely, if ever, take responsibility for their actions, are extremely possessive, and lack empathy for others.[25] Nonetheless, these profiles once again remind us that the perceptions of battered women are not "just excuses" nor are they simply examples of "false consciousness". The realities of battered women must be taken seriously if we are truly to respond to the complexity of the problems and the many levels of victimization that exist in battering homes.

The Social Costs of Wife Battering

Public awareness is growing of the devastating costs of wife battering to battered women in terms of their physical and psychological health, as well as their life chances and overall quality of life. Although public attention has focussed primarily on the women and their suffering, increasingly — and often at the urging of battered women — policy-makers, academics, and people providing services to battered women are starting to look at the larger costs: the costs to the children in the family, the costs to the batterer, and the short- and long-term costs to society as a whole.

The Costs Of Wife Battering To The Women

Many of the psychological costs of wife battering for women are self-evident from the preceding descriptions of actual experiences. We know from studies and from the reports of the women themselves that battered women, after prolonged abuse, suffer from low self-esteem, they stop taking care of their appearance and health, they frequently blame themselves for the violence, and they feel overwhelming guilt. In addition, they are extremely isolated and may use alcohol and/or drugs to cope with the physical and emotional pain. Fourteen per cent of the women in this study's sample reported a history of alcohol dependency and 8% a history of drug abuse. There is no statistical information on the extent of the short- and long-term disabilities suffered by women, but anecdotal information suggests that these figures would be staggering.

In addition, previous research indicates that the costs for the women of trying to get outside help are often extremely high. Women have been made to feel even more guilty or insane for seeking help for a "non-problem", as defined by social workers, doctors, therapists, police, ministers, priests, rabbis, and even friends and family. Women are frequently left feeling dejected, rejected, and without hope. In some cases, seeking help can also increase the violence if the batterers find out about their efforts. And so, ironically, trying to find assistance can compound both the physical and psychological pain. These experiences of "secondary victimization" will be elaborated on in subsequent chapters of this book.

Greater use of violence by women may be another cost of wife battering. Women living in an environment where the threat of violence is always present may also come to believe that violence is the only way to get what they want, or they may be forced to use violence to defend themselves or their children. Most women who use violence feel extreme guilt as a result of these acts. Therefore, learning to use violence also "costs" the women. As one woman said:

> I'm no better than him, am I? I feel like I just can't take it any more and now I'm throwing things back at him when he gets mad. I dream of hurting him, sometimes of killing him. How can I fault him? I'm just like him.

Another woman added:

> I think I'm here [at a transition house] because I realized that I'd get to be just like him if I didn't get out. At first, I'd just take the beatings, when they didn't happen so often. But now, I don't want to lie down and take them. The last few times he's come at me, I've fought back. I even threatened him with a knife. The thing that really hurts is I've even started to slap my kids when they don't do what I want them to. I never thought I was a violent person. What's happening to me?

Transition-house workers also spoke of their increased realization that many of the women who come to them also deal with their anger and frustration through violence. This violence is most commonly directed at their children, but in more cases than were previously acknowledged, the women have been violent toward their husbands or partners, not simply as a reaction to their partner's violence, but sometimes even before any physical violence by their partners started. Violence in these cases is most commonly explained by the battered women as:

> . . . the only way I could cope with all the putdowns, the constant criticism. . . . I just felt so frustrated all the time, so worthless, I just started hitting him and throwing things in a blind rage.

The guilt and repugnance that some women feel as a result of their violence may lead them to turn their violent feelings against themselves. One anthropological study found that battered women in many cultures "are much more likely to kill themselves than women who have not experienced violence".[1]

The Costs To The Children

With an increased realization of the ripple effect which wife battering can have, and the expanding destruction and suffering which it can cause, has come a growing concern about the children who live in families where the women are battered. Certainly they must be considered when estimating the magnitude of the problem.

As described earlier in this report, 70% of the women who stayed in transition houses in 1985 came with children: 26% with one child, 27% with two, and 17% with three or more children. This means that, based on this study's previous estimates of the numbers of women who probably stayed in all 230 shelters across the country in 1985, at least 55,000 children stayed in crisis shelters which accepted battered women. As well, at least another 55,000 were the children of mothers who requested shelter but could not be accommodated. This means that, in 1985, at least 110,000 children were living in homes where the mother sought emergency shelter. Of these, the mothers of at least 86,000 children requested shelter explicitly because they were battered. Most of these children were young. Fifty-two per cent were under five years of age, 32% between five and ten, and 16% between 11 and 18.

The children of battered women not only live in houses fraught with the tension characteristic of abuse and may witness the abuse either surreptitiously or at the explicit demand of the batterer, they themselves are often victims of direct abuse as well. Seventy-four of the transition houses surveyed kept statistics on the relationship between wife battering and child abuse. These houses revealed that 26% of the women who stayed with them reported that their partners abused the children physically, 48% reported that their partners abused the children emotionally, and 7% reported that their partners abused the children sexually. Nine per cent of these abuses occurred daily, 28% weekly, 14% once or twice a month, 38% occurred occasionally, and 11% occurred **only** when the woman was beaten. In addition, research done in the United States indicates that, over time, as the battering continues, the children were increasingly likely to be assaulted. In one study, "children were involved in at least one of the beatings suffered by 54% of the women".[2]

Transition-house workers were also asked to estimate what proportion of the battered women who stayed with them abused their children. The statements which follow are not intended to heap further criticism on the battered women who stayed in transition houses, but rather, to reflect more accurately the potential social cost of wife battering for the families involved and for society as a whole.

Workers estimated that 8% of the women abused their children physically, 3% emotionally, and 1% sexually. In the cases where the women told workers that they abused their children, 12% reported that the abuse occurred daily, 16% reported weekly abuse, 8% reported abusing their children once or twice a month, 45% occasionally, and 20% whenever their husband beat them.

The overall rates of physical and emotional abuse by women were much lower than those reported for their partners. However, this study's research suggests that it is possible that these rates reflect an under-estimate, particularly of emotional abuse or neglect. Emotional abuse and neglect are largely subjectively defined, and women who are battered and who are themselves emotionally abused and neglected may not recognize their own neglect of their children. Certainly in informal conversations with transition-house workers, they frequently alluded to their concern with the poor parenting skills of many of the women and to the fact that they were too emotionally drained themselves to give their children adequate support and attention.

Further, when staff members were asked if they had witnessed any child abuse in the transition house, 56% of the house workers replied that they had and 6% stated that, while they had not witnessed overt abuse, they had witnessed neglect. Only 32 houses gave an estimate of how many cases of child abuse they witnessed in the past year and their estimates totalled only 119 cases, or 3.7 cases per house in 1985. Nonetheless, these findings suggest that the incidence of child abuse could be higher than this study's figures indicate. Children in homes where wife battering takes place are therefore at risk, not only of indirect emotional abuse through witnessing the incidents and living through the characteristic tension build-up to the abuse, but also of being victims of explicit child abuse.

The effects of wife battering on the children are also likely to be long-term. In particular, boys who grow up in a violent home are likely to have adjustment difficulties and to manifest behaviour problems.[3] Research also shows that they are more likely to be violent in their own marital families as adults.[4]

Transition-house workers in the present study said that they are seeing an increased number of very violent children accompanying their mothers to the shelters. This violence is also appearing at a younger age. At one time, most shelter workers believed that only adolescent boys were a real threat in terms of violence, but workers now cite cases of conscious and serious violence by boys and girls as young as five. Transition-house workers are also reporting more and more second-generation violence.

> What really gets me down is seeing the daughters of women we sheltered and counselled ten years ago coming to us as battered wives. Even when their mothers 'got their heads together' and got away from the violence, their daughters are repeating the pattern.

The intergenerational transfer of violence, or violence as learned behaviour, is well substantiated in the literature and will be dealt with in the next chapter of this book. There is also evidence that wife battering is related to the future criminality of the children, and particularly to criminal behaviour involving violence. For example, a 30-year longitudinal study found that reports of ongoing parental conflict and violence during childhood were

> . . . significantly predictive of serious adult personal crimes (e.g., assault, attempted rape, rape, attempted murder, kidnapping and murder), but were not predictive of serious adult property crimes.[5]

The Costs To The Batterer

Many readers will find it difficult to conceive of the batterer as an indirect victim of his own violence; however, wife battering also has costs for the man.

Counsellors for men who batter spoke of the low self-image and frustration of many of the men they deal with. Counsellors reported that these characteristics are generally chronic and were part of the men's psychological make-up long before the battering began. Partly to reduce these feelings, and in an often vain attempt to persuade their wives to return, some batterers sincerely want to stop the violence and feel their actions are wrong, but don't know how to deal with their anger in any other way. For these men, the cost of their violence is even lower self-esteem, greater frustration, and guilt. Men who are violent are chronically isolated and their battering can imprison them in this isolation even more as they become partners with their wives in keeping their terrible secret hidden.

Battering can also result in a criminal record. Men who are convicted can lose their jobs or have their future employment prospects limited.

Finally, as cited previously, men can also pay for their violence with their lives when their wives finally decide they've had enough.

One counsellor commented on the costs to the men:

> I don't want to go too far with this idea of the man as a poor soul. His problems don't come close to the problems he inflicts on his wife and children. But if we are going to get anywhere with our goal of preventing wife battering, we have to realize that these men, like their families, are victims of very narrowly defined social roles for men as well as women. Most battering men are battering for control. They've been told they have to be 'in control', to 'be responsible', all their lives, for their jobs and for their families. But responsibility scares most of these men to death. They are really little frightened boys at heart. And they've never been taught how to be responsible. They assume being responsible is being 'in charge'. They don't feel up to taking responsibility so they're just brutally bluffing their way through it. It's ironic, isn't it? They go out of control to be in control. But how can we teach these men in a few months to take responsibility for their violence when they are so frightened of any responsibility at all?

The Costs To Society

It is evident from this brief summary of the costs of violence to individual family members that the costs to society are high.

> Direct costs include the expense of protective services, such as police and child welfare. Indirect costs to taxpayers include medical, legal and social services to deal with victims and abusers. Citizens also pay a social cost in the form of children too traumatized to learn or develop normally, adult victims unable to function to their full potential and diminished quality of family and community life.[6]

The social costs are by far the most serious because they affect all Canadians and can frustrate our shared hopes for the future. As already shown through the discussions of the social costs to battered women, to their children, and to the batterers, the social costs of wife battering may include more violent crime, social disorganization, lack of trust, fear of others, and a general societal loss of control over social order. The human and social tragedy of wife battering is profound.

Financial costs, while a poor indicator of these ultimate costs, can help to put their magnitude in perspective. However, our ability to estimate financial costs is also extremely limited. There are no national statistics on the number of battered women who seek medical help or counselling for themselves, their partners, or their children. Nothing is known about the duration of counselling sought, even on a local level. Almost nothing is known about the length of hospital stays for physical injuries or psychological problems. In addition, it is not known how many battered women approach private lawyers for help, or how many battered women request court orders. It is not known how many children have to repeat grades at school or have special tutoring because of the stress they live with in their battering family, nor are the additional educational costs known. It is not known how many children are institutionalized by the corrections and child welfare systems as the direct or indirect result of battering. It is not known how many women and children are on welfare, or for how long, because they left a battering man. The list of what is not known in terms of the true magnitude of the social and financial costs could go on and on.

The little that is known, however, suggests that the financial costs of battering could be astronomical, as the following rough estimates of the cost of police intervention and the provision of emergency shelter for battered women reveal.

It has been estimated that, for all police services, "Canadian taxpayers and their governments in 1980 paid over 1.6 billion dollars".[7] While the years and geographic scope aren't comparable, a study done in Vancouver in 1975 found that more than one-third of all citizen requests for police service to the Vancouver Police Department during a six-month period in 1975 were for social service-related calls — a category which at that time included calls related to wife battering.[8] Although a reliable estimate of the proportion of police officers' time spent going to the scene on wife-battering calls is not available, and while there seems to be significant variation by location, most of the police officers interviewed for this study estimated that wife-battering calls accounted for about one-tenth of all so-called "domestic disturbance" and "social service calls", or about 3% of all requests for police service. However, at least in the past, it has been recognized that police have not gone to the scene of many such calls (although this situation is changing). Even if it is assumed that police respond to only about two-thirds of the calls that come in related to wife battering and it is assumed that actual police responses to wife-battering incidents would account for only about 2% of the police officers' time, this still means that, in 1980, Canadian taxpayers and their governments could have paid at least $32 million for police intervention in wife-battering cases and for related support and administrative services. The true cost at present is no doubt much higher. Informal reports suggest that police officers today are going to the scene of a greater proportion of wife-battering calls in many locations and, therefore, responses to requests for help from battered women account for a much larger part of police work. Nonetheless, even this extremely conservative figure emphasizes the high financial cost which is probably incurred as the result of only one form of help available for battered women.

The only other type of services for which there is available financial information are shelters which accept battered women. Only 106 (69%) of the shelters which responded to the written questionnaire for this study reported financial information. The total 1985 budgets for all 106 of these shelters was $18.3 million. On the basis of this figure, the total cost of operating all 230 transition houses and shelters across the country in 1985 can be estimated at approximately $40 million — a bargain to house, feed, and clothe more than 42,000 women and 55,000 children, and to hire staff to assist them and run the houses on a 24-hour basis, but nonetheless a significant dollar amount.

These figures should be treated as only indicators of the overwhelming financial costs of wife battering to society. It should be remembered that these estimates are based on figures from different years, and that, particularly, the police statistics are very rough estimates derived, in part, from anecdotal information. It should also be remembered that the majority of transition houses are being forced to pay their staff extremely low wages, that they have little or no money for house renovations, that they frequently must depend on donations of food and clothing to break even, and that, even with these extremely tight budgets, many of the houses are operating at a deficit. Nonetheless, these dollar estimates have been included to point out that the direct cost of wife battering to the Canadian taxpayers, for only two of the most obvious forms of crisis intervention, is at least $72 million per year.

As a society, we are beginning to realize that, if we are to reduce these heavy financial and social costs in the long term, we will have to escalate our costs for crisis, follow-up, and especially for preventive services in the short term. Policy-makers are increasingly realizing that any attempts to reduce current financial expenditures for services related to wife battering will undoubtedly increase long-term social costs and their concomitant long-term financial implications. Short-term expenditures will no doubt be high and may escalate for some time as preventive and follow-up services are put in place. However, as a society, we have now come to the conclusion that we cannot afford to ignore the problem and to incur the devastating social costs which would result for the long-term future. A drastic reduction of wife battering and an ultimate goal of prevention provide the only hope of reducing the burden of these social and monetary costs.

Through Women's Eyes:
Our Growing Understanding Of Wife Battering

The costs of wife battering to society and to the individuals directly and indirectly involved are undeniable. However, any solution which looks only at the costs is doomed to failure. Our growing knowledge of wife battering increasingly reveals that, by its very nature, because wife battering occurs in the family, because it often occurs in families with children, because it usually co-exists with a sexual relationship, it is surrounded not only by pain, but by hope — the hopes of the women, the hopes of the children, the hopes of the men, and the hopes of society.

The resulting complexities of wife battering have eluded society and have confounded attempts to really understand why wife battering exists, why it happens in some families and not in others, why some women stay and others leave. Increasingly, people concerned with wife battering in our society are feeling that current explanations are inadequate because they focus too often on the costs of battering and on the violence and pain, but not enough on the hopes and the love which are so often intertwined with the battering.

Unless society begins to grapple with this complexity and ambiguity, many service-providers fear that we will not be able to envisage services or a future in which battered women, their children, or the men who batter them will want to participate. Only by expanding our understanding to incorporate hope as well as pain and violence will we move beyond charity to true support and understanding for battered women and their children.

In this chapter, two of the most common "explanations" of why wife battering exists will be examined very briefly and supportive research for the growing understanding of the phenomenon will be cited. The "explanations" focussed on have been chosen because they are the most common and have provided the understanding upon which many of the current service responses are based. In an attempt to stretch our understanding of the adequacy of these explanations, some of the perspectives expressed by battered women about wife battering will be briefly presented. The women's perspectives on the violence and their reactions to it will be placed side by side with explanations which have grown to enhance service delivery to these women. These perspectives will begin to reveal some of the strengths and shortcomings of our knowledge of wife battering and, in particular, some of the shortcomings of our assumptions of how best to help battered women. These insights will be used to set the stage for the discussions of existing service delivery and plans for the future, which follow in subsequent chapters.

Explaining Why Wife Battering Exists

Although society is still far from understanding why wife battering exists, research studies and field experience have taught us much. It is now widely known that very few batterers conform to the easy-to-accept image of a mentally or physiologically deranged person,[1] although there have been physiological studies showing that many wife batterers do suffer from food allergies and abnormally low blood-sugar levels.[2] Further, it is known that, while alcohol or drug abuse may frequently be associated with wife battering,[3] and that unemployment or poverty, like other life stresses, including the women's pregnancy, can precipitate wife battering by lowering inhibitions against it, there is no conclusive evidence that any of these factors **cause** wife battering.[4]

As a result of the growing acceptance of this knowledge, it has become almost a cliché in writings and public presentations about wife battering to state that we are all potentially battered women or batterers. This statement is an important one to reiterate because it can never be stressed too often that research done over the past ten years has repeatedly shown that battered women and batterers can come from all walks of life. They may be working outside the home or in the home. They may be unemployed or have a steady job. They may be rich or poor, well-educated or illiterate, of any nationality or race, young or old, with or without children.

In fact, it is likely that both the fascination and the horror of wife battering for many Canadians lies in the growing recognition that, based on our expanding knowledge, wife battering can happen to any woman, and that there are no easily identifiable causes that can simply be eradicated or avoided.

Despite the difficulty of understanding wife battering, two major types of explanation have emerged over the last decade which have been widely used to respond to battered women, their children, and the men who batter them. Both of these types of explanation will be summarized briefly in the sections that follow.

Power-Based Theories

Theorists from this school have expanded our awareness that wife battering and violence against women generally are socially created. These theorists explain that violence against women is perpetuated by society's power structure which makes men dominant over women through the creation of separate and unequal roles for each gender. This dominance is also reinforced through institutional rules and structures based on male supremacy.

As staff members of the Women's Research Centre in Vancouver have so lucidly stated:

> Wife assault is a reality in our society because men have the socially ascribed authority to make the rules in marriage; and because violence against their wives is accepted in the eyes of society, as an appropriate instrument of control. The social and economic structure of marriage as an institution in which women are dependent on men, requires this assignment of authority to men.[5]

Power-based theories of wife battering emphasizing sex-based inequality and the patriarchal structure of society originated among feminists and have gained wide-spread acceptance by policy-makers and service-providers in this field. This explanation for the existence of wife battering appears in most writings on the subject and helps guide intervention techniques in most services for battered women, their partners, and their children.

Research on the power dynamics in battering families also asserts that power is a more highly valued commodity in battering families than in non-battering families. On the surface, this power may not always overtly rest with the man. However, research findings suggest that, in families where the woman is dominant in terms of decision-making or earning power, or where the woman is perceived to be superior in some other way, violence is often used by the man to shift the balance of power. So, for example, Adler found that, while both partners **might** use violence against one another in their relationships, "the use of violence by husbands was strongly associated with their dominance over their wives".[6] In other words, men tend to use violence to reassert their power and authority over their wives. Violence by women tends to be used most often as a means of protection or retaliation. Other researchers have also found that, when the husband had a less prestigious or lower-paying job, or a lower level of education than his wife, he was more likely "to use force and violence on family members than when the husband had the 'resource' of a higher-prestige occupation".[7] Further, many counsellors reported that many men resort to physical violence when they feel their wives are more articulate than they are. These men frequently complain that they can't win an argument with their wives, so they "shut them up" by the use of force.

These reports and the preceding research findings suggest that, in accordance with the tenets of the power-based theories, the acceptance and social reinforcement of violence in the family is a means to establish and to maintain the male in a dominant relationship over his wife.

Because male roles are socially created as dominant over female roles,

> Wife assault is as much a product of society's traditional attitudes toward domestic violence and toward women as it is a result of a violent assault by one man against his partner. Wife assault arises out of the socio-cultural belief that women are less important and less valuable than men and so are not entitled to equal status and respect. Thus central to the task of dealing with the problem of wife assault is the need to recognize that wife assault is a social problem experienced by many Canadian women each year rather than an isolated inter-personal problem between two particular spouses.[8]

Learning Theories

Learning theorists basically argue that witnessing or suffering violence teaches people to use violence to try to solve problems or deal with stress in their lives.[9] This argument is supported by research and by statements from service-providers which reveal that many batterers come from families where their mothers were battered and/or where they themselves were physically, sexually, or psychologically abused as children.[10] These findings are also corroborated by the statistics collected for this study. Sixty-one per cent of the partners of the women who stayed in transition houses in 1985 had been abused as children. Thirty-nine per cent of the battered women reported being physically abused as children, 24% reported being sexually abused, and 48% reported being emotionally abused as well. It is very noteworthy that, of the women who said they physically abused their own children, 69% said they had themselves been physically abused during their childhood.

Learning theorists also argue that the use of violence as a discipline tool can teach violence. In this vein, researchers report a "strong relationship between parental punishment and aggression" and suggest that,

> . . . increasing evidence indicates that a high price is paid for maintaining order in the family through violence. The norms that legitimate violence assure a family institution and a society characterized by violence for years to come.[11]

Learning theorists also frequently explain the perpetuation of violence, that is, the factor that turns isolated violent incidents into the **persistent** violence which characterizes wife battering, by stating that victims, friends, and society as a whole unintentionally reinforce the violence.

> Oftentimes their violence at home is inadvertently reinforced by what follows the
> battering episode. Many of these men have been experiencing mounting pressure and
> psychological tension. When they become violent, they experience a reduction in that
> physical tension and that drop in physiological arousal can be a powerful reinforcer.
> Sometimes there are other reinforcers as well. The victim after the beating, may indeed
> do as he insists; others may treat him with more respect and often he feels more in
> control. Even if he feels remorseful or guilty about her injuries he (and sometimes the
> victim herself) tends to blame the victim for `causing' him to `lose control'. He denies
> responsibility for the negative behaviour. Due to the tacit acceptance of family violence in
> society and to the lack of clear messages that his violent behaviour must stop, his violence
> is rarely punished.[12]

Finally, learning theorists also suggest that witnessing violence vicariously, as opposed to the direct witnessing of actual wife battering or the experience of child abuse, can teach some men to use violence in their lives whether within or outside the family. This particular tenet has created considerable concern about pornography as a teaching tool for violence.

> Pornography (especially as it is legitimized in mainstream T.V. shows, ads, movies,
> fashion layouts, etc.), socializes some men into thinking that the maltreatment of women
> is erotic, sexually desirable, desired by women and a necessary proof of virility.[13]

This belief was strongly supported by those transition-house workers who responded to the written questionnaire for this study. Unfortunately, 36% did not answer the question: "In your experience, is pornography related to an assaultive process?" or said they did not know how to answer it because they had never asked the women who came to them about the use of pornography by their partners and/or themselves. However, of those workers who did answer the question, 95% answered yes, that, in their experience, pornography is related to an assaultive process. While there is no conclusive evidence that pornography is related to assault, informally they spoke of their observations that men "copy" the violence depicted in the pornography in their relationships with their wives.

These two types of explanations, one based on the structure of power in our society, the other on learning theory, have clarified our understanding of wife battering, and have helped to guide intervention efforts. Yet many shelter workers and other service-providers lamented that, while these explanations seemed sufficiently clear in the past, they no longer seem to provide a complete enough explanation to expand our vision of what battered women and their children need and want. More and more service-providers also worried that "these theories that seem so clear to us just don't seem to ring true for too many of the women who come to us". Many service-providers believe that the answers are more complex. They believe that theories are needed which will make room for ambiguity and for the emotional bond between battered women and their partners who batter them.

"The answers" as to why wife battering exists are still far from being known. In order to better grapple with these persistent questions, and to attempt to incorporate some of the ambiguity of wife battering into an understanding of the problem, the perceptions of the battered women will be re-examined. In the next section, accounts of the battered women's understanding of wife battering will be presented. These accounts are not indirect critiques of the theories presented earlier, but are presented to complement these theories and to draw a fuller picture of our understanding of wife battering.

How Do Battered Women Understand The Battering?

Battered women understand the battering partly in terms of power in their families, but they speak of a shifting, ambiguous type of power. They spoke sometimes of feeling powerless against their husbands or partners. They also spoke of their power in the relationship and of the powerlessness of their partners. Many of them believe that, basically, women are more powerful than men in society, as the quote below elucidates:

> I can't quite make sense of what the women here [at the shelter] are saying about the patriarchal structure of society and about power and society making men more powerful and all that. When I was growing up, my mother was for sure stronger than my Dad in every way but physically. She was smarter, could do more, and more people respected her. I think it's the same with my husband and me. There's no way he's stronger than me, except physically, and that's why he hits me, because he feels so low.

Other women elaborated this theme in terms of a mother-son model of relationships between themselves and their partners.

> My husband and all the men I've ever known are like little boys. We're really like their mothers, underneath. Everyone keeps telling me to leave him; they say he'll destroy me. But they don't know how strong I am and how weak he is underneath.

Others spoke of the power they feel in the relationship.

> Sure I feel sorry for him. He says he would have nothing without me and the kids. I know he's pretty rotten sometimes. But he really needs me. I guess that's why I keep going back. He makes me feel important.

Still others spoke of their partners as victims or losers in society.

> You can talk about men being powerful in our society if you want, but you're not talking about my husband. My husband's never had any power in his whole life. He's never had a chance. He was born poor. He was born Indian. He's never felt better than anyone. He's never felt better than me. It's because he's so low that he hits me.

In these women's words, even if they don't represent the experiences of all battered women, is a perception that, although they don't like being hit, the batterers themselves make the women feel important, needed, even powerful within the relationship. In these women's words as well is a realization that many battered women are strong. Many battered women do not feel like powerless victims, and will not respond positively to services which treat them like victims instead of survivors.

These experiences remind us of the complexity of the realization of power in individual relationships. They also remind us that power in our society is not just gender-based; it is also class-, race-, and age-based.

Many battered women also understand battering as something that "got out of hand", as an extension (at least at the beginning) of a normal part of a normal relationship. Many battered women feel that their relationship started out much like any other relationship and, in fact, some emphasize that they feel they had an unusually loving, intense, and close relationship. In other words, they support the understanding that, over time, wife battering may take on a life of its own and become a pathological syndrome which reinforces or produces certain psychological and behavioural characteristics in both the batterer and the battered woman. However, they argue that, **at first**, wife battering often begins as actions at the extreme end of a continuum of behaviour which occurs in most relationships, particularly in relationships which have a sexual element.

It is important to acknowledge the apparently "normal" context within which most first acts of battering occur to understand why so many women do tolerate battering. This is certainly not to say that wife battering is therefore normal, acceptable, or excusable. Neither is it to diminish the horror of the sadistic and perverted violence suffered by women like Jane Stafford Hurshman, the much-publicized woman who killed her extremely abusive husband. She was initially found not guilty of the murder on the grounds of self-defence but then later, in an appeal decision, was sentenced to six months for manslaughter.[14] However, few cases are so clear-cut. Much of the professional and social ambivalence about wife battering and much of the continuing reticence to act, as well as much of the ineffectiveness of current solutions for many battered women, emanate from the fact that few batterers are clinically definable as sadists and not all women endure the extreme brutalization that Jane Hurshman suffered. The psychological suffering that other battered women experience may be equally intense, but the nature of the brutality is not as clear and the batterer not so obviously violent in every facet of his life as was Jane's husband.

We can understand better what battered women are saying if we consider the nature of intimate relationships in our society. Intimate relationships, by definition, generate a wide range of emotions and responses. The image of romantic love idealized in our society is characterized by highs and lows. Being "in love" is living "on the edge", participating in a kind of emotional aerobics. Our society highly values energy and "living on the edge". The socially accepted use of drugs, the preoccupation with "having it all", with creative stress, the fitness craze, and even our social addiction to soap operas and violent television shows emphasize high energy and intense emotional highs and lows.

For these reasons, wife battering at the outset is often difficult, if not impossible, to prevent, or even to identify, because some violence (rough sexual play and psychological games intended to elicit jealousy) is intertwined with our whole ideal of "being in love" (isolation and possessiveness). In different socio-economic groups, this violence may be more or less psychological, or more or less physical, but the romantic desire to be alone together in a private world and the desire to have constant physical contact with your loved one are simply the "positive" faces of the jealousy and isolation which become part of most wife-battering experiences.

Battered women often talk of the intensity of their love for the batterer. Throughout this study, many battered women made the following kinds of statements: "I've never had better sex with anyone", "I just can't believe he'd hit me. I know he really loves me as much as I love him", "No one's ever loved me the way he does". Battered women also speak of the highs and lows of the relationship:

> You know, life was a roller-coaster with Bill. In the end, of course, that became unbearable — all the tension. But in the beginning, it was just so thrilling. I never wanted to come down.

Many battered women, like so many people in our society, are guilty of no greater "weakness" than being in love with being in love. It's their attempt to stay in love, to retain an idealized vision of their partner, that often prevents many battered women from realizing that they are being battered until the battering has become a part of life.

Women who are battered do not generally define themselves as battered women the first time they are battered. In fact, because wife battering includes emotional, verbal, and financial battering, as well as physical and sexual battering, it may be very difficult to define when the first incident actually occurred, either for the battered woman, or for an outsider. This ambivalence is evident in the words battered women use to describe their early experiences with the batterer. It is not uncommon for battered women to say:

I was flattered by his jealousy at first — I thought it meant he loved me.

He said he would rather stay home, just with me, than go out with friends. I loved the attention and closeness at first. I thought he was the most romantic man in the world.

Even the first case of physical abuse is not always clear-cut. In many cases, the woman is "just pushed". While pushing can result in very severe injuries, depending on the location of the push — down the stairs, over a chair, into a pot of boiling water on the stove, etc. — the push itself can be easily re-interpreted by the batterer and by the woman who is battered as something very minor. The results of the push (a fall down a set of stairs, a scalding, etc.) can be viewed as an accident, rather than as a direct result of the push. Again, battered women speak of this ambiguity:

I was just baffled the first time he hit me. It wasn't really a hit you know, not like a punch or even a slap, he just pushed me really hard. I broke an arm, but it was from falling backward over a chair, not from his push.

Another woman's statement mirrors these sentiments:

I couldn't believe my husband had hit me. I just kept asking, is this the same man who loves me so much that he can't stand it if another man talks to me? It was really easy for me to accept his explanation that he'd had a hard day at work and a little too much to drink. I couldn't see anything else without having to ask if he really did love me, and that was just too painful. It wasn't until much later, years of violence later, that I could see that the way he loved me — his jealousy, his possessiveness — were also part of the violence.

Is this form of "illogic" really so different from the logic used in many relationships, which we call compromising, or "forgiving and forgetting", when it does not involve identifiable or reported violence?

One real problem is that, in many homes, battering begins with a relatively minor incident, at least in terms of the severity of the violence. Another real problem is that, while violence almost always escalates, it may not do so in many homes for months or even years. The result is that women accept the violence as an unpleasant but bearable part of life, given the good things about the relationships (and most battering relationships do still provide sporadic periods of closeness during the honeymoon phases of the violence, even if these become shorter and less frequent as the violence progresses), until they are so enmeshed in the cycle of violence and so demoralized and trapped by it that they can't "just leave".

Many service-providers, and even women who have been battered, counsel that leaving or calling the police "the first time it happens" is the most effective way to ensure that it won't happen again. However, given that it may be hard to define "that first incident", especially since definitions of intolerable violence are culturally relative and since most women have a lot of emotional and practical investment in their relationships, this advice frequently has an unreal, hollow ring to it.

In many battering relationships, certainly in the early stages of the battering, it is the **persistence** of the violence, not always the objectively definable, evident severity which characterizes the violence as battering and separates it from similar isolated episodes of psychological or physical violence in non-battering relationships.

American author Susan Schechter points to the "normalcy" of the early reactions of most battered women, at least in terms of the current "rules" of intimate relationships, in her comment: "Most people feel ambivalent when ending a long-term relationship. Major change is always difficult, often slowly and haltingly undertaken".[15]

There is growing evidence that leaving provides little or no guarantee that the battering will stop and may even escalate the violence. In the present study, 12% of the women were separated or divorced. Anecdotal information suggests that the majority of these women were battered by their ex-husbands, some by new partners. Michael Smith, in his telephone survey of 315 Toronto women, found that, while the rate of abuse for all women interviewed was 18.1%, for women who were separated or divorced, the rate jumped to 42.6%.[16] Similarly, a study done in London, Ontario, to determine the characteristics of women who came to the London Battered Women's Advocacy Clinic found that, even long after the divorce is finalized, the woman is still in danger. Of those women who used the clinic and were divorced, two-thirds had been divorced between six and ten years and yet were still being battered by their ex-husbands.[17] The divorced population in the London sample is small and so these results must be used with caution. Nonetheless, these figures strikingly corroborate this study's finding that separation and divorce do not provide reliable protection. Many battering men share the sentiment expressed by one man to his wife: "You are my wife. You are mine forever and no piece of paper will ever change that fact."

The reactions of most battered women, not only at the beginning of the battering, but throughout their battering experiences, are often strong and logical and must be seen and treated this way if we are to reach out to battered women and provide services for them which "ring true", will be helpful, and will be used by a greater number of battered women. It is easy as an outsider providing an alternative to violence to scoff at, or be discouraged by, the astonished response of many women to the suggestion that they leave their violent husbands: "But he's my husband, and the father of my children. . . . I can't just abandon him". It's easy from an outside vantage point which assumes that the batterer, the battered wife, their relationship, or all three are defective, to dismiss as misguided sentiment the woman's heroic attempts to keep her marriage together, to keep her children from knowing about the violence, to insist that she loves her husband. The woman's actions and statements are easy to dismiss as long as we assume that the battered woman, along with her partner and their relationship, are somehow basically different from us and from non-battering relationships, not just in terms of the violence, but in terms of the basic personality of the man and woman and in terms of the initial quality of the relationship.

However, as this study has established repeatedly, research shows that battered women do not fit one psychological or socio-economic mould. Few common characteristics which are not the direct result of the battering have been cited. In fact, in the one study known to the author where the personality traits of battered women **before** the violence were discussed, Lenore Walker found that women who are battered "perceive themselves as more liberal than most" in their relationships with men[18] — a far cry from the stereotype of the battered woman as a traditional woman totally oppressed by, and dependent on, her partner.

It is **after** prolonged battering, as a result of the battering, that battered women begin to display certain similar psychological traits. After prolonged battering, women suffer from low self-esteem and isolation. They are emotionally dependent on the batterer, are compliant, feel guilty, and blame themselves for the violence, and yet demonstrate great loyalty to the batterer. Not only do they want the relationship to continue, they state that they are staying for the sake of the family. They believe the batterers' promises to change and they frequently believe that the violence would stop if only their partners would get the one lucky break they've always wanted.[19]

To truly understand the women who are battered and what they want, as well as the batterers and what they want, it is important to erase the assumption that battered women are somehow intrinsically different from non-battered women. To understand the actions and perceptions of battered women, it is important to think of how we all act in relationships, what we want, and the extent to which many of us will go to preserve a relationship. As one shelter worker poignantly said:

> Relationships are hard to come by. Sure we should help women know that they have worth outside their marriages, but a marriage isn't just status and a piece of paper . . . it's warmth, belonging, and a future. Battered women don't always get these good things out of their relationships, but most of them did in the beginning, and they just keep hoping it will come back. People will go to any lengths to feel loved, and love is not just waiting around the next corner for every battered woman who leaves her batterer.

Even the majority of women who report the violence do so out of hope — that, by reporting the violence, she and her partner will be helped to return to their pre-violent state. Of course, she may also hope that she will get attention and be listened to because she is frequently lonely and unnurtured as a result of the isolation most batterers impose on their victims. She may also hope he will be punished or "get his just deserts". But behind it all, she often just wants them to be happy again. The importance of these hopes should not be diminished.

Unfortunately, as will be demonstrated in subsequent chapters, many of the services and initiatives which have been created for battered women and for their partners have been built on the assumption, either consciously or unconsciously, that the relationship is not worth saving and ignore or belittle the woman's hopes to save and rekindle it. The hope of the service-providers is most often to save or protect the woman as an individual or to help or change the batterer as an individual in some way. This well-intentioned, institutional hope often buries the woman's pleas for a different kind of help. It is this very basic discrepancy between the battered woman's hopes and the hopes of the service-providers which renders so many of the initiatives taken inappropriate and frustrating for the women who are battered and which contribute to the burnout and despair of the sincere and hopeful people who try to help the women, their children, and their partners.

In the following chapters, society's progress in developing services to meet the needs of battered women will be acknowledged. However, throughout the presentations of these great strides forward will be an assessment of how well the services are addressing the needs and hopes of battered women. In addition, there will be an assessment of how closely they are responding to the directions suggested by shelter workers — the women who have for so long provided the majority of services for battered women and their children in Canada.

By returning constantly to the women's perspectives in order to evaluate progress, an attempt will be made to distill that vision of the future already emerging through existing and planned initiatives which will respond most sensitively to the needs of the widest number and range of battered women in Canada, and which will best help realize the shared hope of battered women, shelter workers, and all Canadians of preventing wife battering in this country.

A Realistic Model of Prevention:

Building a Network of Support

Sheltering

Overview

Profound changes have taken place in the shelter movement in Canada over the past seven years. These changes have originated in two separate, complementary goals and hopes among shelter workers.

The first is the hope of community workers to ensure that sheltering options available to battered women provide more than inexpensive emergency housing for women who live in and around urban centres and who want to escape a violent partner. Certainly, transition-house workers have always provided informal or formal counselling and support in addition to safe accommodation, even if they haven't had adequate resources to support these additional services. However, increased knowledge of the needs of battered women, of the dearth of other services available in the community to meet the range of their needs, and of the tenacity of violence in our culture have stimulated shelter workers (and to a lesser extent, other front-line service-providers as well as policy-makers) to increase their efforts to expand the range of services provided to more fully meet the needs of battered women and their children. This expanded vision emanates from a widespread concern to work toward the prevention of violence and so to move beyond charity and a narrow crisis response.

Accordingly, there has been a growth of "sheltering options". The number of sheltering experiments which provide medium- and longer-term housing through "second-stage housing" has increased, there continues to be a great interest in finding viable sheltering and service alternatives for women who live in rural and isolated areas and, increasingly, shelters are now able to include support, advocacy, and sometimes preventive services.

The second goal which has coloured the progress in sheltering services over the past seven years is the complementary hope of reaching more women and more types of women. Many transition houses are attempting to reach out to the entire range of battered women in their community. This includes: the provision of services for middle- and upper-income as well as low-income women; support, not only for those women who decide to leave their partner, but also for those women who wish to return to or remain with their partners; and services which will feel appropriate and supportive to aboriginal women, immigrant women, disabled women, and women from a variety of religious backgrounds.

These two complementary goals together create a promising vision of expanded services and opportunities which closely mirror the hopes and realities of the battered women they serve. However, they have developed in tandem with two obstacles which frequently contradict this vision of expansion. The first is the concern of most politicians to cut costs within a climate of overall financial restraint and the enduring reality of competing priorities. Financial constraints have created enormous pressure on many front-line workers, particularly in British Columbia and most of the Atlantic provinces, to do more for less, even though transition houses have been operating on shoestring budgets. The second obstacle is the current political fashion of emphasizing program autonomy, with the accompanying reluctance of the federal and many provincial/territorial governments to expand the government-supported social welfare service net. This reluctance has been experienced by shelter workers most concretely as a hesitancy to give long-term government financial support to agencies and programs defined as dealing with social welfare.

As a result, attempts by front-line workers to fulfil their hopes of expanding services have coincided with the rhetoric of restraint and self-sufficiency to create many of the changes and the problems seen in sheltering services today.

Progress/Change In Sheltering Initiatives

Despite these obstacles, significant progress has been made over the past seven years in the provision of sheltering alternatives to meet the needs of battered women. These gains have been primarily the result of tenacious and energetic efforts on the part of shelter workers. However, it should be added that, in some locations, these gains have been significantly facilitated by the work of policy-makers and government officials who share the belief that sheltering options for battered women are important, that the perpetuation of wife battering has far-reaching implications for our society, and that the unique needs of battered women and front-line service-providers point to the poverty of the funding formulae developed within the rhetoric of restraint. Many government officials are also looking for imaginative ways in which services can be expanded without signifi-cantly increasing long-term costs to governments. The successes detailed below show that communication between front-line workers and government officials is improving in many locations, that some government officials are very open to the visions of expanded services being promoted by shelter workers and other advocates for battered women, and that the time may be ripe for service-providers to share their hopes for the future with policy-makers at the federal, provincial/territorial, and municipal levels.

The Number Of Shelters Has Tripled

At the time of writing, there were 230 shelters which accepted battered women across Canada, compared to 71 shelters in 1979. According to the statistics collected through the written questionnaire sent out to shelter workers in this study, 44% of these shelters were interval or transition houses **only** for battered women and their children. Thirty-seven per cent were transition houses **primarily** for battered women and their children but which also accepted women experiencing other types of crises sparked by the need for housing, drug or alcohol dependency, mental health problems, and pregnancy or family problems other than wife battering or child abuse. Eleven per cent were more general emergency or crisis shelters which accepted battered women and other women in crisis, but which did not necessarily give priority to battered women; 3% of the shelters identified themselves as "safe-house networks", that is, networks of private homes which provided very short-term accommodation for several days for battered women; 2% were second-stage alternatives which provided medium-term housing, usually for up to a year; and 3% were simply designated as "other". Since not all shelters across Canada responded to the written questionnaire, this breakdown is indicative only of the range of available sheltering options. Statistics provided by the National

Clearinghouse on Family Violence are similar. Clearinghouse staff estimated that, at the time this report was being written, there were 208 transition houses or crisis shelters, about a dozen safe-house networks, and ten second-stage sheltering alternatives in nine urban centres.

The rapid growth in the number of shelters across Canada reflects increased community awareness of wife battering, extraordinary efforts by community and shelter workers, and increased government financial and philosophical support of services related to wife battering.

Government Support Of Sheltering Options Has Grown

■ Government Support For Crisis Shelters Has Increased

While there is currently a general goal in most governments to reduce government expenditures, particularly in the support of services which fall under the rubric "social services", some provinces have either initiated or are currently studying ways to provide a stable and flexible funding base which will meet the crisis needs of battered women and which will respond to the budget and planning problems faced by shelters. More and more provinces/territories are moving to better funding arrangements with shelters where they agree to provide funding based upon 100% occupancy of the house, regardless of the actual number of women staying in the house. This type of agreement allows shelter workers to continue regular programming despite a periodic dip in residency. Other provinces/ territories have agreed to give the shelters funding on a quarterly rather than a monthly basis, to balance seasonal trends in occupancy.

In addition, a preferred-rate mortgage financing arrangement for emergency shelters has been considered in some areas and some provinces/territories have also provided specified amounts of money to front-line workers and community groups who are trying to start new shelters.

About half of the shelters in Canada are now funded under the "Homes for Special Care" provisions of the Canada Assistance Plan (CAP). This means that the operational costs, including mortgage costs, counselling, information, referral, and child-care services, are rolled up into one sum which is cost-shared on a 50-50 basis with the federal government. Under this arrangement, the provincial or territorial government determines whether a particular home will receive funding; it then requests listing for the home with CAP and submits claims for cost-sharing. An advantage of this arrangement is that the provincial government can also decide to administer a short-form needs test and to by-pass the cumbersome documentation required to list the woman herself for social assistance.

Despite these very significant advances, there are still several crisis shelters which have no funding at all; others only receive funds to cover room and board and not for support services. These shelters are forced to budget from month to month with no assurance of a steady supply of funds. Some provinces/territories do not seek to list any of their homes under the "Homes for Special Care" provisions of CAP. Instead, they base their funding arrangements with the houses on "per diems" which stipulate that, if the shelter is to receive funding to help serve a woman who wants to stay at a shelter, that woman must be a person in need of social assistance. If the woman is found to be "in need" according to the social assistance criteria, then the shelter will be paid the amount of social assistance to which she is entitled, for providing her room and board.

The disadvantages of this method of payment have been detailed by battered women and their advocates in many speeches, articles, books, and pamphlets produced throughout this decade. Under this funding arrangement, lengthy forms must be completed to prove that the woman is in need, to identify what other sources of income she might have, and to identify all of her dependants. Battered women and their advocates find this approach demeaning, inappropriate, and unnecessarily time-consuming, and have strong fears about the loss of confidentiality and the stigmatizing of battered women which it perpetuates. In addition, under this arrangement, because the money is allotted, not for house operations, but for the number of "needy" women staying in the house (which can vary), it is also more difficult for shelter workers to plan and fund a flexible, in-house program for counselling, children's services, outreach, and follow-up programs.

■ Governments Are Interested In Supporting Safe Homes And Other Rural Alternatives

Safe homes and/or safe-home networks existed in seven provinces and both territories at the time of writing — Newfoundland (in Labrador), Nova Scotia, Ontario, Manitoba, Saskatchewan, Alberta, British Columbia, the Yukon, and the Northwest Territories. Safe homes are private homes where the residents have agreed to take in battered women and their children on a very temporary basis until they can be transported to a transition house, to another more secure residence, or to the home of a friend or relative.

A number of provinces are also experimenting with other options to protect and support battered women in rural areas. For example, Ontario has developed multipurpose family resource services with a residential component. Saskatchewan has implemented a pilot project in a rural location using a day centre to serve women staying in a wide network of safe homes. In this option, women in rural areas who cannot be transported to a transition house or who do not wish to leave the area, can stay at a safe home for the night, but each day are driven to the day centre for counselling, emotional support, referrals, and advice about their options. The day centre maintains links with the closest transition houses. In addition, training and per diem payments are provided for safe-house operators. Saskatchewan has also established six family crisis centres in rural areas of the province to coordinate existing community-based resources. In Prince Edward Island, a pilot project has been funded by the federal Solicitor General to explore the feasibility of a comprehensive program in a rural area combining emergency shelter, self-help support groups, a toll-free crisis line, a network of volunteer intervenors and community contacts, and therapeutic counselling groups for men who batter.

■ Government Support Is Also Growing, But More Slowly, For Second-Stage Housing Alternatives

Direct government funding and/or subsidized housing through the Canada Mortgage and Housing Corporation (CMHC) has been provided to support most of the second-stage housing which currently exists. Second-stage housing provides an interim residence for battered women and their children between their stay at the transition house and setting up their own homes. Most transition houses can only accommodate women and their children for a few weeks and many battered women who choose not to return to their partners do not feel ready to live on their own after their brief transition-house stay. However, they need somewhere to stay where they will still receive the counselling and support characteristic of their transition-house experience; second-stage houses have been created to meet this need. It should be noted that not all these second-stage housing alternatives are separate houses or apartment complexes accommodating only battered women and their children. Second-stage housing can also be available as one or more designated units in an apartment building or as part of a mixed development for battered women and other low-income single women. These units are usually equipped with special security devices to help ensure the safety of the residents.

■ Governments Are Beginning To Provide More Affordable Long-Term Housing For Battered Women And Their Children

Ontario has introduced a new category on its priority rating form for subsidized housing which allows points to applicants who have been forced to live in emergency accommodations. It is also generally agreed by government officials that more accessible, affordable long-term housing with community support services is essential for battered women. CMHC is exploring ways to facilitate battered women's access to subsidized housing.

- Some Governments Are Also Supporting Specialized Shelters For Aboriginal And Immigrant Women

At least two provincial governments — Ontario and Manitoba — have supported urgings by front-line workers to create separate shelters for aboriginal women. In Toronto, there is also a shelter specifically for immigrant women. In several provinces, the hiring of aboriginal staff is stressed, and in areas with a high concentration of immigrants, shelters are also encouraged to hire staff who reflect the cultural/language mix of the community. Front-line workers in other provinces, including Saskatchewan and Alberta, are trying to encourage their provincial governments to provide additional funding for separate services, and/or the hiring of workers for existing programs, to better meet the special needs of aboriginal and/or immigrant women.

Community Support Has Increased Considerably

All house workers interviewed for this study spoke of the pronounced increase in community involvement in, and commitment to, resolving the issue of wife battering. Increased support seemed to be particularly pronounced in isolated areas in northern Alberta, in some traditional rural areas in Saskatchewan and Prince Edward Island, and in urban areas where a perceived "community" exists, for example, parts of Vancouver and Toronto. Some transition houses have even adopted the slogan for public education presentations: "Wife battering is not just a woman's issue — it is a community issue".

Community support has financially benefitted houses in some locations. On average, 5% of the budgets of transition houses was provided by community agencies (e.g., Rotary and Kiwanis clubs) and another 10% through private donations from community members. In addition, 79% of the communities provided non-monetary support to crisis shelters. Eighty-five per cent of the shelters received some free food, 56% received clothing, and 49% received furniture and other household items. Community members and businesses also donated free labour, entertainment vouchers, free taxi rides, and office supplies. One house in Calgary was even able to pay for much of a new shelter through community support by soliciting community services to "adopt a room", that is, to pay for the building and furnishing of one room in the house.

Community involvement has also benefitted shelters and battered women in terms of easing their liaisons with additional needed services. Other aspects of the wider community involvement in helping to address the problem of wife battering will be elaborated on in a later chapter.

Shelters Have Greater Stability

- Many Shelters Have Received Some Increase In Funding

Similar to the growth in community concern, the growth in government concern with the problems of battered women has benefitted shelters financially as well, even though funding problems still plague many houses. On average, shelters reported an annual operating budget of $172,597, and 67% said that their annual operating budget was higher in 1985 than in 1984. This increase still has not provided sufficient funds for such a critical service. This positive news should be placed in the perspective of the funding problems described in other sections of this chapter.

- Many Houses Now Benefit From Reduced-Rate Mortgages And Rents

Fifty-eight per cent of the shelter workers who responded to the questionnaire reported that they were buying their house and more than 80% of these houses had a CMHC reduced-rate mortgage. In addition, almost half of the houses which were renting said they would **not** buy their houses if they had the opportunity because their rents were so low. Several houses said that, in effect, the use of the house had been donated to them and they were simply paying a nominal rent.

- Houses Are Not Having To Close Their Doors As Often

The increased stability of funding, combined with community support, is reflected in an apparent increase in the longevity of shelters in Canada. Half of the shelters responding to the written questionnaire in this study had been in operation more than five years, and 68% had been in operation more than three years. In fact, the average time shelters responding to this study's questionnaire had been in operation was six and one-third years. However, it should be noted that, since this survey did not follow shelters over a long time span, the houses which have been forced to close their doors over the past seven years have not been identified. Therefore, this survey does tend to over-represent shelters which have been successful at keeping their doors open to battered women and their children.

- Almost All Houses Are Now Open 24 Hours, Seven Days A Week

Improvements in funding and increased experience among shelter coordinators have helped ensure that almost all houses (98%, according to the written questionnaire for this study) are now open on a 24-hour basis seven days a week.

The Philosophies And Goals Of Shelters Have Changed

Increased community and government support has been both a facilitator and a product of changes in philosophy among many shelter workers, as the descriptions below suggest.

- Shelters Emphasize Service Delivery

Shelter workers reported an increased concern to ensure that they were truly meeting the needs of a wide range of women in their communities, whether or not these needs meshed with workers' expectations. As one worker said:

> Within each woman there is an answer. It may not be an answer I would choose, but we have to respect her life and her decisions. We've come to realize that many of the options we talk about — retraining, good jobs, careers — are realistic primarily for young, urban, middle-class women.

Other workers spoke of a change in the motivating force for staff in their houses. One worker explained:

> At one time it was politics, an ideology of empowerment and feminism that held us together and kept us going. Now we focus more on the service, the quality of the service, and how well it meets the needs of the women. We haven't given up our feminist ideals, but we feel we have to provide a really professional service to gain the trust and support of battered women and of the community.

Another worker echoed this theme:

> We need feminist ideals to understand and deal with wife battering, but now we realize that we are first and foremost a social service agency. Now we ask what the women really need. . . . We can't use battered women to fight political battles. . . . When politicization is an issue, the women often lose.

This assessment of changes in goals and philosophies, which has led to a stress on service delivery while retaining feminist ideals, appears to be widespread. Seventy-six per cent of the houses reported that their primary goal was to provide safe shelter, but 47% of these houses still included empowerment of women as one of their three major goals. Forty-three per cent of the houses also reported that they had made a major change in the organization or goals of their houses since they first opened. Of these, one-quarter said they now provided broader, more professional services, and another 25% said they had increased the number of specialized staff.

Some workers spoke of the difficulties of meshing a commitment to feminist ideals with a genuine desire to provide a service.

> We try to remember that we are dealing with some very traditional women with very traditional values. Even if we want exactly what the woman wants, if we don't speak her language, we may lose her trust.

■ Shelter Workers Increasingly Consider The Whole Family

Shelter workers also spoke of a shift in attitude toward the batterer and toward the family.

> When we first started this house I guess in retrospect some of us just assumed that if a woman came to us, she must want to leave her husband. We also thought that if she didn't want to leave, she should because no woman should live with brutality. We didn't want to make decisions for her, to force her to do anything she didn't want to do. We just wanted what was best for her. Most of us have softened our position on the men and we've done it for the sake of the women — to be closer to them emotionally. We now know that most of the women we see aren't ready to leave their husbands and may never want to leave. We've tried to see the men through slightly more sympathetic eyes, in the way their wives see them. We've tried to emphasize that we're not out to destroy families. We want to save families, or at least those that can come to exist without violence, but above all, we want to encourage women to be decisive.

■ Relationships Among Shelters Have Improved

One major benefit of these shifts in philosophy, in addition to the easier acceptance of transition houses by most governments and communities, is the improved relationships among houses. In the late 1970s and early 1980s, shelters were mainly of two types: those started by feminist groups, and those started by women who had been active in services offered by their churches and who started their shelters with initial church backing or ongoing support.

The changing goals and philosophies of shelters have brought these two types of houses closer together and have given workers from houses enough commonality to gain a unified voice in some provinces and territories. Since 1979, the shelters in eight provinces and one territory have created provincial/territorial associations of transition houses and/or shelters to increase the coordination and communication among transition houses and to strengthen the power of transition houses in realizing their goals.

Many church-based houses have become more secular and more focussed on the particular problems of battered women. Eleven per cent of these houses explicitly said they had become more feminist. Conversely, most of the houses which saw themselves as feminist, although they have not abandoned their feminist convictions, had made concessions in their terminology, public explanation and education of the issue, and counselling of battered women to ensure that they were more in tune with the women in their communities.

■ Many Shelters Have Changed Their Funding Philosophy To Maximize Sources Of Support Available To Them

The desire to be more a part of the community in order to serve women better also has manifested itself in a shift away from the hesitancy of some houses in the late 1970s to accept money from agencies which did not share the philosophical orientation of house workers. Most houses currently accept money or support from a variety of government and community sources, and see broad-based fundraising as a method of increasing public awareness and ensuring greater financial autonomy.

Major Changes In Staffing Have Taken Place

These changes in philosophy are reflected in a change in the type of staff hired and the organization of the staff in shelters.

■ A Shift From Collectives To A Hierarchical Staff Organization

The model of egalitarian collectives — in which there is no formal hierarchy established, but instead action is based on sharing, dialogue, and cooperation — was prominent in feminist-oriented houses in the 1970s, but has become less common. Currently the collectives which do exist are concentrated in Quebec, with a few in British Columbia and Ontario. However, 84% of the shelters across the country reported having a team leader or director. Eleven per cent of the houses reported consciously shifting their organization from a collective to a hierarchical structure. While this does not seem like a large proportion, it should be remembered that few houses that started **after** 1980 **began** with a collective orientation. Since there were only 71 houses in existence in 1979, and not more than half of these houses were collectives, this means that the majority of houses which began as collectives are now based on a more hierarchical model with more distinct definitions of duties.

It is not uncommon for a house to have at least a director, several crisis staff for dealing with the battered women, a child-care worker, and an administrative officer. In addition, several houses have an assistant director, a maintenance worker, a public relations worker, a volunteer coordinator, and a housekeeper or cook. This is a pronounced change from the model where each staff member did "anything and everything". While the division of labour in most houses is not as discrete as these separate positions would suggest, nonetheless staff are generally assigned specific duties.

■ A Growing Emphasis On Professionalism Has Emerged

Along with a shift in structure toward clearer task divisions has come a move toward the hiring of staff with more formal educational credentials and professional qualifications. Many workers spoke of the dedication of the workers in their houses, and of the fact that the workers were highly qualified and could earn much more than they were earning in the shelter if they were willing to take jobs unrelated to wife battering. Eighty per cent of the house workers responding to the written questionnaire said that they felt the staff in their house were underpaid in terms of their education, and 90% said their staff were underpaid in relation to their experience. This emphasis on education is a major change from the earlier concern of the houses to avoid "professionals" because the services they represent were frequently seen as perpetuating the victimization of the women, or even imposing a kind of secondary victimization through rules, delays, and perspectives which are part of the ideology or structure of mainstream health, social, and legal services.

Many workers welcome this change because it has tended to increase the credibility of shelter staff in the community and has made the creation of links with other professional agencies easier. However, others spoke of the dangers of domination by professionals in what was once a dedicated grass-roots movement. As one worker who had worked in the same shelter for almost ten years explained:

> There has to be change. I accept that. That's good. But it does worry me some when I see other women start work here who know so much less about the suffering of battered women than I do and the other "old-timers". They've never been battered. They don't have the years of experience talking to battered women and counselling them that we have. They can get the experience, of course, but I'm afraid that most of them just want

to use this job as a stepping-stone to a better job. I don't mean to be critical of them. They do care about battered women, and why shouldn't they be thinking about a career that pays them well — for sure they're not going to get that here. But once people like me are gone, will there still be enough drive in the workers who see themselves first as professional social workers, psychologists or whatever, and as transition-house workers only after that, to continue to fight for the rights and needs of battered women and all women? Will they still have the commitment to this issue to keep the transition houses open?

■ Increased Experimentation With Different Types Of Staff

Many houses are now hiring some male staff. Several houses reported consciously seeking out male staff to coordinate children's programs or to assist with child care. Men are also used as casual staff or volunteers by some houses to provide transportation and do house maintenance work.

In addition, funding problems, combined with an expanded attempt to reach out to the community, have led many houses to experiment with the use of ''fine-option'' workers to help supplement their staff. Fine-option workers are people who have been convicted of a crime and sentenced to do a certain number of hours of community work. They can be placed to work in the transition house by the courts, as part of their sentence, at the request of the transition house. These workers have generally been used to help with house maintenance, heavy cleaning, and secretarial work. Most houses reported a good experience with this program.

■ Boards Of Directors Have Taken On A New Role In Shelters

The increased academic qualifications of shelter workers and the shift to hierarchical structures has been accompanied or perhaps preceded by the changing composition of the boards of directors for many shelters.

Funding for almost all houses contacted was dependent on the house having a board of directors, or an organizing committee which might have staff members on it, but which is mainly separate from the staff. This funding stipulation, defined by provincial/territorial government departments responsible for funding transition houses, also existed in the late 1970s. However, the tenor of the board and its relationship to shelter staff has changed dramatically.

Most boards seven years ago were essentially extensions of the staff and were made up of friends of the staff and other community members who shared the philosophical orientation and goals of the staff. This type of board still exists in some houses. However, even for these boards, there is a greater attempt than there was seven years ago to have a wide range of professional skills, so that lawyers, accountants, teachers, and social workers are often included on these boards.

In many houses, boards are being seen less as extensions of friendship networks, and more as power brokers. Board members for these houses are chosen very deliberately for the influence they wield in the community, rather than for their pure philosophical commitment to the issue or for their friendships with staff members. These boards are fashioned on a business model. They are seen as political tools for increasing the visibility of and support for the house, and, more generally, for the issue of wife battering, in the community. One house worker spoke of the benefits this new board model had brought them.

> *The success of our funding drive and our program is largely attributable to our board members. They are connected in the community. The professionalism of the board has gone up and up. The board now prepares our plan of action for each year. They set policies. Even though this worried staff initially and did cause some tension, it has helped us greatly to become viable and respected.*

■ Volunteers Are Used Increasingly By Most Houses

The promotion of business-like, cost-effective houses encouraged by many boards has meshed with the emphasis on restraint by some provincial/territorial governments to create a fairly high use of volunteers in many houses. On average, 13 volunteers worked in each shelter in 1985, and each of these volunteers worked six hours a week.

The Scope Of Services Offered In Shelters Has Changed

Along with an attempt to reach out to more women has come an expansion of the range of services delivered in shelters. In the late 1970s, the majority of houses provided safe shelter, informal or formal counselling for the women who stayed with them, and referral and advice regarding social, financial, legal, health, and housing options available to battered women.

As in the past, all the houses surveyed provided assistance in dealing with social, financial, legal, health, or housing services. They also offered protection, referral to other services, and crisis counselling for resident women. Ninety-five per cent also accompanied those women who went to court, and 80% would accompany women to their homes to get their belongings.

In addition, however, over 90% of the shelters now provide some crisis counselling to women who do not stay at the transition house. Almost 75% provide family counselling for women and children. Eighty-five per cent of the houses provide counselling for some of the children who stay with them and a quarter of them counsel virtually all the children who stay with them. Almost 80% of the houses have an activity program for children, 10% provide family counselling including the partner, or couple counselling. Fifty per cent have a parenting program. Eighty-two per cent have some sort of follow-up program. Sixty per cent provide sexual assault counselling and 70% provide incest counselling. Ninety-five per cent do some public education.

A few of the more general crisis centres also provided alcohol abuse programs, and sometimes drug abuse programs, for women as well as for men. These programs are offered to battered women and batterers but are not exclusively for their use.

The Women's Perspectives: How Shelter Workers View The Changes

Changes in philosophy and service delivery in general have engendered a good deal of pride and optimism among shelter workers. When workers were asked whether there were any particular features of their house which contributed to the success of their program, 12% cited the high professional quality of their in-house programs, 14% cited the ability to treat each woman more individually as a result of expanded services, 8% spoke of their follow-up and outreach programs, and 5% mentioned the quality of their public education program.

This pride, however, is mixed with some fear that shelters are becoming part of the mainstream services which can perpetuate and compound the victimization of women.

Shelter workers are caught between a longing for a "more innocent" past, focussed more centrally on committed women working with women, and an appreciation of the benefits of professionalization. On the whole, however, shelter workers are optimistic about an expanding future rooted in community concern with wife battering. Some even state that the idealized past some mourn as lost never existed, and that workers are forgetting all the conflict that was created by attempts to run a service within a loose cooperative structure.

Nonetheless, there is a large number of workers who, despite their optimism regarding the potential for expanded service delivery and their gratification regarding the growth in community support, are fearful that professionalization may be jeopardizing the relationships between battered women and shelter workers. As one worker said:

> In the past, our strength was that we always reached out to women on an emotional level. We really listened and we really heard what they had to say. Battered women used to tell us that we were the only ones who understood. We may be losing this. We've had three client grievances in the last three weeks. They've accused us of being hypocritical. They've said that we're telling them to reduce the power differential between themselves and their husbands but then we do it with the staff.

Challenges For The Future

The problems experienced by shelter staff almost all revolve around the question: Who owns the issue of wife battering and how does this ownership create or change the definition of the problem of wife battering as well as the type and quality of services provided to battered women? While, technically, no one can "own" a social problem, social reactions to that problem and service development are largely decided by who controls the money.

Funding Problems

Funding continues to be the primary and perennial concern of shelter workers. Similarly, the amount of funding remains an issue for many houses and there are still houses which are threatened with dissolution by funding problems. Ten per cent of the houses reported that they were unable to provide basic crisis counselling services, house maintenance, or 24-hour staffing because of lack of funds. These houses depended primarily on per diem funding. Twenty-five per cent of the workers reported that, at some time, they had required and received "bail-out" funding from the federal government and their provincial/territorial government because they were threatened with having to close their doors. However, this experience does not seem to be as common as it once was, especially since more of the house structures are now owned outright, provided rent-free, or at a reduced rent or mortgage.

The major funding problems of shelters today fall into two categories. First, funding is still mainly short-term. Second, it is based on occupancy rates, even though costs associated with house maintenance, staff salaries, and services do not change perceptibly with occupancy rates. Therefore, houses are still unable to plan ahead because their budgets for the next year are rarely known until the year is upon them. Staff also spend what they feel is far too much time soliciting funds. Houses reported that at least one staff member on average spent one-quarter to one-third of her time each year raising funds.

■ Funding Based On Occupancy Rates Restricts Services

The emphasis on occupancy rates means that houses still receive the majority of their funding through per diems; that is, through payments for room and board for women who are eligible for welfare. As a result, houses perennially find that they do not have enough money for house maintenance, staff salaries, or the creation and delivery of services which promote prevention and change. Seventy-four per cent of the house workers reported that, because of inadequate funds, they were prevented from providing certain types of services at all, or from providing as comprehensive a service as the needs of battered women and their children would warrant. Adequate child-care and counselling services were mentioned most often (by 38% of the workers), but follow-up, outreach advocacy, and more community education were also frequently cited. On average, house workers estimated that each of their houses would need another $46,000 added to their annual budgets to be able to offer these needed services.

The persistence of funding problems for many shelters, as the next sections of this chapter will demonstrate, affects staffing decisions, staff satisfaction, the goals of shelters, the types of services offered in shelters, and the types of new shelters created. The type and amount of funding provided can reduce the ability of workers to put in place or coordinate the diverse services that shelter workers know are needed by battered women. The type and amount of funding provided can keep houses understaffed and so fail to permit shelter workers enough time to be able to communicate their knowledge of needed services to the general public, to other professionals, or to policy-makers. Inadequate funding and inappropriate funding regulations can thereby undermine the influence of shelter workers in the wife-battering service movement and can deny them any real control over the evolution of services for battered women and their children.

This potential loss of influence seems particularly unfair to shelter workers and also tragic for the progress of service delivery because, to date, shelter workers have provided the most in-depth knowledge about wife battering. Shelter workers have worked most closely with battered women and have been the major influence in bringing wife battering to public attention. Low levels of funding not only reduce the credibility of shelter workers in the community, they can also undermine the public perception of the importance of services provided by shelter workers in a society which values people by, among other things, their level of pay.

- The Special Needs Of Different Houses Are Not Always Recognized By Funding Agencies

One of the policies which potentially creates a loss of control by shelter workers is the policy model for funding, used by some governments, which divides houses and their funding needs by the number of beds in the house. In a typical policy of this sort, a house with ten beds might be expected to function with six crisis workers, while a house with 20 beds would be allowed 12 crisis workers. This formula appears logical on the surface, but does not take into account the fact that no matter what size the house, staff must still be available for 24-hour coverage; daily house maintenance does not differ significantly by size; fundraising still takes virtually the same amount of time; and the costs of services are not always directly proportional to the number of people using them. Smaller houses are therefore severely penalized by a logic which does not take the reality of house operations into account.

Another source of inequity, mentioned particularly in the poorer sections of the Atlantic provinces, arises from government funding formulae which insist that municipalities contribute a fixed percentage of a shelter's operating budget, even though the financial ability and willingness of municipalities to contribute money vary considerably. Government policies increasingly emphasize community participation and financial support in determining levels and conditions for funding. While, philosophically, this ideal is shared by most shelter workers, this condition has resulted in a number of shelters in poorer or in less progressive areas being unable to open because of their inability to raise funds locally.

- Funding Is Inflexible

Many shelter workers reported that the funding level they applied for when they first opened became their basic funding level for the life of the shelter. It is largely because this base level is used as a perennial benchmark that funding discrepancies among houses grow even though the size of the shelters and the scope of services offered may become more similar over time.

■ Fundraising Is Restricted

Most houses have discovered over the years that they benefit from a diversification of funding sources. Diversification increases their autonomy by making the houses less dependent on one funding source for survival. Diversification also allows the houses to broaden their connections in the community. Some houses, in particular those which rely on United Way to provide a portion of their funding, are restricted in their freedom to raise funds in the community. United Way funding regulations specify that member agencies may not seek further funds from the community since the United Way has already approached the community for global support of services and charities.

■ Funding For Shelters Which Serve A Large Aboriginal Population Is Particularly Unpredictable

Shelters which potentially, or actually, serve a large aboriginal population report many problems collecting per diems for aboriginal women and their children because payments must be collected from Indian and Northern Affairs Canada. According to shelter workers, this means that Indian and Northern Affairs must approve the woman's stay in the house and has the authority to shorten the length of the woman's stay from that approved under the funding regulations for the shelter. Thus, an aboriginal woman staying at a transition house where women are allowed to stay for six weeks could be told that she can stay for only three weeks.

Another related problem mentioned in interviews is that band councils, who ultimately distribute the money for aboriginal women living on reserves, ask shelters to reveal the woman's treaty number before they will pay for the woman's stay. Since this removes the woman's anonymity, shelters generally won't agree to this stipulation and so must absorb the cost of the woman's stay. If the house is unable to absorb this cost, the house may be accused of refusing to accept aboriginal women, the reputation of the house may be compromised in the community, and the house's ability to serve aboriginal women in the future will be jeopardized.

■ Funding Alternatives May Compromise Ideals

As mentioned earlier, while few houses were overtly concerned with the problem of receiving money from private agencies or from government, and instead saw diversified fundraising as a form of public education, some workers did express dismay at having to use government make-work programs to provide services which could not be covered under their basic operating budgets. One worker clarified the problem:

> We wouldn't have had child care without hiring Canada Works people, but I hate to support this program because what we're really supporting is the concept of getting people off welfare for three months at a time. By supporting this program, we're helping to lock people into short-term, poorly paid jobs, and we're helping to ensure that they'll never really be able to plan their future.

■ Sustaining Grant Funding Is Also Needed For Transition-House Associations

At the time of writing, shelters in all provinces and territories except Nova Scotia, New Brunswick, and the Northwest Territories had successfully worked together to create a provincial/territorial association of transition houses. While not all houses in all provinces/territories belong to these associations, the process by which they were formed in all provinces/territories was through sustained dialogue among the houses to weigh the benefits and disadvantages of such an association, and to work out the logistics of the association, followed by subsequent applications to federal and provincial government funding sources to support the association. (Manitoba is the one exception; in that province, the government took a more prominent coordinating role.)

Shelter workers interviewed across the country spoke of the important role played by transition-house associations in terms of the information-sharing and coordination they encourage among the houses, the time they save shelter workers by helping them with fundraising and public education, and the morale-boosting that results from the constant reminder provided by these associations that no house is isolated in its problems.

Despite the important role these associations play for transition-house workers, for government funding agents (by helping to rationalize applications for funding across the province/territory), and for the general public (by helping to coordinate and more actively disseminate, across the province or territory, information packages developed in local houses), most association coordinators reported that they are constantly scrambling for funds. New funding agreements are rarely announced until funds for the old year have already run out. Association staff sometimes are forced to work out of their homes. There is little money for transportation to keep in personal contact with shelter workers, or for publications or the dissemination of information to shelter workers across their jurisdiction.

To enable transition-house associations to carry out the important coordinating and planning function which most shelters need and want, federal and provincial/territorial governments must recognize that they need sustaining grant funding. This type of funding will allow each association to maintain an office, pay for long-distance telephone calls, travel within its jurisdiction, occasionally meet with association representatives from other provinces/territories, and produce and distribute information to shelter workers in its province/territory as well as to workers in other provinces/territories.

Staffing Problems

Funding problems also affect staffing in a variety of ways.

■ The Number Of Staff Is Often Inadequate

On average, each shelter responding to this study's questionnaire had five full-time staff, two part-time staff, and seven relief staff. While 14 staff members may sound ample, it should be remembered that almost all houses are open on a 24-hour basis and most houses need three shifts of workers. Relief and part-time staff, by definition, are not available to take their full share of the shifts. In addition, the attempt by houses to broaden the number and types of services they provide places enormous pressure on staff members to "do it all". Ironically, the increased specialization of staff duties potentially increases the responsibility load for each worker, since there may be no one available who would know how to do another worker's job and so no one who could assist another worker with a particularly heavy workload.

These reported problems are supported by this study's findings. Eighty-seven per cent of the shelter workers considered their house understaffed. On average, they felt that they would need three additional full-time staff to have a truly workable staff/client ratio. Workers were specific about the duties they would like additional staff to fulfil. Seventy-six per cent of the houses would like a child-care worker; 44% would like more crisis workers; 37% want advocacy and follow-up workers; 25% want more night-time relief; 17% would like a secretary/bookkeeper; and 11% want a coordinator of volunteer workers.

■ Staff Training Is Also Inadequate

All of the shelter staff who responded to the written questionnaire said they felt staff would benefit from additional specific forms of training if time, funds and/or training resource people were available. Sixty-four per cent of the houses wanted additional training in crisis counselling; 34% wanted training in child care. In addition, 14% wanted more information on funding options; and 27% asked for a course on the legal system. Forty per cent of the houses felt that their training program was not adequate for paid staff, and 31% felt it was not adequate for volunteers.

■ Staff Salaries Are Not Competitive

On average, the director/coordinator of a shelter in Canada earned $398 a week, or around $20,000 a year in 1985. Full-time staff made $308 a week, part-time staff $46.48 a day, relief staff $48.87 a day, and child-care staff $186 a week, or less than $10,000 a year. In all houses, these salaries were recognized to be far below the salaries that these workers could command at other jobs requiring similar expertise and involving a similar level of responsibility, but unrelated to wife battering. As a result, 80% of the shelter workers who responded to the questionnaire felt that the staff in their houses were underpaid in terms of education, and 90% considered their staff underpaid in terms of experience.

■ There Is A High Level of Frustration Among Staff Members

The effects of inadequate funding are the major causes of staff discontent and frustration reported by staff members. Fifty-four per cent of the respondents said that overwork was one of the main problems which contributed to discontent or frustration among staff members, 43% identified low wages, 9% noted a lack of benefits, and 38% pinpointed the limited resources in the house. According to responses to the questionnaire, 42% of the houses reported that the frustration had become so great that staff had quit because of these problems. In 58% of the houses, these problems were seen as contributing to staff illness and 73% of the respondents said that these problems created unnecessary tension among staff members.

Some workers felt that greater professionalization tended to increase both staff frustration and staff turnover as workers attempted to enhance their careers by seeking new opportunities.

■ The Increased Reliance On Volunteers Has Created Problems In Some Houses

As established earlier, low levels of funding and increased pressure by government to use volunteer workers has forced most shelters to use volunteers whether or not they would have chosen this option. This is not to imply that the practice is bad, but only that funding constraints limit the staffing options open to shelter workers. In fact, many shelter workers interviewed reported that the presence of volunteers has had some very positive consequences. It has helped increase the diversity of workers connected with shelters. Women in high-income brackets, more rural women, and more women who learned of the shelters through their church involvement said they felt much more comfortable applying to work as a volunteer than as a paid worker in the shelter. Volunteer work can be extremely rewarding for the volunteers themselves, and certainly can play a public education function. As one volunteer said:

> I shouldn't really admit this, but I had no idea people lived so differently from me until I came to work here. It's opened my eyes and made me more tolerant of people and more aware of the world.

However, despite the positive results of the widespread use of volunteers, some shelter workers worried that volunteerism could seriously under-rate the value of women's paid work, and might ultimately erode the public and government perception of the importance of the work done in shelters. The ultimate danger for shelter staff, according to their reports, is that funding agencies may want paid staff in shelters replaced by volunteers. Shelter workers said that governments are increasingly encouraging the use of volunteers as a form of "community involvement". Most houses have attempted to curb this danger by insisting that volunteers never be used to replace a paid staff member, but instead be used to do jobs specifically allocated to volunteers, usually child care, secretarial/clerical work, and transporting women to the transition house, to court, to welfare offices, etc. Nonetheless, the fear of this danger lingers.

In addition, workers spoke of problems with continuity created by the short hours most volunteers work, and the fact that few volunteers can agree to be on call. Volunteers may be very committed, but because the job is unpaid, they are more likely to leave their shelter positions after a relatively short time. As one worker explained: "Many of our volunteers are unemployed or are just out of school. They leave as soon as they can find a paying job."

This fact increases the real cost to shelters of training volunteers. Most houses provide some formal training for volunteers, and 36% of the houses use the same training program for paid staff and for volunteers.

Other workers pointed out that, no matter how committed the volunteer, there is a risk that the quality of the service provided will be compromised by using volunteers just because there is less continuity and because most houses can't afford to give volunteers the same in-depth training they give to paid personnel. Some workers worried that even using volunteers for transportation can compromise the quality of the service provided because the drive between the woman's home and a safe home or a shelter is a time when important counselling can take place. Even if the volunteer is adept at counselling the woman, it is unlikely she or he will have the time to communicate all she or he has learned from the woman to other shelter staff. As well, battered woman may feel cheated that the volunteer, to whom she has just told her life story, is now leaving her.

■ Board Members Can Undermine The Influence And Credibility Of Shelter Workers

While relationships between board and staff members in most houses tend to be very good, one major source of tension frequently arises from the fact that the boards generally have final control over the goals set for the house. Therefore, if there is a clash between the perceptions of staff and board regarding appropriate ways to operate and administer the transition house (and these can vary widely), this can create irreparable divisions and erode the future influence of staff members in goal-setting exercises. An outright schism or a foreshadowing of such a division can lead to an organizational decision which may severely limit the power of the staff. For example, the staff in two houses were prohibited by the board from attending board meetings because of anticipated disagreements over goal-setting. Such an exclusion can, of course, reduce the knowledge of board members regarding the changing realities of battered women, can reduce staff awareness of constraints on the board, and can ultimately reduce the effectiveness of the services delivered in the house.

■ Unionization Has Had Ambiguous Benefits

The chronically low pay and poor benefits available to shelter workers has prompted the staff in a few houses to seek unionization. Like the professionalization of boards, unionization can promise many benefits in terms of appropriate rewards for work done and job security. Unions can also make a strong philosophical statement that shelter workers will not accept the ghettoization of women's jobs. However, at the same time, workers who have considered unionization or have become unionized have had to deal with the question: "Would we strike and walk off the job over a pay issue and so jeopardize our service to the women?" Since workers invariably answered "no" to this hypothetical question, workers in unionized houses had to acknowledge the limited power that their unionization gave them. Other workers were against unionization because they saw it as an essentially male organizational concept with no room for women's reality.

Despite these concerns, unionization has improved the lot of some shelter workers. In one house, as a result of unionization, the salaries of front-line workers were boosted from $12,000 to $18,000, they received an excellent benefits package, and their work week was reduced from five to four days. Nonetheless, the unclear benefits of unionization symbolize the ambiguous position shelter workers frequently find themselves in when they attempt to assert their expertise and establish their influence over services for battered women.

A Shortage Of Funds Has Increased Competition Between Shelters

Overall funding levels and staff salaries vary widely across Canada, within provinces/territories, and even within cities, towns, or municipalities. For example, in one city, the child-care workers in one house were paid $8,000 a year, in another $18,000, even though in both houses the prerequisite for getting the job was a degree or diploma in early childhood education. These discrepancies have made the staff in many shelters resistant to the idea of joining a provincial or national association of transition houses. As one worker deliberated:

> In the long run, I know such an association could give us power and certainly could save us some time in terms of public relations and fundraising. But we're sure that the first thing the government would do is to reduce us all to the lowest common denominator . . . find the house that was doing the most work for the least money and set this house as a standard for us all. All our hard-won gains could be lost. It just doesn't seem worth the risk.

Competition for funding not only occurs among transition houses, it also exists across different types of services. Thus, in the last few years, despite the support most transition-house workers have expressed for more programs for children and counselling services for batterers, service-providers have voiced some anxiety that the growth in counselling programs for men, or increased services for children, or the creation of safe homes, could mean a serious reduction in financial and philosophical support for transition houses. As well, service-providers have stipulated that programs for children and batterers require built-in evaluation processes.

The rhetoric of restraint creates an either-or mentality. Wife battering is a complex problem which requires a variety of simultaneous responses. Restraint rhetoric is creating, whether intentionally or unintentionally, resistance to change, territorial jealousy, and an increased perception of powerlessness among many service-providers.

Restraint May Have Compromised The Type Of Additional Shelters Created

Some shelter workers feel that the rhetoric of restraint has also negatively influenced the type of new services created. Particular concern was expressed about the dependence on "safe houses" as the major rural option being supported by some provincial/territorial governments across Canada.

■ Are Safe Homes Unsafe?

Several years ago, safe-house networks were generally lauded as an innovative and low-cost means of providing protection to battered women in rural areas. However, the safe-house experiment has been perceived by the majority of shelter workers as unsuccessful and unsafe for the battered women who come to the houses and for the permanent residents of the houses. Despite the concerns expressed by transition-house workers to government representatives, workers reported that safe homes are being considered by some funding agencies to be appropriate alternatives to transition houses in rural areas.

The quality of services provided in safe homes has come under attack. Workers have said that transportation is not always readily available from safe houses to transition houses. Transition-house workers said that, in their experience, safe houses generally do not provide the counselling, peer support, information, or referrals that battered women need. Many battered women report that they feel uncomfortable in these predominantly middle-class, husband-wife homes and say that seeing the couple together made them feel even lonelier for their husbands or partners. (It should also be mentioned, however, that other battered women found it enlightening and uplifting to see a family interact without violence.) Women spoke of feeling like intruders in a private home and said they worried about the noise their children made.

There have been suggestions that many of the safe-home operators are strongly religious people and that the battered women feel uncomfortable with the emphasis on religion which they can encounter in these houses. As one woman said: "I felt like they didn't want to help me. They wanted to save me."

Other problems with safe homes mentioned by other service-providers are that they are difficult to monitor, so standards are hard to set and maintain. Safe-home operators often are not available in peak periods of violence because these periods coincide with holidays. Other shelter workers wondered if safe homes are even "safe". One worker raised the following question:

> Safe homes are most needed in smaller, isolated communities. But in these communities, everyone knows everyone. How can these safe homes guarantee the woman the anonymity she needs to protect herself?

In addition, safe-home operators risk personal harm by accepting battered women into their homes. Because they are often located in isolated areas, help would rarely be readily available if the batterer should come to the house. They risk ostracism from the community if their location becomes widely known, and few of these operators receive pay for these risks.

Despite the serious concerns expressed by transition-house workers about safe houses, most concur that they can provide a useful temporary measure if the woman is simply taken to the safe house until transportation can be arranged to a shelter. Transition-house workers are not against other options for battered women. They are, however, concerned about options which ignore the wisdom they have gained based on their extensive experience with battered women. They are concerned about choices being made in some locations which downplay the importance of transition houses, and they are concerned about government officials making choices which will restrict options for battered women in the interest of cost reduction.

Future Directions

Overall, shelter workers expressed the hope that sheltering standards, our knowledge of what battered women want, the need for expanded, high-quality service delivery, and the deserved recognition of the expertise of shelter workers would not be compromised in the legitimate quest by government representatives for ways to keep costs down.

Shelter workers expressed the concern that currently, restraint is creating fear of change and competitiveness among some service-providers who should be working cooperatively. If the desire to provide a wider scope of services and so to reach more battered women in Canada shared by so many service-providers were emphasized instead, perhaps restraint could be encouraged creatively without fostering concern over ownership of services for battered women, and without potentially jeopardizing responses to battered women.

So, for example, funding formulae could emphasize the service-delivery role rather than just the sheltering role of transition houses, crisis centres, safe homes, and second-stage shelters. The current emphasis on their sheltering roles means that they are serving a narrower population than they might otherwise reach. Women who come to transition houses for shelter generally have endured violence for several years and are poor. A greater emphasis on the outreach and non-residential service component of transition houses is needed to encourage higher-income women to benefit from the expertise of transition-house workers and to enable workers to help women at an earlier stage in the battering. While many of these services could be located in transition houses, it may not be appropriate for all these services in all communities to be delivered by transition-house workers, or to be located in transition houses. However, to take full advantage of the expertise of shelter workers and to provide an easily identifiable focal service for battered women, it will be important that these services be developed in consultation with transition-house workers, coordinated with other shelter services, and that shelter workers have some influence in deciding which agency/service is most appropriate to provide a given service.

The per diem funding model is particularly tied to a shelter emphasis and to a crisis-oriented model which does not allow room for creative outreach and preventive services. Because it is essentially a welfare model, the per diem model perpetuates the image of services for battered women as charity. Shelters, consequently, are often perceived by battered women and other community members as an escape for the woman, but not as a potential tool for change.

The current per diem model places shelter workers who attempt to help aboriginal women in the position of having to act as collection agencies negotiating with band councils or with Indian and Northern Affairs Canada. Not only does this waste the time of shelter workers, it also perpetuates the perception of differences between aboriginal and non-aboriginal women and militates against the comfortable integration of aboriginal and non-aboriginal women in transition houses.

Funding models and restraint goals should not be used to foster competition among service-providers. Funds should be made available to encourage greater cooperation among shelters and other non-residential services. Workers in services for battered women, their children, and their partners need to share information to increase their influence and effectiveness. Women working in shelters can also be guilty of under-rating their own power and influence. This power can be increased if a common bank of information about procedures, funding, terminology, and services could be created and shared. Many house workers spoke of the benefits which computers in their transition houses could make possible in terms of the gathering and sharing of information. Other workers hope for funds to create a national association of service-providers concerned with wife battering. Transition-house associations also should be given sustaining grant funding to enable them to foster cooperation and information-sharing across programs.

The expertise of staff in shelters could be given more deserved recognition through the institution of pay and benefit levels more in keeping with a professional scale, through the involvement of shelter workers in planning exercises for services related to wife battering, and through recognition by other employers of the professional status of jobs in shelters. Shelter staff need ongoing training to enhance professional upgrading and to give them the flexibility to expand their careers.

Community involvement in sheltering initiatives should be encouraged through multi-disciplinary community committees and through public education. However, shelters or committees trying to start shelters in communities where the public awareness of the problem is low, or where the community is very poor, would benefit greatly from provincial/territorial and federal government recognition that not all municipalities can or will contribute the same amount of money to support a shelter.

Safe homes and other service options which have come under attack should be more carefully evaluated. Even more importantly, any service option should be presented within a wide constellation of possible options in order to avert the problems currently experienced by service-providers. In this way, safe homes, like other services, can potentially be retained as valuable elements in a broad scheme of options including transition houses, day centres (non-residential counselling and referral services), follow-up support groups, multifaceted community services, counselling, outreach programs, advocacy services, public education initiatives, and longer-term secure housing options.

Overall, the expertise of shelter workers, as well as the value of sheltering services and of the non-residential programs which can be provided through and in conjunction with shelter services, must be recognized through more predictable, stable funding. Furthermore, this funding must be based on the delivery of counselling, support, referral, information, outreach, and follow-up programs, **not** room and board. Short-term crisis funding is inadequate and inappropriate for a problem so deeply rooted in our society. A long-term commitment to long-term funding is needed to address prevention and support needs as well as crisis services. As one shelter worker puzzled: "Why do we need bake sales to provide women with the right to live in dignity and freedom from fear?"

Programs For Children

Overview: Why Services For Children Are So Important

Data on the expanded range of services in shelters, presented in the last chapter, revealed that one of the most profound changes in the last seven years in service delivery is the growth of concern and program development for the children of battered women. Shelter workers, because they may care for both the battered women and their children, have always been concerned with the welfare of the children. However, seven years ago there was a legitimate fear among shelter workers that, by acknowledging this interest openly, money which was crucially needed to shelter, counsel, and support battered women would be diverted to their children alone.

Our increased knowledge of the linkages among many forms of violence, both inside and outside the family context, has begun to raise our consciousness beyond competing interests. Increasingly, it is being recognized that the problems of the children **are** the problems of the mother. It is also widely acknowledged that we must look to prevention, and so to the children of battered women, if we want to help reduce the number of battered women in the future. As a result, shelter workers and other professional and community workers dealing with battered women almost universally express the desire to reach out to the children, because:

> These kids have so many needs. They are sad. They are angry. If their mother is staying at our house, they are probably uprooted from their school and friends, so they are lonely. Hell, they're all lonely anyway. And there's nothing more demoralizing for workers than getting a woman on her feet, helping her to get some dignity and to really do it on her own, only to see her daughter come back to us five years down the road because she's just been battered by her husband or boyfriend.

In addition, as demonstrated in earlier chapters, children living in battering homes may suffer a higher risk of direct physical or sexual abuse and many are neglected. In one study of 630 children who stayed at WIN House, a shelter in Edmonton, Alberta, in 1985, "87% of the children 3-18 years of age were found to be abused or neglected."[1] Some mothers

> . . . are virtually forced into neglecting their children by men who demand full-time attention themselves or who numb the women with serious violence so greatly that their care of other family members suffers.[2]

Many experts agree that there are three stages which characterize the battering cycle: the tension build-up phase, the crisis stage, and the honeymoon stage during which the husband may be contrite, apologetic, attentive, and loving.[3] Most children living in battering homes experience anxiety, fear, and confusion as they attempt to cope with these different stages and try to understand why their parents act so differently toward them at different times. "Children in abusive homes learn to expect unpredictable criticism, abuse, and neglect and cope as best they can, terrified of being abandoned."[4] Many of the children become withdrawn, some become suicidal. Others become violent toward the people around them. These children also frequently feel constant and overwhelming guilt that they are the cause of the violence.

As one shelter worker so lucidly stated:

> These children really are the innocent victims of a major war being fought in many battles across the country. These kids are prisoners of that war. They are trapped in the actual violence while they are little and can't get out on their own, and they may be trapped in it psychologically for the rest of their lives. We've got to get amnesty for these children. One way we might just get a reprieve for the children and for the adults as well, is by showing the parents what the battering is doing to the children. Sometimes this is the only thing that can bring the parents up short to look at what the final result of the violence is — it's ruining their children's lives, not just their own.

This last point made by the shelter worker is an important one and may hold the key to the directions for the ideal, non-violent future envisioned by front-line workers and battered women.

The Women's Points Of View:
The Hopes of Battered Women For Their Children

The primary hope of all battered women interviewed for this study is that their children will escape the violence and will not repeat the battering cycle of their parents. The needs of their children are usually paramount in the minds of battered women. Most battered women feel tremendous guilt about what their children have endured as a result of the battering, and agonize over how these experiences will affect their futures.

"Doing the right thing for the children" is often the prime concern of battered women in their decision whether to leave home or to stay. The woman's perception of "the right thing to do" is frequently complicated by the ambiguous or negative feelings many children who live through or witness violence feel toward their mothers. While "most children in violent homes feel responsible for the violence, for the unhappiness, for their own suffering and that of their parents",[5] children in battering homes may vent their anger and frustration on their mothers. Children in battering homes often blame their mothers for being too weak to protect them-selves or their children. They may accuse her of "starting the fights". They may even become accomplices with their father in the violence against their mother. Under these circumstances, the women usually feel that the children would not want to leave with them. And so some women stay with their batterers because they feel they would lose everything, including their children, if they should leave. Even if they do leave, those women with children who have emotional and/or behavioural problems are more likely to return to their husbands. In the study done at WIN house, cited earlier, 70% of the mothers of children with such problems returned to their batterers.[6]

In other cases, particularly where the children are small, women hope the children are unaware of the violence, and that they are not being affected by it. But even the women who are convinced this is true worry about the future, when their children are older and it will not be so easy to just "put them to bed" when the tension is reaching the breaking point.

Battered women want the violence to stop, mainly for the sake of their children or their children's children. When battered women were asked what they would recommend as the most important program for the future, one typical response was:

> . . . to teach all children about violence, about how to live without hitting and being cruel to each other. . . . I don't feel like there's much hope for me, but I don't want my children to go through what I've gone through all my life.

Even though we must continue to recognize and emphasize the needs of the battered women, to be receptive to the hopes of the women, we must acknowledge that the women's and men's concern for their children's safety and futures may provide the catalyst to help stop the violence in individual families, and certainly should be one focus for the ultimate goal of prevention.

Progress To Date

While concern with the children of battered women has grown considerably in service and policy circles, it has not been manifested in a wide range of service options. Of course, interest in and responses to explicit child abuse have grown enormously during the last few years, but the programs in place are targetted at children who are victims of physical and/or sexual abuse, and do not generally address the frequent link between wife battering and child abuse. Thus, children who are psychologically battered or neglected, but not physically or sexually abused, would not be helped through many of these programs. In addition, abused children would not necessarily be identified and helped even if their mother sought help for her own battering. Conversely, it is not common enough for a battered woman to be identified and helped, even though her children are known to have been abused.

The progress which has taken place to address the varied needs of children who live in homes where the woman is battered and where the children may or may not also have been the direct victims of violence has been limited to a valiant attempt to provide services for these children in transition houses, despite overwhelming resource obstacles. These needs are also being indirectly addressed by a few curriculum reviews and developments in the schools across Canada.

Fifty per cent of the transition houses which responded to the written questionnaire for this study said they had a specific program in place for children, usually including care, activities, and some counselling. In these houses, at least one worker was on staff primarily or solely to deal with the children and their needs. The creation of these programs in many cases reflected a major change in the goals and organization of some houses. Twenty-five per cent of the houses, when asked to identify changes in the organization of their houses since they first opened, cited the expansion of the services they provided and most often this expansion was focussed around the provision of services for the children of battered women.

As established earlier in this report, while only 50% of the houses reported that they have a specific program for children with at least one staff member assigned to this program, 80% of the houses in Canada now provide at least some counselling for resident children, usually by crisis workers who also work with the women. However, only 29% of the houses were able to provide this service to **all** the children who stayed with them. Thirty-eight per cent of the houses provided some counselling for non-resident children as well, usually as a follow-up for children who did stay at the shelter at an earlier time. Seventy-five per cent of the houses provided some organized activities for the children, either through a child-care worker or through crisis counsellors who also work with the women, and, in 40% of the houses, this program was provided for all or almost all the children. Sixty-five per cent of the houses had a special play area for children inside and sometimes also outside the house.

In addition, 51% of the houses provided a parenting program to offer general information on childhood developmental stages, advice on coping with different types of behaviour, and information on nutrition. These programs are offered either in-house or through a formal liaison with another agency. Forty-two per cent provided specific counselling on child-care options for the mothers. Nine per cent of the houses estimated that they used their parenting and/or child-care counselling programs with the majority of the women who stayed in the house.

A number of individual houses have also developed innovative programs to help meet the specific needs of certain groups of children who stay with them. For example, in the Sheriff King House, in Calgary, music therapy sessions led by a trained therapist are held twice a week for the children in the shelter. Another example is Kirby House, in St. John's, Newfoundland, which has launched a video project for adolescents who live in battering homes. Through this project, the young participants make videos, gain skills using the equipment, observe men and women working together cooperatively, and have an opportunity to share their feelings and experiences with others who are also living with violence.

Besides programs for children run through transition houses, in most provinces/ territories, one or more school courses which include material concerning family violence are being developed for secondary and primary students. As well, in some provinces, courses are actually being piloted in secondary schools and in the upper elementary grades. Training and awareness programs for teachers are also in existence in most of the provinces and territories.

In addition, in Alberta, it is possible for a shelter to apply for a special institutional status which would allow and provide financial support for the provision of educational services within the shelter. In this way, the children of battered women may be spared the additional upheaval and anxiety of changing schools while they are staying at the shelter.

It is noteworthy that, at the time of writing, of all the provincial/territorial governments, only Ontario was allocating specific funds for new community-based counselling services, not only for battered women and for batterers, but also for their children. However, it could not be determined what proportion of the funds had actually gone into counselling programs specifically for the children.

Challenges For The Future

It is evident from the limited progress in the creation of specific programs for children that the widespread ideological commitment to the needs of children among front-line workers, other professionals, and government workers is not yet strongly or consistently backed by concrete government funding. As a result, the effectiveness of the commitment of transition-house staff to the needs of the children is often seriously hampered by inadequate funding. Many houses reported that they had to rely totally on donations for toys, books, and child-sized furniture, and that this limited their ability to choose durable and safe equipment. It also curtailed purchases of therapeutic toys (such as anatomically correct dolls used to assess and help counsel children who have been victims of sexual assault), which would rarely, if ever, be donated.

Because funding specifically for programs for children within shelters is low, or even nonexistent, child-care workers in transition houses are generally paid the lowest salaries of all shelter workers. As established in an earlier section of this report, the average salary reported by paid child-care workers in this study was just $186.00 a week, or less than $10,000 a year! There are also considerable discrepancies among salaries paid to child-care workers within provinces, between provinces, and sometimes within a city or town. The minimum reported salary for a child-care worker was just $100 a week, the maximum $414. In addition, as noted in the chapter on shelters, there is a fairly big gap between the average salary paid to child-care workers and the salaries paid to workers who deal primarily with the battered women. To reiterate, the average salary paid to full-time general crisis staff in 1985 was $308 a week compared to the $186 paid to child-care workers.

In many houses, because of the shortage of funds, child-care workers must work on a volunteer basis if a program for children is to exist at all. Some houses reported that the only way they could get funding for child-care workers was through federal grant programs aimed at encouraging employers to hire unemployed people. While most houses were more than happy to hire unemployed workers, the stipulation for the most common type of grant at the time of writing was that the workers hired must be untrained people. By definition, they could have no experience in working with children. As a result, coordination, training, and supervision were generally required and this placed an added burden on the other house workers.

Shelter workers report that all these factors contribute to chronic demoralization among child-care workers and a very high turnover rate. The shortage of child-care staff also means that there is frequently no time for these workers to connect with the mothers. Therefore, the children are often worked with in isolation from the mothers. The fragmentation of programs which battered women and shelter workers have attempted to battle for so long has become a logical outcome of inadequate funding.

The majority of houses which have a children's program operate it with no full-time staff member or only one full-time staff member whose primary function is to deal with the children. Only 38% of the houses with some services for the children had a staff member who acted primarily as a children's program coordinator; generally this staff member was the only person who provided services related to children.

Occasionally, professional jealousy, discrepant pay, education or training levels, or even a concern with confidentiality can contribute to structured isolation across staff groups. In three houses where staff members were interviewed, child-care workers were denied access to information regarding the mother's background and were not allowed to attend staff meetings because individual women could be discussed. Therefore, in the interests of the battered women, child-care workers can become second-class citizens in shelters, and a more holistic approach which responds to the needs and hopes of the women is sacrificed.

These problems clearly illustrate the consequences of inadequate funding for shelters. However, even if additional funds were allotted to transition houses, this alone would not allow the shelters to provide the entire scope of services needed for the children who stay with them. As well, transition houses don't reach the many children living in homes where the woman is battered but never stays at a transition house. The problems created for the staff and residents of transition houses by the lack of funds, and the problems experienced by battered women and children who never stay at transition houses, are exacerbated by the lack of other community programs for children. These problems are particularly pronounced when shelter workers and parents try to deal with the needs of adolescent children or of very violent children of all ages.

The consensus reached by many shelter workers is that there are no services outside transition houses for adolescent children living in battering homes, or for teenagers being battered by parents or boyfriends, and that there are no services for violent children of any ages.

> These poor kids just have to suffer and cope as best they can until they get old enough to either run away and become teenage prostitutes or until they follow the pattern, commit their first violent offence and can then be handled by the prison system.

The feelings expressed by one transition-house worker concerning the ramifications of this lack of services for shelter workers and residents were echoed by many others:

> We can't cope with the really violent kids that we're seeing now. The other week we had a seven-year-old who had to be just about constrained constantly. If he was out of our sight for a minute he was beating up on the other kids, kicking and hitting staff and residents, sticking pins in babies — he almost smothered one baby yesterday — really doing destructive and violent things. His mother can't cope with him and neither can we. We need one full-time person to work only with him; we just don't have the staff. But what can we do with him? There's just no residential programs out there for children like him.

Even identifying those children coming to transition houses who are potentially very violent has become difficult since the passage of the *Young Offenders Act*, which prohibits access to information about the criminal behaviour of young people. As a result, these children are not identified when they arrive at the house and are not dealt with appropriately. Mothers hesitate to reveal their children's criminal records for fear their children will be stigmatized, or worse, refused admission to the shelter. Thus, the safety of transition-house staff and residents is jeopardized.

The child welfare system, according to transition-house workers, is overburdened and frequently unclear or too narrow in its intervention philosophy. Many shelter workers said they realized that child welfare workers were extremely overworked and had to deal with frequently contradictory demands and social norms. However, shelter workers felt that the extreme pressures on child welfare workers frequently resulted in a lack of decisiveness on the part of many of these workers. This can have very negative ramifications for the children in the battering homes, for their mothers, and for shelter workers, in the opinions of the shelter workers concerned with this issue. As one worker said:

> They usually jump in if the child is physically abused, but they are very reluctant to deal with emotional problems or neglect that doesn't amount to outright abandonment, and most of them won't acknowledge sexual abuse either.

These general criticisms of the entire system of services which currently exist for children and adolescents are also reflected in the assessments given by transition-house workers of their relationships with family and children's services. Sixty-five per cent of the houses reported that they rarely, if ever, received a referral from family or children's services, and 70% described their relationship with family and children's services as poor or just adequate on a scale ranging from poor to excellent. Battered women, according to their reports as well as those of shelter workers, do not trust the child welfare system either. Many of the women who stay in transition houses have had direct or indirect experiences with the child welfare system either in their childhood or adult lives, and their first concern when they come to the transition houses is often: "Will I lose my children?" In fact, this fear is not without foundation. In the majority of provinces/territories, the children can be removed from the home by child welfare authorities if there is violence in the home. Whether or not this does happen, the perception of many battered women is that child welfare is not there to help and support the family or individual members in it, but rather to break an already injured family apart. This fear is exaggerated by some batterers who threaten that they will call child welfare and have them take the children away if the battered women leave home.

The perceived inadequacy of child welfare and parent aid services is also reflected in the fact that some women are seeking shelter in transition houses primarily to protect their children from abuse, not to protect themselves. They have come to the shelters because they say they don't trust that the child welfare system will give the child adequate protection without taking the child away from the mother. Approximately 1,380 women who stayed in shelters in 1985 gave, as their major reason for needing admission, the abuse of their children by their fathers or step-fathers. Another 92 women sought shelter to obtain help for their own abusive behaviour toward their children. These women reported that they came to transition houses for help, at least in part, because the orientation of most transition houses today is to help both the woman and her children, while the orientation of child welfare services, in the eyes of many women, is to split their families or to help the children only, with no regard for the women.

Nonetheless, despite the good work being done and planned by transition-house workers, it is important to remember that transition-house workers generally have contact with the children who stay with them for a short period (two weeks or less). As well, there are many abused and neglected children living in homes, where the mother is also battered, who will never stay at shelters. It is therefore imperative to recognize that, while the efforts of shelter workers to meet some of the needs of the children of battered women should be supported, these workers cannot provide all the services needed by children in violent homes.

Unfortunately, according to shelter workers and the battered women who stay with them, adequate community services do not exist outside transition houses to help the children directly. Neither do they exist to help the battered women deal with their children and the problems of their children related to their mother's battering. Many provincial departments and local agencies or services do offer parenting courses, but they are generally on a voluntary basis. The public education programs which exist are not good enough to reach women isolated by battering. These programs need better outreach components if they are to help the very women at whom they are targetted. The general ability of professionals in all types of services to identify members of battering families is currently poor. Therefore, these women are not directed to the parenting courses which exist for high-risk families.

Inadequate funding and limited community services for children also mean that few, if any, follow-up services are provided even for the children who stay at transition houses and so can be identified as being in need of continuing help. Transition-house workers feel that this is essential to prevent these children from repeating the pattern of violence they have witnessed.

Better follow-up of what happens to these children when they come into contact with professionals outside transition houses may also be important simply to protect the child. One very central problem in this regard reported by many transition-house workers was that judges are still permitting fathers to have visiting rights, even when there is evidence that the father abused the children. Further, transition-house workers reported that recommendations made to child welfare services regarding the need for protection of specific children are not always responded to, mainly because the child welfare workers are overworked.

A final but major problem identified by transition-house workers, other service-providers, and battered women was the problem of teaching respect for women to children who live in battering homes. Not only does wife battering teach children to behave violently, it can also seriously undermine the child's perception of women as equal and valuable members of society. As one researcher noted of the children who stayed in a shelter in Cleveland, "the children . . . stopped listening to their mothers or to any of the female staff because their fathers have devalued all women in the eyes of the children".[7] This problem has potentially enormous ramifications for the life chances of women in the present and future and for the entire future structuring of society.

Future Directions

The hopes and obstacles outlined above provide a strong argument that the problems of battered women and those of their children must be dealt with in tandem. They show that more preventive, crisis, and follow-up services are needed for these children. They show that major changes are needed in the goals and delivery of services within the child welfare system, and that better identification tools are needed to target children in battering families. They show that the education of children, professionals, and the general public about wife battering, child abuse, and how to get along with others is essential to help prevent violence and to increase the respect of men and women for one another. Some more specific directions for action suggested by women and men working in the field of wife battering and by battered women themselves are summarized below.

Short-Term Goals

Workers consistently expressed the hope that the needs of children who stay in transition houses will be more adequately recognized by funding agencies through the support of crisis counselling for these children, follow-up services, and activity programs provided or coordinated by shelter staff. All the shelter workers who answered this study's mail-out questionnaire said that, if they had the funds, they would like to develop a program specifically geared to the needs of children.

To ensure the success of these services, and the safety of the residents in shelters for battered women, workers feel it is imperative that they be given specific training to help them deal with aggressive or overtly violent children. Thirty-four per cent of the shelter workers who responded to the written questionnaire for this study also identified training in child care as a major need.

The importance of non-threatening parenting courses geared to the needs of battered women was also stressed. As one worker lamented:

> Too many parenting courses are oriented to middle-class women and don't deal with such basic issues as valuing the child and nutrition. Parenting courses should not be used as tools to threaten or coerce the battered women by making them fear that they will lose their children unless they attend.

Other workers felt that, even if the parenting skills of many of the women who stayed with them were poor, this problem should not be used to conclude that they do not love their children. Shelter workers were emphatic that these women, and many of the batterers as well, really care about their children. Therefore, workers hope that we might be able to stop the violence in some families by making the parents more aware of the neglect and emotional abuse of the children that occur in most battering relationships. Workers also believed that some of the guilt and depression many women feel regarding their children could be reduced if battered women were helped to understand that the children's anger is usually directed at the parent who is the victim of violence, and that this parent is almost always the mother.

The role of schools in providing support for children was also considered paramount. Teachers are in an excellent position to disseminate, through the children, information on services available to battered women and their children, as well as information on drug and alcohol abuse, which could benefit the whole family. Information on wife battering, child abuse, and interpersonal skills could also be communicated to all children if courses incorporating these topics were developed at all grade levels.

Most shelter workers felt that children staying in all transition houses would benefit from the model created in Alberta of providing teachers from the local school boards to give instruction to the children during their stay in the transition houses.

Service-providers also recognized that education should not be directed only at children. Many people working with battered women and their children spoke of the need to provide special training courses to professionals in the criminal justice, health, recreation, social service, and child welfare services, to enable them to identify and sensitively respond to children who live in homes where battering exists. Judges in particular were identified as requiring education on the psychological and physical dangers to the child of allowing men who have abused their children, and are separated or divorced from their wives, to have unmonitored access to their children. It is also the hope of people concerned with wife battering that these same professionals will be encouraged to develop protocols outlining procedures to help them identify and respond sensitively to children living in homes where their mother is battered.

Long-Term Goals

Shelter workers and other service-providers also spoke of their hopes for the development of improved residential and counselling services for very violent and self-destructive children of all ages. These services are particularly needed for adolescents who are abused or are participating, usually with their fathers, in battering their mothers. These workers also stressed that children living in violent homes need a variety of community-based drop-in programs which could incorporate counselling within a non-threatening, non-stigmatizing, recreational environment.

To help parents offer their children a life without violence, service-providers asserted that more parental support is needed through more widely available, high-quality, subsidized child care in a wide variety of settings, including child-care centres, but also including care in a neighbourhood private home and in the child's home; through support services for single parents in both rural and urban areas; through subsidized emergency child care and health support services in the home for use by mothers when sickness makes alternative care essential; and through the provision of remuneration for women caring for their own children in the home. Workers interviewed also identified the need for outreach programs to identify and help support mothers isolated in their homes.

Above all, workers stressed that, through all these programs, every attempt should be made to promote and support the valuing of children and of women in our society. One worker summarized this hope:

> So many of the problems we try to deal with are the direct result of children never feeling loved, never feeling special, never feeling worth anything. So many kids in our society are desperately grasping at straws of affection. . . . They'll take any tenderness even if it's preceded by a beating or sexual advances. We could do so much towards reducing violence of all kinds in our society if only, as a society, we would communicate that we value our children, and that we value women.

Criminal Justice Initiatives:
The Law As A Symbol Of Change

Overview

One of the most important roles the criminal justice system plays in our society is a symbolic one, through which it reflects, and may help promote, emerging values. It also symbolizes what we as a society will tolerate and what is beyond tolerance.

It is this function, more than its correctional or punitive functions, which has given the criminal justice system such potential to be an important ally in promoting change in societal attitudes and responses to wife battering. In the last few years, through significant reforms, particularly in the police and legislative responses, the criminal justice system has clearly announced society's unwillingness to tolerate wife battering.

Reform in the criminal justice response to wife battering is, in part, a reflection of a larger process of internal change and questioning within the criminal justice system itself. This questioning has centred around a number of concerns: a growing attention to the victims of crime; an ongoing attempt to make the *Criminal Code*, sentencing, and the criminal justice system generally more responsive to current social norms and problems; a search for more coordination among police, court, prison, and probation workers; and a growing interest in the preventive and even the "curative" role of the criminal justice system.[1]

However, progress in the criminal justice response has also been significantly stimulated by the demands of advocates for battered women. Battered women and front-line shelter workers have played a central role in bringing the inequities and limitations of the criminal justice response to the attention of policy-makers and criminal justice system agents.

To put these reforms in context, the concerns of battered women and their advocates which have stimulated change will be briefly discussed below. While reforms have been impressive, many of the concerns of women have been only partly addressed. A reiteration of the concerns of battered women's advocates can therefore serve as a reminder of the need for additional changes in the criminal justice system.

Women's Central Demands For Change
In The Criminal Justice System

Above all, the advocates for battered women have demanded that the criminal justice system recognize that wife battering is a crime. As early as January 1980, the CACSW recommended that:

Above all, the advocates for battered women have demanded that the criminal justice system recognize that wife battering is a crime. As early as January 1980, the CACSW recommended that:

> . . . *any direction for change in legislation should be guided by certain principles:*
> (a) *that assault is a crime, whether it occurs within or outside the home;*
> (b) *that victims of assault have a right to protection;*
> (c) *that women who want to leave a violent situation have a right to be given every assistance to do so;*
> (d) *that the community has an obligation*
> > (i)   *to do everything possible to protect all its members from violence, regardless of age, sex, marital status, or where the violence takes place;*
> > (ii) *to encourage long-range prevention through educational programs, information campaigns, and the presentation of family models in the media which do not perpetuate an image of women as dependent;*
> (e) *that the long- and short-term interests of women who are battered must be considered in any proposed solution or change;*
> (f) *that any proposed changes to reduce the incidence and negative effects of wife battering be developed in conjunction with women's groups who work in the field — most notably, transition house workers.*[2]

This recommendation has been reiterated in many subsequent recommendations, including two passed by the World Conference to Review and Appraise the Achievements of the United Nations Decade for Women. These recommendations urged "appropriate governmental agencies to pay special attention to violence against women and to treat such behaviour as criminal" and called upon

> . . . *states to develop laws and procedures, where they do not already exist, and to strengthen enforcement processes, including those of the police and courts for the proper protection and support of women and to hold violent men legally accountable for their violence.*[3]

The very clear demand by battered women and their advocates that wife battering be recognized and treated as a crime has been coupled with a demand for increased sensitivity by criminal justice agents toward battered women and a greater recognition of their needs. This demand for changes in attitudes and procedures has, in the past, been misinterpreted by some criminal justice agents, since it frequently has been expressed in the apparent ambivalence of some battered women toward **their own use** of the criminal justice system. One battered woman, quoted below, summarizes the feelings shared by many women, some of whom have also lobbied for change in arrest policies in wife-battering cases.

> *I've thought so many times about calling the police. If truth be known, I've thought about it for years — to teach him a lesson, to make him see what he's doing. But I always figured it would do more harm than good. My husband works as a security guard. Right in his contract it says he can't have a criminal record. So I call the police, and bang, he's out of a job, and jobs aren't so easy to come by here. Then where are we at? Things'll just get worse. We'll have no money. He'll start drinking more. He'll be even more angry at me and he'll hit me more. So where's the sense in calling the police?*

For this battered woman, and others, a criminal justice response which emphasizes only punishment does not offer the solutions she considers appropriate. As documented throughout this report, some battered women explain their partner's behaviour as a "sickness" or understand the man's violence as a reaction to unendurable life stresses. For these women, the traditional, punitive response of the criminal justice system seems totally inappropriate. Many women also worry about the stigmatizing effect on their children of involving the police. Others assert that any criminal justice penalty which involves a fine or an indirect loss of money through loss of employment can also jeopardize their security and that of their children.[4]

Other battered women are ambivalent toward the police once they arrive at the woman's home because these women do not really understand the ramifications of criminal justice involvement when they call the police. These women called the police for immediate protection, for transportation to a crisis shelter, or to teach the batterer a lesson, but they weren't prepared for any long-term follow-through. One woman elaborated:

> I was really afraid one night. I was afraid he'd kill me if it got any worse, so I called the police. He'd been so down ever since he lost his job — he just didn't seem in his right mind. I needed someone to stop him, just so he could see some sense. But when they got here, they started talking about arresting him, about me going to court. Well, I didn't want to do that. I didn't want our names in the paper. I didn't want this thing to drag on and on. He's just going through a bad time. I don't want to hurt him more. I want to help him.

While these feelings are not shared by all battered women, research which documents the number of times battered women experience violence before they call the police or seek outside help suggests that, in the early stages of the battering, many women do not automatically look for a criminal justice solution. One study found that, on average, women spoke of enduring ten physical assaults before they sought outside help.[5] Another study found that, while most women do seek outside help at some point, they are most likely to approach family, friends, doctors, nurses, or lawyers.[6] In the same study, when women were asked what they considered the best way to stop men from being violent, only 6% suggested involving the police and pressing charges.[7] Most felt that leaving the batterer or having him attend counselling sessions would be most effective.[8] Further, in this same study, when women were asked what more should be done to help battered women, only 12% suggested increasing the effectiveness of police or the legal system as a first priority. Twenty-three per cent suggested it as a second priority. Public education and sheltering far outweighed criminal justice alternatives as effective solutions in the women's minds.[9]

Thus, while women have demanded strong, clear, and decisive action by the criminal justice system, at the same time, they have alerted the system to the fact that its traditional responses may not always be appropriate in wife-battering cases. Women have therefore lobbied for **fundamental** change in the predominantly punitive, adversarial approach endemic to our criminal justice system.

To reiterate, the apparent ambivalence expressed by some is, in fact, an attempt to inform criminal justice agents of their lack of understanding concerning the characteristics of wife battering and the traditional dearth of sensitive responses to wife battering within the legal system. Dissatisfaction with the criminal justice response has also been more directly communicated through specific identification by women and their advocates of slow police response, or even the failure of police to respond to a battered woman's call for help, combined with a lack of coordination among the police, court, and corrections sections of the criminal justice system.

The authors of a Quebec provincial government document commented on criminal justice system inefficiencies which may discourage women from seeing police and courts as effective sources of protection:

> Police intervention in matters of conjugal violence has certain disquieting facts attached to it. For instance, few actual investigations are undertaken, the intervention is often reduced to a mere report of the happening, certain cases are directly referred to the crown attorney without a request to influence proceedings. . . . The crown attorney is very badly equipped to find an acceptable judicial solution. In fact, the cases are frequently referred to him without investigation by the policemen and it even happens that the data indispensable to the laying of an information [charge] are absent from the record.[10]

These problems are reflected in the generally poor assessment of the criminal justice system, **prior to recent policy changes**, reported by many women who chose to call the police. In most studies done on the satisfaction of battered women with the criminal justice system, **prior to the widespread endorsement of a more aggressive charging policy**, the level of satisfaction expressed was very low. In one study, only half the battered women surveyed were satisfied with the response of the justice of the peace, and only 31% were satisfied with the Crown attorney's intervention. The reasons they gave were that the Crown attorneys didn't spend enough time explaining the situation and court proceedings, they offered no support or understanding, there were long delays between the incident and the final court disposition, and, even though 85% of the women worried about being attacked by their spouse during this time, no special protection was offered or provided.[11]

In fact, in another early study,

> . . . 14% of the women interviewed felt that using the police as a source of help had increased their difficulties, and 32% of those who contacted police thought the police were very ineffective.[12]

In addition, two-thirds of the shelter workers responding to the written questionnaire for this study reported that about one-quarter of the women who stayed with them expressed concern that police might charge their husbands. One counsellor elaborated on the dilemmas many women expressed about involving the criminal justice system:

> Women say that they feel victimized by the police, by their friends and neighbours, even by society, when they call the police in. Even though police are supposed to lay the charges, many still put subtle pressure on the women to do it. Even if the police do lay the charges, the community is still not aware of the change in the charging policy, so her friends and relatives may accuse her of being vindictive, of ruining her husband's life. With all this pressure, ironically the woman often feels that her husband is the only one giving her support because he's begging her not to lay charges, he's promising her he'll change and he's telling her he loves her. In addition, it usually isn't until the woman stops loving the man, is worried that he'll hurt the children or that he'll kill her, that she is really committed to seeing him charged. Very few women I see feel vindictive towards their husbands, and they see pressing charges as a vindictive act.

Progress To Date

Many criminal justice system workers and policy-makers have taken the concerns of women, summarized above, very seriously, and have responded with decisive action. The resulting changes in policy have been dramatic. The summary which follows is an attempt to highlight major criminal justice system initiatives related to wife battering which reflect these basic changes, and which promote the role of the criminal justice system as a symbol and sign of change in society's values regarding violence against women. No attempt will be made to provide an exhaustive catalogue of all relevant criminal justice-related initiatives.

Legislative Changes

Two major legislative changes have taken place in recent years which communicate societal recognition that wife battering is a crime. As of 1983, in Canada, the sexual assault legislation was changed so that a husband could be charged with raping his wife. In the same year, amendments were made to the *Canada Evidence Act* which expanded the situations in which a wife (or husband) could be compelled to give evidence against her/his spouse to include offences related to wife battering and child abuse.

Changes In Police Charging Policy

No change initiated by the criminal justice system has announced society's unwillingness to tolerate wife battering as strongly as the decisions by federal and provincial/territorial ministers across Canada to support and encourage police and Crown attorneys to adopt a more aggressive charging policy in wife-battering cases.

On July 15, 1982, a letter was sent by the federal Ministry of the Solicitor General to the Executive of the Canadian Association of Chiefs of Police requesting their support and cooperation in dealing with violence in the family, and encouraging all Canadian police forces to lay charges. The Royal Canadian Mounted Police (RCMP) subsequently consulted with provincial Attorneys General and developed a national charging policy in February 1983. In conjunction with the federal Department of Justice, the Solicitor General issued guidelines for police and prosecutors in the Northwest Territories and in the Yukon in December 1983.

Since 1982, all provincial/territorial governments have issued directives to the police, and in most cases to Crown attorneys as well, encouraging rigorous investigation and prosecution of wife-battering cases. In most directives, the police have been instructed that, while they must have reasonable and probable grounds to assume that an assault has taken place, as a result of amendments to the *Criminal Code* proclaimed in 1983, they do not have to actually witness the incident.

Police Training Has Been Upgraded To Stress Sensitive Intervention In Wife-Battering Cases

All Canadian police education and training centres now report that they include a segment on wife battering in their training courses for police recruits. A number of courses have been substantially revised following the issuing of directives encouraging more aggressive charging policies; in some locations, these revisions were made with the input of women's groups. Training manuals have also been upgraded in some jurisdictions. As well, in Saskatchewan (where a core training package has been developed for the use of a variety of professionals), representatives from the RCMP, municipal police forces, prosecutions, and corrections are being encouraged to attend training sessions.

The Number Of Domestic Crisis Intervention Teams Has Grown

Crisis intervention teams represent an attempt by police forces to coordinate a more sensitive, multi-disciplinary response to wife battering and to other cases termed ''domestics'' by police forces. Crisis teams are generally made up of police officers and social workers, but some use volunteers as well as police officers.

These services attempt to respond to the needs of victims of domestic and neighbourhood disputes, as well as people suffering personal crises and mental health problems. They provide crisis intervention, short-term counselling, emergency referral, and sometimes emergency property repair through specially trained police officers or trained civilian personnel. These programs emphasize inter-agency referral, consultation, and communication. They also depend heavily on police discretion and definitions of appropriate or needy clients.

Battered women have also benefitted to some extent from the growth of police-based services developed for all victims of crime. Such services are primarily oriented to providing information on the progress of specific cases, information on crime compensation, crime prevention, and practical information regarding court appearances, as well as criminal justice system procedures. These services also offer referrals to other services which can help victims with their financial, health, and social service needs.

Unfortunately, most general victim services operate only during business hours. As a result, these programs are of limited benefit to most battered women since they are not designed to meet the battered woman's needs for emotional support or protection, which are usually required outside these hours. Nonetheless, like all victims of crime, battered women gain from criminal justice programs which help to integrate victims into the criminal justice process by providing information and emotional support.

Improved Criminal Justice System Data Collection

The RCMP and several provincial, territorial, and municipal police departments have redesigned their statistics collection systems so that wife-battering cases can be differentiated from other forms of assault, and so that the outcome of the case, as well as some demographic characteristics of the suspect and the battered woman, can be identified. Improved statistical collection will enable police to estimate more accurately the proportion of assaults which are in fact wife-battering cases, will help them more consistently assign trained officers to these cases, will increase society's recognition of the magnitude of the problem, and may expedite the design of court-based programs and sentencing alternatives to meet the special needs of wife-battering victims.

Some Progress Has Been Made In Attempts To Improve The Protection Of Battered Women

A perennial concern of battered women and their advocates has been the ineffectiveness of court orders instructing batterers to keep the peace and/or to have no contact with their wives and/or children. While police policy in all jurisdictions states that police are to enforce all court orders which prevent a man from seeing or harassing his partner, police have been criticized over the years for failing to adequately enforce breaches of court orders.[13] To address this concern in Ontario and British Columbia, studies and discussions are underway to determine ways to increase the effectiveness of court orders as a means of providing better protection to women who are victims of wife battering.

In addition, to shorten the time period currently required by police to write up and to serve an accused batterer with a peace bond and to help ensure that the wishes of the battered women are recorded by the police officer in such a way that they will be accurately interpreted by the judge, the Alberta government has asked the Alberta Law Society to consider implementing a common wording format for all restraining orders.

Police officers interviewed for this study also reported informally that they are now taking court orders much more seriously and are reacting more decisively when a man disobeys a court order. As one police officer commented:

> The number of breaches of bonds is constantly going down. . . . We don't treat it lightly. We've found that counselling the batterer on the terms of the order in front of the woman who holds the bond can make it more meaningful for both of them.

Many police officers have also tried to assist and protect battered women by routinely providing transportation to a crisis shelter, to the home of a friend or relative, or to a motel if they consider her to be in danger.

Sentencing Patterns Are Being Investigated

There has been some concern demonstrated in the criminal justice system regarding the effectiveness and fairness of sentencing procedures in wife-battering cases. For example, Saskatchewan undertook a survey to determine the number of offenders sentenced for wife battering. As part of a larger study on sentencing, the federal Department of Justice is also examining the notion of mandatory minimum sentences for offences in general. In addition, changes to data collection techniques mentioned earlier will facilitate research on sentencing patterns.

While there are currently no national statistics on sentencing patterns in wife-battering cases, informal interviews conducted for this study with shelter workers, police officers, and Crown attorneys suggested that there are fewer absolute discharges or dismissals in wife-battering cases today than there were seven years ago. The most common sentences, according to these informal reports, are a conditional discharge or a $200 fine. It was estimated, through these informal reports, that about 40% of the cases are dealt with by conditional discharge and about another 35% by fines. Approximately 20% of the batterers receive jail or prison sentences.

In locations where counselling programs for batterers exist, judges can demand that, as part of his sentence, a batterer receive counselling, and some judges are passing sentences which include mandatory attendance at these programs. As the number of these counselling programs increases, and as the awareness of judges regarding their existence grows, it is probable that requiring the batterer to accept treatment as part of his sentence will become more common.

Developments In Court-Related Programs

One of the most widespread changes in court-related programs has been the creation of Crown attorney positions which are specifically designated to handle wife-battering cases. Known as designated Crown attorneys, they are usually given special training about wife battering to familiarize them with the victim's perspective and to educate them about the realities of wife battering. These prosecutors are appointed to deal with all cases involving wife battering which go through their courts.

Most designated Crown attorneys, according to several interviewed, try to meet with the battered women before the cases, and to speak personally to battered women who want to drop charges. Some also reported that they make the woman's wishes regarding sentencing known to the judge before sentence is passed.

In most provinces/territories where designated Crown attorneys have not been appointed, instructions have been issued to all Crown attorneys regarding the handling of these cases, encouraging them to handle these cases more sensitively, to provide emotional support to the women and, at the very least, to meet with the battered woman before the case is presented in court.

In addition, a number of experiments with court options are being conducted to improve the efficiency and sensitivity with which courts handle wife-battering cases. In the fall of 1984, Manitoba established a wife-battering court with a special judge and one Crown attorney assigned to it to deal with cases where the batterer pleads not guilty and asks to be tried by a judge alone, not by a judge and jury. The relative benefits of using family courts,[14] as opposed to criminal courts, to handle wife-battering cases are also being assessed in some provinces/territories. Ideally, family courts tend to stress negotiation among the parties involved, to make referrals to social agencies for counselling or needed support, and to attempt to reduce the conflict among the parties involved through an inquiry conducted by the family court judge without the cross-examination characteristic of a criminal trial. Criminal courts are more public, and are based on an adversarial model in which one party is deemed the winner and one the loser. In Alberta, for example, a trial coordination project is underway to determine whether family or criminal courts are preferable for hearing trials concerning wife battering. In addition, Nova Scotia has a family court which has been granted the authority to deal with criminal assault charges punishable on summary conviction, laid under Section 245(b) of the *Criminal Code*. Ordinarily these cases would be dealt with through criminal courts.

Efforts are also being made to address two of the most common problems mentioned by battered women regarding cases which go to court. These problems involve the inordinately long delays often experienced between arrest and the beginning of court hearings, as well as the delay between the start and finish of the trial. An attempt to improve the efficiency of the court process is being made in Saskatchewan, where the Regina Prosecutions Unit is piloting a project in which cases of wife battering are assigned a special priority similar to the priority given to cases where the accused is held in jail awaiting trial. The aim of this project is to shorten the time between the arrest of the batterer and the prosecution of the case in court.

The Women's Points Of View On Criminal Justice System Changes

The significant changes which have taken place in criminal justice intervention in wife-battering cases are generally lauded by women across Canada as major victories in asserting society's abhorrence of wife battering and in promoting better protection for women against wife battering.

Eighty-one per cent of the shelter workers who responded to the written questionnaire for this study stated that their shelter is in favour of the current more aggressive charging policies. Most of the remaining 19% answered negatively only because they felt these charging policies were not being enforced adequately. That is, they were in favour of the policy but were critical of its current implementation. In addition, shelter workers estimated that, of those battered women who stayed with them in 1985 and who were aware of the new charging policies, 72% of the women felt they were good policies. Only 10%, in the estimation of shelter workers, saw them as bad. The remaining 18% simply saw them as currently ineffective.

Eighty-nine per cent of the shelter workers also reported greatly or somewhat improved relationships with the police and, as a result of this improvement, 79% felt that they had a good or very good current relationship with the police officers in their locations.

Other recent studies do show that, in the period following the changes in arrest policies and police training programs cited above, battered women are more satisfied with the police response. In one study, almost three-quarters of the respondents expressed satisfaction with the police handling of their cases.[15]

However, findings from the current study indicate that women are most positive about criminal justice intervention when the criminal justice system is seen as a preventive and protective, rather than a punitive, system. So, only 24% of shelter workers felt that more women would want the police to lay charges if they knew that their partners would be sent to jail. However, 64% estimated that women would be more favourable toward charging if the women and children could be guaranteed 24-hour protection until the man was put in jail or taken to court, and 81% felt the women would be more in favour of charging if they knew that the man would be ordered by the courts to get special treatment.

Other recent research also documents the benefits of criminal justice system changes for women, particularly the changes in charging policies. As one researcher writes:

> Domestic assault victims reported a significantly higher level of satisfaction with police handling of their complaints [when charges were laid]. . . . Those who had charges laid . . . were more likely to estimate a decrease in future assaults.[16]

Challenges For The Future

All the findings detailed above indicate great support among Canadian women for the recent criminal justice changes. Criminal justice system reforms have helped clarify society's position on wife battering and have benefitted many battered women. Nonetheless, many challenges still remain before the effectiveness of the reforms that have been achieved can be maximized.

Implementing More Aggressive Charging Policies — The Challenges

This study reaffirms that women need and want more aggressive charging policies because women who are battered need the reassurance that society is behind them, that they're not alone. Women need the safety net from retributive violence provided by being able to say to their husbands: "I didn't lay the charges, the police did". However, both the short- and long-term effectiveness of more aggressive charging policies depend on implementation of these policies. Simply because police have been directed to arrest does not mean that all police are complying with these directives. A recent report prepared for the British Columbia government noted that:

1. *The policy is being implemented unevenly across the province, particularly with respect to police and Crown Counsel.*

2. *Attitudes of police and Crown Counsel in relation to the policy cover the whole range from opposition to support and from cynicism to hopefulness.*

3. *Knowledge and understanding of the policy on the part of system personnel varies from good to a complete lack of awareness of its existence.*[17]

Similar concerns and observations were expressed by service-providers across the country. In addition, only 1% of shelter workers who responded to this study's questionnaire believed that police enforce the charging directives all the time, and only 16% felt they enforced it most of the time. In addition, workers estimated that, in about one-third of the cases where no charges were laid, the women would have liked the police to lay charges. Even more telling are shelter worker reports that 88% of the women who laid charges themselves would have preferred the police to lay charges.

In general, police interviewed for this study were favourable to the charging policy, but gave several reasons for its uneven application. One was that they didn't feel the policy was explicit enough on operational procedures, such as whether police have the right to remove the man from the family home. Second, they raised the perennial problem of coordination within the criminal justice system. As one police officer said:

It's fine for us to be firm about charging, but the lawyers and judges aren't up on the policy, so they keep giving these guys discharges and that can be pretty frustrating, so some of the police get discouraged and stop charging.

Police in some jurisdictions said they won't lay charges unless they think the case will result in a conviction, because they are often reprimanded or penalized for a low "success" rate. Finally, police explained that the additional paperwork which accompanies the new guidelines is so time-consuming and confusing that it tends to discourage police officers from getting involved in the wife-assault cases.

■ Police Training

While the quality of police training related to wife battering has improved, almost all the training is given to recruits. Police and shelter workers stressed that **ongoing** training is needed for **all** officers, including commanding officers and middle management, to encourage consistency in the application of policies relating to wife battering.

Police also expressed frustration at the fact that training for lawyers and judges is almost non-existent. This perception is supported by this study's statistics. Only 15% of shelter workers said there had been training programs or awareness seminars concerning wife battering for judges or justices of the peace, and only 29% knew of such programs for Crown attorneys.

■ The Need For Increased Sensitivity Among Judges And Crown Attorneys

The fact that there is almost no training about wife battering for judges,[18] and very little training for lawyers, speaks eloquently to the lack of sensitivity of judges and lawyers reported earlier in this chapter through the words of battered women and their advocates. This lack of sensitivity helps make many battered women hesitant to see court as a viable course of action, and can lead to additional victimization of battered women. A current glaring example of this lack of sensitivity is the practice, in some Canadian locations, of charging women with contempt of court if they refuse to testify against their partners. As one shelter worker warned:

> We can't become too purist about the effectiveness of criminal justice system intervention, or the criminal justice system will simply become a major way to victimize women. For example, the current trend in some jurisdictions to charge women with contempt of court if they refuse to testify is victimizing women. Oh, I can see why it is necessary from a purist point of view. It's necessary to impress on the women as well as on the men that wife battering is a crime, and that it is not alright to just drop charges in wife-battering cases, any more than it is alright to drop charges in other criminal cases. But wife-battering cases aren't just like other cases. How many individual women are we willing to sacrifice for symbolic and ideological purity? Should women be sacrificed to make a point?

Women in this study, as well as some designated Crown attorneys, concurred that battered women were more likely to testify against their husbands if they were told what to expect in court, were given some emotional support by the prosecutor, and were allowed to express their misgivings to the Crown attorney and have the Crown work through these concerns with them. Through a sensitive, human approach to battered women, then, Crown attorneys could frequently prevent the problem of women refusing to testify, and so deflect the unnecessary and harsh use of contempt charges against women who are feeling frightened, vulnerable, and confused.

■ Data Collection Challenges

Police record-keeping systems still do not, in all locations, permit police officers who are responding to a wife-battering call to know whether there has been a history of assault in that family and, if so, the nature of these previous incidents and whether weapons have been involved. This serious gap in the availability of data decreases the ability of police officers to be properly prepared to handle all wife-battering cases appropriately and so potentially increases the danger to both police and battered women as a result of police intervention.

■ Crisis Teams Can Put The Appropriate Role Of Police In Question

Most police are very positive about an increased emphasis on crisis teams. They stress the benefits for police as well as for the victims, of programs in which police work with social workers, volunteers, or others who work with victims. Nonetheless, these programs, as well as other victim-oriented programs which emphasize a social service approach to victims, currently create uncertainties for some police officers who are concerned with the modification of their roles away from a law enforcement focus. These officers worry that they will suffer a change in status through affiliation with victims' services and that they will spend far more of their time dealing with inter-agency disputes. Police also reported that they were concerned with the implications of these new responsibilities for their collective agreements, with escalation of intra-departmental friction, and with increased pressures on time and budget allocations.[19]

The Continuing Challenge Of Providing Adequate Protection

According to reports collected for this study, adequate protection of battered women is not available to women who report the battering to the criminal justice system. Even though different governments are attempting to make more effective use of peace bonds and restraining orders, which instruct batterers to stay away from their wives, battered women and shelter workers spoke of the fear of retribution many women experience if they report the battering to the police. As one woman said:

> If I report him, he'll come after me to kill me, but the police won't help. I have a friend who asked them to have a car posted in front of her house, but they just smiled and said, 'All you've got is a verbal threat — we can't babysit you'.

Section 745 of the *Criminal Code* does provide that threats of death, of serious injury, or simple threats accompanied by an act or gesture of violence are criminal offences. But,

> . . . the peace officers must determine if the threats suffered by the victims are an offence against one of these sections of the Criminal Code and take the indicated action if a criminal offence has been committed. However, certain threats . . . although few in number . . . are not considered as a commission of a criminal offence. We are referring here to a situation where there is a fear that violence will erupt: tempestuous arguments between spouses and family quarrels are sometimes of that order.[20]

Current interpretations of threats under the law, therefore, do not seem to provide adequate protection for battered women in Canada. As one police officer concluded:

> Section 745 has to be totally rethought. It gives a total false security to the woman. What the man gets out of it is meaningless, especially if he's been through the mill, has been in trouble with the law before. We're trying to do something preventive in a system that is inherently reactive.

■ The Challenge Of Handing Down Fair Sentences

Shelter workers, and many other social and legal service-providers across Canada, concurred in their perception that sentences handed down in wife-battering cases are often arbitrary and inappropriate. Appropriateness is not necessarily equated with harshness of sentence by these workers. As the staff at the London Battered Women's Advocacy Clinic write:

> If the batterer's problem is the use of violence as a control mechanism, does it really make much sense to place him in a hostile jail setting where the use of power and dominance to maintain control is exercised not only by the system itself but also by the underground power structures maintained by prisoners? If the court seems to flex its muscles to control his actions, could this not seem to the batterer to validate his use of power to control his partner? If the court imposes heavy financial penalties, does this not also penalize the family which the batterer often supports?. . . Often a harsh penalty will confirm a batterer in his hostility toward the victim; he may believe it is her 'fault' because she used the system as a weapon against him and he feels justified in punishing her with further abuse or harassment.[21]

However, at the same time, shelter workers and other service-providers generally agree that appropriate sentences are certainly not sentences which seem to absolve the batterer or which blame the victim for her own victimization.[22] Unfortunately, current sentencing practices often convey these messages. As mentioned earlier, informal reports suggest that the most common sentences in wife-battering cases are still absolute or conditional discharges, although fines of $200 are becoming more prevalent. The apparent leniency of these sentences can be made more unfair if they are based on the judge's unfounded and stereotypical assumptions about the battered woman. The case cited below graphically demonstrates this problem.

> One particular case involved a charge of sexual assault of the estranged wife. In handing down the sentence the judge said: 'In this particular case, there was a sexual assault done on a woman that was the accused's wife. The sexual assault was minor. There were no previous convictions. Though the crime on the face was very serious, the circumstances bring it down considerably.'[23]

Sentences are needed which will protect battered women and their children, give the batterers the counselling they need, where appropriate, and clearly convey the batterer's responsibility for his actions.

Making Legal Aid More Helpful To Battered Women

While no reliable statistics were collected for this study on the use of legal aid by battered women, informal reports uncovered a number of complaints and problems. Most women mentioned during their interviews that there are not enough legal-aid lawyers. Some spoke of the need for battered women to have the chance to get a legal-aid lawyer if both parties qualify for legal aid. This need arises from the fact that, in many cases, because the woman may be coping with her injuries and moving her children out of the home, the partner is likely to request a legal-aid lawyer before the wife does so. In these cases, if the woman lives in a location where there are few lawyers who will accept legal-aid clients, the woman may be unable to find any legal-aid lawyer at all, or may be forced to take a lawyer she does not feel will adequately represent her interests. Women also reported that, because of the shortage of legal-aid lawyers, these lawyers often have a heavy case-load and so there are longer than normal delays in bringing their cases to court.

■ The Challenge Of Accepting The Reality That Arrest Is Not A Solution For All Battered Women

A final challenge remains for criminal justice agents and policy-makers as they attempt to implement the major policy changes which have been realized, and to interpret the results of evaluations linked to this implementation. The challenge involves accepting that, while clear and more aggressive charging policies are of great benefit to many battered women, not all women will choose to turn to the police or courts for help with battering. This fact should not be used to diminish the importance of a strong arrest policy, nor should it be used to argue that the necessity for uniform enforcement of this policy across Canada is questionable.

Criminal justice services are only one part of a wide constellation of service options which should be available to battered women. Battered women share with all of us a human urge to hope. Their anguish may be long term, but their vision of the future is even longer term, and this vision frequently includes the hope that the violence will end and that their marriages will stay together. As a result, some battered women may reject what they see as short-term solutions which may dash their long-term hopes. Therefore, the arrest option and reliance on the criminal justice system is, to **some** women, a very unpalatable solution because they perceive that the intervention of the law will increase the chances of the marriage ending. In addition, the law gives her no assurance that the violence will end. Most battered women want help which will give them long-term hope. They do not want to sacrifice potential long-term solutions, no matter how seemingly "illogical" to outsiders, for short-term solutions, particularly when the level of effectiveness of these short-term solutions is so uncertain. This seeming ambiguity is not limited only to the attitudes of battered women towards the criminal justice system. As Susan Schechter reminds us:

> In its assessment of reforms, the movement must ultimately face other layers of contradictions. Many women want to use neither shelters nor courts. They do not want police to arrest; they just want the violence to stop. For another group of women, leaving their husbands or communities is unthinkable, and going to court feels like cutting themselves off from their only base of support.[24]

These apparent contradictions must not be used to downgrade the importance of recent reforms within the criminal justice system for battered women. Criminal justice system reform is a necessary component in any multi-dimensional solution to the problem of wife battering. However, it is important to acknowledge that it responds to only some facets of the problem, and to the hopes and needs of only some battered women.

The continuing feeling among some women that the criminal justice response is inappropriate should, in part, be accepted as inevitable and natural in a diversified society. This perception among some battered women should, however, also provide a constant reminder that criminal justice personnel must deal with wife-battering cases sensitively, and with a recognition of the uniqueness of these cases.

Future Directions

Throughout this chapter, it has been demonstrated that criminal sanctions to stop wife battering are a vital part of any response to the immediate crisis problems of battered women, and that they provide an important symbolic statement on which to base any long-term program to prevent wife battering. It has also been repeatedly stated in this chapter that, while the importance of changes in the criminal justice system should be stressed, it must also be recognized that:

> The criminal justice system can't really provide a solution to violence. If we are really trying to make people better people, this can't be legislated or punished into existence.[25]

The changes in the criminal justice system are impressive, but they are very new, and they are based on a quest for larger reform within the criminal justice system which is still tentative. Reforms related to wife battering, accordingly, must be seen as experimental. We do not yet know the effectiveness or consequences of many of the changes. As yet, not all criminal justice officials at the working level are even implementing the policy directives on a routine basis. It is therefore important not to be impatient for dramatic results; not, for example, to define the success of these policy changes in terms only, or even primarily, of increases in the number of wife-battering cases reported. The implementation of criminal justice reforms should be closely monitored and evaluated not only in terms of their effects on official statistics, but also in terms of their effects on battered women, their children, and the batterers; in terms of the perceptions of battered women, service-providers, and the general public concerning these changes; and in terms of costs, both financial and social.

These evaluations should also ask some difficult questions. For example: Are we limiting the choices of some women through a too rigid application of criminal justice procedures (for example, charging women with contempt of court for refusing to testify against their partners)? Already, some shelter workers speculate that because, under the law, children can be removed from a home where violence has occurred, women may be discouraged from reporting the violence. Is greater criminal justice intervention going to force some women back into hiding, particularly if women fear that this intervention will lead to the removal of the children? Could changes in operational guidelines for police, reached through consideration of this problem with child welfare and shelter workers, help allay this concern? It must also be asked: Do we want to bring more people to court?

Canada's court system is already overburdened with too many cases of all kinds and, as documented earlier, we know that the effectiveness of criminal justice intervention in wife-battering cases diminishes over time. Therefore, will more court cases benefit women? These and other questions must be seen as the backdrop for the short- and long-term goals expressed by service-providers as well as battered women.

Short-Term Goals

The need for evaluation of the implementation of new charging policies was repeatedly emphasized by shelter workers, researchers, and criminal justice officials, as was the importance of reducing the time between charging and the court appearance. Many people interviewed felt that the potential benefits of using family courts versus criminal courts should be reassessed. As one worker said:

> With the emphasis on making wife battering a criminal offence like any other criminal offence, the potential of expanding the role of family court has been de-emphasized, but, in many cases, battered women are more comfortable with family court and feel it better meets their needs.

Shelter workers want legal aid to be restructured and criminal injuries compensation systems to be more responsive to the needs of battered women. Some workers also spoke of the need to make women aware they can sue their partners for compensation. These workers believe that substantial financial penalties may be the most effective way of stopping violent behaviour, particularly among middle-class men. In addition:

> Being a plaintiff in a civil suit implies an offensive approach. Using such assertive and even aggressive behaviour helps women express their anger at having been victimized in a socially acceptable manner. For many of our women, winning was less important than the whole process of feeling as though the balance of power had changed, and knowing they could control their tormenter.[26]

Shelter workers also spoke of the need for more advocacy clinics across Canada to assist battered women in their dealings with the criminal justice system, and for advocates to accompany them to court. Ideally, advocacy workers would also have links with social, health, and financial services to help women deal with these problems together with their legal problems.

Long-Term Goals

Three major long-term goals and hopes were shared by most women and men interviewed across Canada. First, there was a desire to ensure that criminal justice programs are being developed and used in such a way that women's options will be expanded, not narrowed. Finding ways to increase the ability of this system to protect women was a major priority, as was looking very closely at the practice of charging women with contempt of court when these women do not want to testify against their partners.

The second hope shared by battered women and workers inside as well as outside the criminal justice system was that, through training sessions, discussions, and information dissemination in their associations, judges and Crown attorneys will make a concerted effort to increase their understanding of wife battering. In addition, it was hoped that judges and Crown attorneys will consider ways to increase their sensitivity to the needs of battered women through more appropriate sentences, more contact with the women prior to court appearance, less aggressive treatment in court, fewer unnecessary court delays, considerations of court options (like those, mentioned earlier, being experimented with in a few locations in Canada), and a reduced time lag between charging and court appearance.

The third and most enveloping hope expressed was that criminal justice agents, along with other service-providers and the general public, will increasingly recognize that access to justice for victims of wife battering depends on the coordination of social, health, and financial support services with more sensitive criminal justice programs and responses, innovative prevention programs, and a unique, broad-based information and referral system. This hope expresses the recognition that the realization of justice for battered women, as well as the strength of the criminal justice system, is ultimately rooted in the community. As Susan Schechter concludes:

> Although criminal sanctions to stop abuse are a vital part of a solution to battered women's immediate problems, in the long run, the community, not just the criminal justice system, must understand that violence against women is rooted in male domination. Only by developing a philosophy of and struggle for gender equality will a movement change public consciousness which in turn will force individuals and institutions to treat violence against women as a serious offense.[27]

Programs For Batterers

Overview

Implicit in criminal justice initiatives related to wife battering is the assertion that men who batter, like all those found guilty under the *Criminal Code*, are responsible for their actions.[1] This assertion is also at the root of the rapid development, across Canada, of counselling programs for men who batter.

Most programs for men who batter grew out of a commitment, based on a number of observations, to the prevention of wife battering and to the protection of battered women. The first observation is that most batterers will not change their violent behaviour without some outside pressure and guidance. As one counsellor for batterers explains:

> It has been my experience that most violent men who come to our group and stay long enough to make a change are there because they have to be. That 'have to' is either a court order or their wives saying they won't return unless the men get some help. This does not mean that most men want to be violent . . . [but that] outside pressure is needed to keep them in the group past their usual tolerance level for self-confrontation.[2]

The second observation, which helps explain why most batterers won't change on their own, is that violence, and particularly male violence, is accepted in our society except in its most extreme forms. As Maria Roy, noted U.S. author on this issue, states:

> Societal acceptance of male violence is strong. We are not shocked by it, except in its more heinous forms, such as brutal killings that are clearly psychopathic. In general, violence by men has become an expected, if not accepted, form of behavior. . . . The man is seen as acting out of his natural instincts which are uncontrollable and unchangeable.[3]

The third observation is that violence is learned behaviour. Counsellors for men who batter challenge the belief that male violence is "natural" or that battered women are "masochists".[4] They point out that men who batter often make a series of rational decisions about the violence, including whether to hit their wives where it shows or where the bruises will be invisible, whether to hit or punch her "a little", or whether to use a weapon and risk killing her. As one counsellor from Emerge, a counselling group for men in Boston, points out:

> At first, men tend to say they 'lost control'. . . . I hear it said over and over again and I can't believe that that many men are pathologically out of control. When you ask a

man 'Why didn't you stab her with a knife instead of hitting her?' he'll say 'Oh, I didn't want to kill her. . . . It just feels right to control women.'[5]

Counsellors conclude from these observations that, if men can control the ways in which they are violent, they can also learn how **not** to be violent.

The fourth observation on which the growth of programs for batterers is based is that abuse is one tool men use to ensure that women do what men want them to do. This belief fits with the research, cited earlier in the report, demonstrating that men batter for control.

The logic of these observations has convinced many counsellors, other service-providers, and policy-makers that counselling groups for men who batter are an essential component of any constellation of services aimed at the reduction of wife battering in individual families and at the ultimate prevention of wife battering in our society.

Progress To Date

At the time of writing, there were 45 programs in existence across Canada for men who batter. These programs are supported by a wide variety of community services. Counsellors for men who batter, interviewed in this study, said they receive referrals and requests for information from many different sources, including churches, family services, military bases, shelters for battered women, doctors, and employers. It is noteworthy, however, that, in a comprehensive 1984 study on programs for men who batter sponsored by the National Clearinghouse on Family Violence, the positive relationship between women's shelters and men's groups was specially highlighted.

> *In many cases there are official liaisons between the men's group and the shelter by means of a board member, membership on a coordinating committee, use of women's shelter staff as advisors, or belonging to the same parent agency. Frequently, men's group staff had given workshops or talks at the shelter.[6]*

Formal links with the criminal justice system vary widely among groups for men who batter. Some programs are located within correctional institutions and serve only offenders, including those incarcerated for offences related to wife battering, as well as those who have a general problem controlling their violence. Other men's groups accept court-mandated offenders who have been ordered to attend the group as part of their sentence or as an attempt at diversion from the criminal justice system, as well as men who come voluntarily. Finally, there are groups where attendance is purely on a voluntary basis. Counselling is free for participants in most groups and the cost is either absorbed by the hospital, prison, church, or other service in which the group is situated, or the group is supported by government funds. In a few groups, the participants are charged fees which cover the entire cost of counsellors and facilities, but these fees are usually adjusted on a sliding scale according to the participant's ability to pay.

Even though not all programs accept court-mandated clients, most group leaders feel that counselling groups for men who batter can provide an effective sentencing alternative to imprisonment or fines. Some group leaders have made a conscious attempt to increase the number of referrals from the courts by informing judges of the existence of their program, and have organized workshops to help criminal justice, social service, and health service professionals develop better skills in working with men who batter.

An increasing number of counselling groups for batterers are being developed within a constellation of inter-related counselling groups which are either already in existence or are planned for imminent start-up. This development is based on the recognition that there is a need for a parallel group for the battered women, and another group for their children. Public education, follow-up groups, and in some cases, couples groups or family therapy groups to be used with some families after the batterers' groups have been completed, are often all components of these planned service constellations.

The development of networks of services reflects the growing awareness among service-providers that no one element or individual can be the exclusive focus in society's attempts to reduce wife battering. Addressing the responsibility of the batterer and of the community as well as the effects of battering on the battered women, their children, and the community is increasingly being seen as necessary to improve the success of individual programs.

Coordination across programs is also promoted by many groups being co-sponsored by several agencies; for example, by probation services and health services. An increasing number of groups have also chosen to use one male counsellor and one female counsellor to assist men in developing different ways of dealing with women and to facilitate the men's willingness to talk about their feelings, since some counsellors have found that men are more at ease discussing emotional issues and admitting to weakness when dealing with female counsellors.

While evaluation is still not a built-in feature of most groups, there are at least three evaluations of individual programs currently in progress, and the federal government is planning a long-term evaluation study to be supported by three federal departments.

The Women's Points Of View

Research has repeatedly shown that most battered women want counselling for their husbands. Meredith and Conway, in a study of the needs of battered women, found that:

> . . . the most frequently expressed need [91% of the victims interviewed] was for professional help for their assailants. Such help can take the form of alcoholism treatment and/or counselling programs specifically for wife batterers. . . . Most victims do not want their assailant punished so much as they want the abuse to stop and they want their assailant helped.[7]

These conclusions are supported by the finding for the current study, reported in the previous chapter, that 81% of shelter workers felt that more battered women would want the police to lay charges if they knew that the man would be ordered to get special treatment.

Informal conversations and letters from battered women elucidate this finding. As one woman said:

> Why can't they see that he's sick? Sure I get mad sometimes and want him punished. He deserves to be punished and it does smarten him up for a while. But he's not going to change really until he gets some help for his drinking and until he learns how to control his temper.

Another woman added:

> You know, sometimes I think he just doesn't know any other way to act. He gets frustrated, like all of us do, but instead of just yelling a bit, or going for a walk around the block, he has a few drinks and hits me, just like his father used to do.

While it is evident that counselling for batterers responds closely to the needs of battered women, counselling can have unanticipated consequences for both the women and the men which are not always experienced as positive by the women.

Some counsellors spoke of cases where counselling indirectly led to the man leaving his wife. In one such case:

> He came to see through counselling that he was responsible for beating his wife up and he admitted that his actions were wrong. But at the same time he began to feel that he

was basically unhappy in his marriage, and he decided to leave his wife. . . . She blamed us for turning him against her, but that's a risk that is inevitable if you open up a relationship to analysis.

Counsellors and battered women spoke of another unanticipated consequence — the surfacing of the woman's violence as the man's violence declines. Most counsellors felt that the woman's violence was likely to begin or to increase for one of four reasons.

First, as she begins to feel safer in the relationship, her resentment at all the past violence she has suffered may surface as overt aggression. Second, and closely related to the first reason, the woman may learn when the man stops beating her that she, too, knows of no other way to deal with anger and frustration except through violence. While he was beating her, to a large extent, she had to simply suppress these feelings. When she feels less threatened, these feelings may again start to surface and she may resort to violence, partly in retaliation, but partly because she doesn't know any other way to deal with these feelings. One counsellor elaborated on this point:

Women who are used to violence have learned that violent patterns are part of husband-wife relationships. It is unlikely that they are going to unlearn this brutal lesson overnight, particularly if they have never experienced anything else.

The third factor mentioned by counsellors to explain the surfacing of women's violence was that, while the husband's physical aggression may decrease through his participation in the counselling group, in some cases he simply replaced his physical violence with the greater use of psychological, verbal, or economic violence. For many women, these forms of violence are even more painful because they are less predictable and more enveloping, and because they lower already battered self-esteem. In an attempt to stop the escalation of psychological cruelty, some women lash back with physical violence.

Fourth, women who have lived with violence all their lives may experience the termination of violence in an inverted way as an increased absence of attention. Some women report that they initially feel elated, but then somewhat empty as they realize that their partners aren't going to start lavishing positive attention on them once the partners stop giving the women so much negative attention. These feelings do not make women masochists. While they are enduring the battering, many women hope that, if only the violence would stop, they would have a happy relationship with their partners. When they discover that this is not going to come true, many women feel hopeless, and fear that they will never be loved again. Some women temporarily long for any attention, a shouting match, even a beating, to make them feel that they could be loved again, to make them feel alive. As one shelter worker said:

It takes a lot of positive strokes to equal one good shouting match. When you're living with someone who never or rarely gives you any positive reinforcement, a good fight can at least make you feel like he knows you exist. Being ignored makes so many women feel dead. If the only attention she ever gets from her husband is hitting, she may miss the attention, even though she's relieved the violence is gone. We have women who stay with us who say after a few days: 'Won't somebody please yell at me?' It's just like abused kids. They need to feel like someone knows they're alive and being yelled or even being hit is at least some kind of recognition of this fact.

Despite these unanticipated consequences and the resulting distrust some battered women express toward counselling groups for men, many women feel that counselling groups provide their major hope for change in the relationship without alienating their husbands and dissolving their families. Counselling groups for some battered women have provided an unanticipated source of power in the relationship. Counsellors concurred that many men who voluntarily come to counselling groups for batterers, do so because their wives threaten to leave them unless they do. While this motivation may mean that the man will simply use the group as a tool to get his wife back, some men may change in the process.

Many counsellors for men who batter consciously try to enhance the influence of battered women in their relationships. Counsellors perceive battering as a means of controlling the woman to maintain the man's dominance in the relationship. Through their counselling, group leaders attempt not only to teach the man not to hit, but to reinforce the equality of the woman in the relationship. Accordingly, an increasing number of group leaders make a conscious effort to communicate their belief in the woman's credibility and to convey their concern for her safety. Some groups measure the success of their programs largely through the women's reports. Many meet with the women at the assessment stage, when they determine if the men will be suitable for their program, to confirm the characteristics of the violence, and to make sure the women have an adequate protection plan. As more counsellors initiate contact with the women and attempt to link their service with parallel counselling services for the women and children, programs for men who batter may increasingly give battered women a tool which can help enhance their ability to influence change in the relationship.

Challenges For The Future

Despite the general support of battered women, government officials, and community agencies for programs for men who batter, a number of concerns surround the apparent benefits.

The most prominent concern expressed has focussed on the fact that it is not yet clear whether these programs work. While wide-ranging evaluation studies are planned by the federal government, evaluation to date has been minimal. Reports by battered women which reveal an escalation in psychological, verbal, and economic violence as the physical violence decreases, raise the question of what the benefits of these groups really are. As one shelter worker asked: "Are men's groups just teaching batterers to use more sophisticated forms of cruelty?"

It is also widely recognized by counsellors for men who batter and by shelter workers, as mentioned earlier, that many men agree to attend counselling only because they believe this is their last hope to get their wives back, or to avoid jail terms. While it is conceivable that some of these men will be positively affected by the program, how many simply "use" the program to return to their wives and then revert to their previous patterns of brutality? A high drop-out rate might occur partly because men leave the group if their wives take them back and partly because so many of the men who attend these groups seem to move frequently.

The misuse of counselling programs by criminal justice officials is another factor. Some counsellors reported that, if the man is there on a court order, some probation officers will allow the man to drop out if he has shown good faith by attending a number of sessions deemed sufficient by the probation officer. In other cases, if there is a long waiting period between the court order and the start-up of a new group, the man's probation may run out before the course of counselling sessions is complete. It was also pointed out by some critics of men's groups that these counselling groups are likely to be less useful for the many men who are not accustomed to verbalizing problems or feelings. The verbal nature of most group therapy may tend to bias "success" toward more middle-class participants with a relatively high education level. To balance this criticism, it should be noted that some counsellors refuted this assumption, and said that their highest success rates had been with working-class men.

Some battered women also express limited faith in the effectiveness of these groups. One Canadian study on therapy groups for batterers found that:

Just over half the women interviewed expressed strong doubts about the effectiveness of the group. From their perception, it was unlikely that violent behaviour that had 'developed over a lifetime' could be changed in six months.[8]

The authors of this same study found that the wives of men who went to the groups voluntarily were more positive about the groups, but that the wives of the men who had been referred by the courts "were more likely to talk about group as a diversion from the man's just deserts".[9]

Other workers in Canada and the United States have wondered whether men's programs are subtly perpetuating wife battering, rather than preventing it, by easing the batterer's feelings of guilt and even by helping him express his violence in more socially acceptable ways. They also wonder whether "the preoccupation with counselling fails to motivate men to make changes in the social relationships which reinforce their violent behaviour."[10]

Linked to the scepticism some shelter workers feel regarding programs for men who batter is a concern that government support for the growing number of men's programs will divert funds from much-needed women's programs. This concern is identified in the report on men's groups sponsored by Health and Welfare Canada,[11] and is well summarized in a recent report on batterer's programs in the United States:

> *Feminists believe that women and children should be cared for first . . . and that if men want to work on stopping domestic violence, they should raise funds for shelters. After all, men in our society generally have better access to monetary resources than women. Moreover, the men's organizations or programs should be careful that they are not competing for power as well as for funds. The women in the shelter movement often perceive the emerging men's services as a means of usurping their leadership and negating their anger.*[12]

A third and related concern arising from this expressed anxiety about the allocation of scarce funds is that, despite good relations between most men's programs and shelters for battered women, too few programs for men are closely coordinated with programs for women. It is recognized by many counsellors for men, as well as by other service-providers, that the man is more likely to change if the woman is also given support, is helped to understand the changes which may occur in her husband and their relationship as a result of the counselling, and is helped to deal with her own reactions to these changes.

A fourth concern is that presenting counselling groups as the major programs available to help men reduce their violence diverts attention and planning from other potential ways of dealing with men. The option of routinely removing the men from the home to residential facilities, instead of removing the women and children, was mentioned most often as another potential way to deal with batterers which is not being accorded the credibility or consideration it deserves.

Currently, throughout Canada, when the police are called to a scene where they ascertain that wife battering has taken place and that the wife and children are in continued danger, the police often take the women and children to a safe place outside the home — a transition house or safe home if one exists, a motel, the home of a friend or relative. Even if the man is arrested, since he is generally released on bail, alternate accommodation which removes the women and children from the home is still seen as the only way to ensure their safety.

But removal from the home may itself be seen as a form of punishment for the women and their children. Many women feel that they cannot subject their children to the reduced standard of living which would result if they went to a shelter, when they are used to a greater degree of comfort. Typically, the shelter is not in the same neighbourhood as their house and so children must change schools temporarily. The women and children are also deprived of the support of neighbourhood friends and of the familiarity of their home and possessions.

The "punitive" nature of leaving home may have the effect, therefore, of deterring many women, particularly middle- and upper-class women, from involving the police. Why not, instead, some ask, remove the man to a residential facility incorporating counselling for his battering, and treatment, if necessary, for his alcoholism and/or drug abuse. Proponents of this option assert that the changes in the assault provisions of the *Criminal Code* have simplified the process of removing the batterer from his home, since if they have reasonable and probable grounds to believe an assault has taken place, the police may arrest and remove the man. The reluctance of the individual police officer to jail a man for a "family" offence has been reinforced by the absence of available alternatives. Some shelter workers and police officers argued that the man could be arrested and removed from the house and then released on a "promise to appear" in court, on the condition that he stay in the residence and not go near his wife or family or even contact them except through the residence staff. If he did not obey, he could be arrested for the breach and jailed until his court date, since the breach would be a criminal court matter. There is currently a great deal of disagreement about the legality of this position. There is also widespread interest in having the legality clarified and variations on the option of removing the batterer from the home explored.

Schechter writes of a program in Duluth, Minnesota, which realized this goal:

> There, by utilizing probable cause arrest, when there was some visible injury, protection orders, eviction orders, court-mandated counselling for abusers, combined with stayed jail sentences, and shelter and support groups for women, activists report that for the first time the onus is placed on the man and community institutions, rather than on the woman. The abuser must move out of his home, face a counsellor who says he is responsible for the violence and in approximately 25% of the cases, a judge who will send him to jail if his wife or a counsellor informs the court of threats or recurring violence.[13]

Proponents of this option claim that residences for men would be much less costly than imprisoning the men, and would be a strong statement that the violence is the man's responsibility. Proponents emphasize that these residences should **not** be seen as replacements for transition houses and other crisis shelters for women since women would still need a place they could go for support and to "get away". However, it is possible that, over time, residences for men could reduce the residential role of crisis shelters for women and enhance their non-residential service roles.

Of course, not all service-providers favour this option. Some women warn that, since the batterers would not be imprisoned, but would merely be participating in residential counselling after their work hours, the batterers could still harass their wives, so the women's safety would not be guaranteed. One city which did try to institute a residential counselling program found that men would not go voluntarily and that the criminal justice system was not comfortable with using court orders to force the man to stay in the residence. Nonetheless, there remains a pronounced interest among service-providers in exploring other options for reinforcing men's responsibility for the battering, instead of relying so heavily on counselling groups for men which still have an unproven outcome, and on removing women from the family home.

The final major concern conveyed by service-providers with men's groups was their anxiety about the use of men's groups as a form of diversion from the criminal justice system. Many workers feel that men should not be able to have "an easy out" by attending counselling groups. Sentiments on this issue are very mixed. Some shelter workers did report that they like programs run on a pre-charge basis where charges can be dropped if the man completes the counselling "successfully", according to the counsellors' criteria. These shelter workers favour such programs because the man has better motivation to take the counselling seriously and because this avenue avoids the lengthy delays frequently associated with the court process, which can undermine the commitment to change demonstrated by most men after they are charged. Some battered women are in favour of this process as well, because they believe it will save their husbands from a criminal record. But many shelter workers disagree strongly. As one spokeswoman for this position states:

> We are emphatic that counselling must not be considered a 'diversion' from criminal proceedings. The batterer must not see the counselling option as a way to 'get off' and the courts must not view counselling as a way of diverting wife-battering cases away from prosecution.[14]

Future Directions

Programs for men who batter provide one example of the growing concern with prevention and with asserting the batterer's accountability for his actions. The concerns, as well as the support expressed for counselling groups for men who batter, suggest, however, that more decisive ways of emphasizing men's account-ability and of encouraging prevention by changing men's behaviour should be considered.

Short-Term Goals

The findings presented in this chapter converge in the realization that not enough is known about the influence of these groups. A definition of "successful" comple-tion of counselling must be agreed upon. Since ultimate success would be long-term freedom from physical and psychological violence, either in the relationship in which the man was involved when he entered the group or in subsequent relationships, counsellors will have to decide if this ideal goal is realistic and, if so, how "success" will be monitored. Consistent, coordinated evaluation of all men's programs is thus a primary need. To address the debate about diversion noted above, these evaluations should compare the rates of completion of the program and the "success" rates in terms of reduction or absence of the use of violence for batterers who are ordered by the courts to attend counselling before their sentence is pronounced (and who are therefore diverted from the traditional court system), with those who are ordered to attend counselling as part of their sentence. Comparisons should also be made between the "success" rates of men who attend voluntarily and those who attend as part of a "penalty".

Most service-providers hope that existing programs for men will establish strong links with other community services, particularly with sheltering and counselling services for women, and that comprehensive treatment models, linking counselling for men with parallel programs for women and children, will become more widespread.

Counsellors for batterers, and many other front-line service-providers, also hope that more programs for batterers will be created, particularly in those areas where no such programs exist. Any new programs should, of course, have a built-in evaluation to correspond with the concerns discussed above. But, even though more must be known about programs for batterers before their real effect can be gauged, some workers feel strongly that we need to take a risk and increase the number of these programs across Canada. As one counsellor said:

> With any new program you take a chance. We may be going in the wrong direction. Yes, it's possible that every man who attends the group is really just 'conning' us to get his wife back or to get out of going to jail. But I feel strongly that we have to start somewhere. We have to at least **try** to change the attitudes and behaviours of these

*men. Tougher arrest policies may deter some men, but it won't reach others, particularly those who have been in trouble with the law before. Judges also need options so that they can pass fairer sentences. People always talk about changing the attitudes of judges. Well, in my experience, judges are interested when they see a program that can help them pass down a good sentence, and not fill up the jails. Through counselling programs for batterers, judges **are** learning about wife battering.*

But what about the concern of many transition-house workers that the creation of more groups for batterers will take money away from transition houses and other programs for battered women and their children? James Browning, the author of the study on counselling groups for batterers funded by the National Clearinghouse on Family Violence, has suggested a number of guidelines for funding men's groups which may help overcome this anxiety.

He suggests that the existence of a women's shelter in the community should be seen as a prerequisite to the establishment of men's programming, that service delivery should be integrated to allow a

. . . reasoned, collective decision about the apportioning of resources for support and therapy services, and that men's groups may avoid competing for funds with women's services by viewing the problem as criminal in nature and prevailing upon the provincial corrections system for support.[15]

Some shelter workers have also expressed the hope that all existing and emerging groups for men will follow the lead of some groups in Canada which are trying to expand their emphasis beyond teaching the man not to hit. As one worker said:

I know it's unlikely that we'll ever teach all batterers to become nice guys, but more emphasis on a wider range of violent acts including psychological violence would make these programs more valuable if their ultimate aim is prevention.

Long-Term Goals

While sentiment regarding residential treatment centres for men was mixed, there was general agreement that the types of programs currently being offered for men should be expanded. Perhaps residential programs could be tried on an experimental basis as one new option. It has also been suggested that counselling for batterers be merged with other forms of treatment, where needed, including treatment for alcohol and drug abuse.

Finally, and most importantly, workers across Canada stressed that, through public education, through the media, through education of children, through places of employment, we must start reinforcing new roles for men based less on competition and violence and more on cooperation and sharing. Batterers need to learn not to hit, but at least as important is their "need to unlearn their over-bearing sense of rigidity, domination and control that they associate with manhood".[16]

Community Support

Overview

One of the most pronounced developments in service delivery related to wife battering in the last seven years has been the overwhelming growth in community support. This support has come not just from women's organizations, or from community-based services specifically targetted to battered women, but from traditional men's service groups (for example, Kiwanis and Rotary Clubs), local health, social, educational, and criminal justice services and, perhaps most noticeably, from spiritual organizations.

Communities, as a whole, are now far more aware that wife battering exists and that it affects every community, at least potentially. Community members also increasingly accept the idea that, to empower battered women, that is, to give them the ability to make rational decisions related to the battering they experience, women must know they have emotional and diversified program support in the community.

The centrality of community support has been recognized in all the preceding chapters on service delivery through two consistent themes: the importance of coordination among services, and the importance of wide-ranging community support for battered women. As one shelter worker wrote:

> If only one goal could be set to deal with wife battering, it would have to be to coordinate all community services, not just those which focus on wife battering, so that we could deal with all the woman's needs and with the family as a whole.

This goal expresses the almost universal realization that concurrent and coordinated programs are needed. These must include programs which deal with individual women, children, and men; programs which deal with the family as a unit (where appropriate and desired by all family members); programs which support and coordinate community involvement; and programs which try to influence attitudes and behaviour in society as a whole.[1]

Progress To Date

Data collected for this study portray the widespread growth in community support. In the mail-out questionnaire sent to all shelters for battered women across Canada, workers were asked to rate the quality of their relationships with different types of service agencies and to assess whether their relationships with these agencies have improved. Responses were very positive about the majority of services. Eighty-nine per cent of the houses reported a greatly improved or somewhat improved relationship with police, 75% reported a greatly improved or somewhat improved relationship with spiritual organizations, 70% gave the same responses for hospitals and public health nurses, 63% responded that their relationships with schools had improved, and 41% said their relationships with Crown attorneys and other lawyers had greatly or somewhat improved since their houses opened.

Unfortunately, not enough responses were received from shelter workers on their relationships with private physicians, psychologists, or psychiatrists to provide a reliable statistic. However, workers revealed in informal conversations that these professionals tend **not** to be sensitive to the problems of battered women and their children and are **not** aware of services which could meet their needs, nor are they generally prepared to make referrals. As one worker lamented:

> We've come so far with many of the professionals in the community, but family doctors who aren't with the big hospital here are still doing a lot of damage. Believe it or not, they're still telling women to try to be a better wife and their husbands will 'behave' and they're still prescribing Valium.

Paula Caplan, author of an Ontario study on battered women who had received therapy from traditional and feminist therapists, found that "traditional therapists actually made them feel more depressed and helpless". Ms. Caplan explains that this "is partly because traditional therapists are taught to help their clients look inside themselves for the causes of their problem".[2]

While shelter workers considered only their relationships with other shelters to be excellent, three-quarters of the houses considered their relationships with police to be good or very good, two-thirds felt their relationships with lawyers or Crown attorneys, spiritual organizations, social services/welfare, and schools were good or very good, and 50% of the houses had a good or very good relationship with court officials other than judges, with whom relationships were frequently non-existent.

The generally high rate of improvement in relationships between shelter workers and other community services, as assessed by shelter workers, is largely attributable to and illuminated by marked development in six types of initiatives which have major impacts on community-based support. These initiatives can be categorized as:

- the growth of committees to promote coordination among community services;
- the development of information-sharing mechanisms;
- the development of health service protocols in hospitals which better meet the health-related needs of battered women;
- the growth in self-help services for battered women;
- the creation of more professionally run counselling programs geared specifically for battered women, their children, and batterers;
- the promotion of public education initiatives.

Developments in each of these areas will be described briefly below.

The Growth Of Coordinating Committees

Women working with battered women have, since the mid-1970s, stressed the importance of community coordination to meet the varied needs of battered women. Through the development of transition-house associations in most provinces/ territories, women's shelter workers have put this principle into practice within their own services.

Governments at all levels and professional associations have more recently followed their lead. As more community services have begun to take an interest in the problem of wife battering, the necessity of coordination has increasingly been recognized as self-evident. Government stimulation has supported and broadened this recognition.

For example, over the past few years, most levels of government in Canada have moved closer to, or explicitly adopted, a philosophy which advocates that governments should support and enhance community initiatives and should, as much as possible, work in conjunction with the community to address social issues. This philosophy has resulted in federal, provincial/territorial, and municipal government stimulation of community coordinating networks and/or of more isolated community inter-service coordinating committees in some locations. The purpose of these committees generally is to share information and to ensure that procedures and regulations of one service are compatible with those of other services.

Governments have strongly encouraged an emphasis on community involvement by making community support and/or coordination a prerequisite of much of the funding available at both the federal and provincial/territorial levels. In addition, in some provinces, like Manitoba and Saskatchewan, the government has explicitly approached different professional groups to ask them to coordinate their activities.

Government attempts to stimulate coordination have also extended to an interest in integrating the education of professionals who deal with battered wives, their children, or their spouses. As a result, Saskatchewan has developed a core training package which can be adapted for the use of various professional groups. Other provinces, including Manitoba and Ontario, have developed training modules for specific professional groups in their provinces, and most provinces/territories have sponsored workshops aimed at different professional groups.

Government concern with coordination has also manifested itself **within** and between governments through the proliferation of task forces, government working groups, and interdepartmental committees on wife battering or family violence.

It is evident from the findings of this study that the efforts of shelter workers and governments to promote community cooperation, combined with increased community concern about wife battering, have resulted in improved service coordination in many locations. For example, almost 50% of the houses responding to this study's questionnaire said that staff members participate in a multi-disciplinary community service advisory or planning group. Seventy-three per cent of the houses had members of other community groups on their boards of directors, and shelter staff in 58% of the shelters participated on the boards of other community groups or agencies.

The Development Of Information-Sharing Mechanisms

The development of information-sharing mechanisms, like the development of coordinating committees, has largely been the result of initiatives taken at the federal or provincial/territorial government level and so is not a direct community-based activity. Nonetheless, the promotion of information-sharing holds profound benefits for community groups by giving them the tools to be aware of other related initiatives across the province or across the country.

The first far-reaching attempt to promote information-sharing was the creation of the National Clearinghouse on Family Violence in 1982. It was established in response to a recommendation made in the national plan of action on the status of women, entitled *Towards Equality for Women*, published in 1979 by Status of Women Canada. According to Clearinghouse staff, it operates on a model of a two-way flow of information. That is, each request for information is not only seen as a demand for service, but also provides vital information about activities in the field. As well, information requests are also used to identify gaps in the knowledge base and to guide the development and acquisition of new information. The National Clearinghouse provides valuable support to shelters for battered women across Canada. All shelter workers interviewed for this study spoke highly of the Clearinghouse and said that they used it frequently and found the information provided by the Clearinghouse to be very helpful.

In 1984, following the publication of the report of the Federal/Provincial Task Force on Justice for Victims of Crime, the Solicitor General created the Victims Resource Centre within the Programs Branch of the Ministry. While this service does not focus solely on wife battering or on other forms of family violence, and so was not as widely known or used by respondents to this study's questionnaire, it is another means for community services to retrieve and share information relevant to the development and operation of their programs.

Concern with information-sharing has also stimulated Alberta to create a provincial clearinghouse on family violence in an attempt to promote information-sharing among its services. Other provinces/territories, including Ontario, British Columbia, Saskatchewan, Manitoba, and the Yukon have also appointed officials to provide an information coordination and dissemination function.

As indicated in the section on legal changes, significant efforts have been made to coordinate and upgrade information on wife battering collected through the criminal justice system. In addition, Alberta and Nova Scotia, in conjunction with transition-house workers in their provinces, have developed standardized systems for gathering data from transition houses.

The Development Of Health Services

In research done for *Wife Battering in Canada: The Vicious Circle* (1980), it was clear that many medical doctors had a tendency to isolate an individual's symptoms from her suffering and to define wife battering as a "personal" problem outside the scope of medical expertise or concern.[3] In general, seven years ago, the assistance provided to battered women by medical doctors was minimal. While this problem still exists, as mentioned above, many doctors today, particularly those affiliated with hospital emergency departments, are beginning to take an active role in identifying, treating, and preventing wife battering. Hospitals in at least half the provinces/territories have developed protocols to help staff provide sensitive, thorough assistance to battered women and their children. Protocol development is also being undertaken by public health nurses in some locations.

As well, training sessions on wife battering are being developed and provided to medical staff in hospitals in most provinces; in Manitoba, a pamphlet on wife battering has been developed for and distributed to physicians. There is also an emerging interest among health professionals and psychologists in how health services, including mental health services, could be better used to assist and support battered women, their children, and battering men. Counsellors and other health service providers across Canada spoke of a quiet revolution in health care and particularly in mental health services. As one psychiatrist noted:

> We are becoming more and more aware of the overlap among different problems, and of treating suffering more holistically. We are seeing that problems we used to define as 'social' and so outside our purview, are often different manifestations of problems which are very much the concern of mental health professionals. If we are to remain relevant, we're going to have to come up with a new model of mental health which recognizes the psychological dimensions of 'so-called' social problems, a model which allows us to work with other professionals, to stretch our ways of thinking and a model which does not shrink from the recognition that people can simultaneously be victims in one situation but show great strength in other facets of their lives.

The Growth In Self-Help Groups And Other Counselling Alternatives

It is still not possible at this time to report national statistics on the number of self-help groups or other counselling alternatives for battered women and their children across Canada. These statistics should be collected. (Statistics collected through this study do not fill this gap.) Nonetheless, most shelter staff interviewed in urban areas spoke of at least one self-help group in each of their locations. Shelter workers also spoke of increased interest in non-residential counselling programs for women and their children, among transition-house workers, some private counsellors, other women's groups, social service agencies, spiritual organizations, and among counsellors who run the programs for men reviewed in the preceding chapter.

In rural locations, shelter workers reported that any counselling available is likely to be offered through the local churches. While some shelter workers criticized these programs as overly focussed on the individual and therefore as perpetuating the isolation of battered women, there were also reports of a great shift in church-based counselling toward counselling based on group support as churches become more sensitized to the realities and needs of battered women. In general, support among shelter workers of initiatives being taken by spiritual organizations was high.

The Promotion Of Public Education

The number of public education initiatives taken in the past seven years are too numerous to tabulate, and so only a few examples will be given. Multi-media campaigns have been funded or are planned in a number of provinces/territories across Canada. Information pamphlets on wife battering have proliferated. In 1984, Ontario launched a successful media campaign across the province, and the Ontario Women's Directorate extended this campaign in 1987. Commercial and non-commercial films have been produced. At the federal level, an insert on wife battering was included in 1.2 million family allowances cheques in 1982. The National Clearinghouse on Family Violence, until the fall of 1986, prepared a quarterly newsletter, Vis-à-vis, which provided a constant update on information related to wife battering. The Canadian Council on Social Development has now taken over publication of this newsletter. In addition, most shelters for battered women, and many professionals involved in this area, define public education as an integral part of the service they provide. The strong emphasis on public education has resulted in the vast changes in public awareness and interest in wife battering witnessed over the past seven years.

The Women's Points Of View

Community support is of paramount importance to battered women. Research consistently shows that battered women, like other victims of crime, look first to friends and family before they turn to official agencies.[4] In interviews for this study, battered women also emphasized the importance of community support. One woman reflected:

> The police were really nice to me. They were nothing like what I had heard to expect. One of them put his arm around me and let me cry for a while. They spoke really softly to me and tried to act like friends. But in a way that really hurt, because it just made me feel worse that I had no friends to turn to. My own mother told me to go back to the bed I made. My best friend makes me feel it must be something I did that made him beat me. I just ache inside for my mother and my friends, but especially my mother, to do for me what the policeman did. It doesn't seem right that a stranger has to be the one who gives you the most kindness.

Another woman said:

> If there had been somewhere to go to ask questions right here, right close to where I live, I would have done something sooner. You know, if I could have just been out taking the baby for a walk and could have dropped in to ask some advice, my husband wouldn't have been the wiser and I would have known my rights. It was just too hard to find out the information I needed. It took too much planning, so that when things weren't so bad I figured it wasn't worth it and when things were really bad I didn't have the energy it took to go to the city to find out what I had to do.

Women who are doubly or triply isolated by race, ethnic origin, or geography often have an especially great need for community support, but most battered women are torn apart at the thought not just of leaving their homes, but of leaving their geographic and/or cultural communities. For some women, it is the strong desire to stay in their communities that influences them to return to violent partners.

Lee Bowker, in his book *Beating Wife Beating*, said:

> . . . it is important to obtain advice, assistance and moral support from one's neighbours, relatives and friends, because these people can offer assistance in the form of specific suggestions, aid in settling disputes, and often physical sanctuary. Straus points out that the beaten wife who avoids involving these people gives her husband a psychological advantage by insulating him from shame and the criticism of his community members.[5]

Challenges For The Future

Despite the well-deserved optimism that surrounds community-based programs and service coordination efforts, a number of warnings were raised throughout this study, to temper but not to dampen this optimism.

The first is that we not fall prey to the myth that coordination is all we need. Steubing comments on this myth concerning victims' services generally, but his comments are definitely applicable to services for battered women in most locations.

> The myth . . . that the community already possesses a full and adequate range of public and private social services for victims which requires only effective coordination . . . was debunked. At present, victims' services were revealed as constituting a patchwork quilt system, full of gaps and holes and lacking either effective referral or follow-up.[6]

Steubing's comment is also supported by findings for this study summarized in the chapter on sheltering, that shelters feel they have to provide many services, particularly outreach, follow-up, and counselling services because no such programs exist in the community. Shelter workers also mentioned the absence of badly needed residential programs for violent children, residential programs for adolescents, and services geared to the particular needs of children who are not physically or sexually abused, but who live in a family where their mothers or step-mothers are battered.

The second challenge is not to underestimate the difficulty of establishing working relationships among groups which have no history of working with one another. It must be well recognized, if discouragement is to be avoided and the goal of coordination is to be pursued, that different services have different philosophies, are structured differently, and have different referral processes. In addition, some professional groups still have a very low awareness of the realities of wife battering, and this can make their inclusion in a coordinated network of services very frustrating. For example, the data collected from this study's mail-out questionnaire singled out two groups of professionals which have continuing poor relations with the majority of shelter workers and physicians in private practice and judges. Relations with judges not only were reported by shelter workers to be poor, they were considered by 10% of the workers to be deteriorating. Four per cent of respondents also felt their relations with children's services were deteriorating, but, in most houses, relations with children's services were not reported to be poor. Deteriorating relationships were not reported for any other group.

A third challenge is that service coordination and even most community-based service models are essentially urban models. Services still tend to be clustered in core areas of urban centres. More innovative rural models are needed to ensure that community support, so vitally important in rural and isolated areas where access to professional help is limited, is given at least the same stimulus as initiatives in urban areas.

The fourth challenge is to recognize that, ironically, the creation of community service networks can, without an umbrella organization, foster isolation by implicitly encouraging community services to stop looking outward to other communities, and so reducing the current attempt to increase information flow across the country.

Future Directions

The goal of enhanced community involvement and coordination is at the root of society's desire to reduce and ultimately eliminate wife battering. Strong community disapproval of wife batterers, combined with support of battered women and their children, are essential in reducing the acceptance of violence in our society.

Service directions are needed which will integrate the woman into the community, and not create service ghettos for battered women. Services must address the varied needs of battered women, their children, and the batterers, without using the sum of these problems to stigmatize these individuals through labels like the "multi-problem family" label which was so popular in the 1950s and 1960s. Despite the difficulty of coordination, and the difficulty of merging competing ideologies, service directions must retain a philosophy which both reflects the needs and hopes of battered women and builds on the wisdom gained through community initiatives in the last decade.

Short-Term Goals

In the short term, service-providers across Canada want greater support for coordination efforts, including support for information coordination. Shelter workers are very interested in the upgrading and coordination of information available about wife battering. Almost all shelter staff interviewed for this study said they would like to computerize their data, if computers or access to computers, as well as funding for training in computer use, could be provided. The majority of the shelter workers also expressed interest in trying to develop a unified data collection form which could be used by shelters throughout Canada, and which would, ideally, be coordinated with data collection systems being developed or planned in the criminal justice system, in hospitals, and in social service agencies.

Shelter workers expressed a desire for increased training and awareness seminars for private physicians and judges across Canada. These two professional groups are seen as creating real barriers to the effectiveness of existing and planned programs through their lack of awareness of the realities of wife battering and through their frequent lack of cooperation with programs which reflect a more sensitive under-standing of the needs of battered women.

More stimulation of community-based coordinating committees is also needed, according to shelter workers. Communication with successful committees could assist other communities in promoting coordination in their locations.

Many workers felt that community coordination could be stimulated through the creation of multi-agency resource centres similar to the one in operation in London, Ontario, where women can receive advice, support, counselling, and referrals on a variety of different problems. Such resource centres could provide assistance to women at many stages in the battering, promote earlier identification as well as help, and provide support to battered women after they leave emergency shelters. Such resource centres could also provide a focus for the creation of self-help groups and other support groups for battered women and their children.

Workers also emphasized that even though it is known that alcoholism and drug abuse do not cause wife battering, there is still a relationship between substance abuse and violence. Many workers felt that this relationship should be recognized through the coordination of alcohol and drug treatment programs, crisis shelters, mental health programs, and counselling programs for batterers, battered women, and their children.

Workers suggested that community coordination be promoted around practical issues, rather than initially enmeshing different service-providers in ideological debates. Transportation of women in rural and isolated areas to emergency shelters, hospitals, or police stations was frequently identified as an excellent organizing focus, because such transportation is badly needed and because many existing services could participate in a unified transportation plan as part of the routine activities of their employees.

Long-Term Goals

The long-term goals of shelter workers are more far-reaching and have been well-summarized by one worker:

> Ideally we need a whole change in the system of legal, social, and employment assistance for women, which supports the real-life needs of women across Canada, which supports them in a variety of choices including the currently unpopular choice to stay at home and raise children, so that women won't be isolated and made more dependent by rational choices which are not supported by our social system. Ideally, professional jealousies should be overcome so that the whole community can in fact work together to meet the goals we all want . . . to reduce violence and suffering.

Conclusion:

Prevention Through Caring, Continuity, and Support

Applauding Our Progress

Seven years ago, it could not have been imagined that progress toward meeting the needs of battered women and reducing wife battering in our society would be so extensive and far-ranging. Much has been accomplished.

Progress has been most visible in the growth of services and initiatives to deal with the crisis aspect of wife battering. In seven years, the number of crisis shelters has more than tripled to 264 shelters across Canada. The federal government and every provincial/territorial government have adopted policies to encourage police to charge wife batterers with assault. Designated Crown attorneys have been appointed in many locations across Canada to deal sensitively and knowledgeably with wife-battering cases. Hospitals and social workers are developing protocols to identify and serve battered women more effectively.

There have also been significant strides made toward our goal of reducing and ultimately preventing wife battering. Legislation has been passed making sexual assault in marriage a crime. There are now at least 45 counselling programs for batterers across Canada. Fifty per cent of the transition houses in Canada have programs for the children of battered women. The coordination of services in many communities has grown and is being further promoted by an expanding number of community coordinating committees. Public awareness has been raised considerably through a plethora of public awareness campaigns. Through curriculum development, wife battering is beginning to be introduced as a topic of discussion in schools. Churches, synagogues, and temples are also coming to the support of battered women. Overall, across Canada, wife battering is increasingly seen as a community concern, as a problem which affects all Canadians.

Knowledge of the important role of transition houses and other crisis shelters for battered women has grown:

- more than 42,000 women stayed in crisis shelters in 1985, and they brought 55,000 children with them, half of them under five years of age;
- another 42,000 women and 55,000 children sought shelter in transition houses but had to be turned away because of lack of space;
- most of the women who stay in transition houses are trapped in a cycle of poverty, and have low education and little job experience;
- shelters usually provide the only service which responds to the wide range of needs of battered women and their children;
- increasingly, women are asking shelters to respond to an ever-widening range of needs by filling the service gap created by governmental deinstitutionalization of health and other residential services.

Society has also learned in the past seven years that the costs of battering are high. For the women, it means depression, isolation, physical injury, reduced life options, and sometimes death through homicide or suicide. For the children, it means terror, pain, behaviour problems during childhood, the likelihood that the cycle of violence will be repeated in their future families, and a higher risk of becoming violent even outside the family in adulthood. For the children, it also means a higher probability of being physically or sexually abused and a virtual guarantee of being emotionally abused or neglected. For the batterers, it can reinforce a low self-image and lead to limitations on their jobs and mobility options if they are arrested and convicted for their violence.

For society, the social and financial costs are high and far-reaching. Financially, the cost of policing and crisis-shelter services alone in our society is estimated to be at least $72 million a year. The social costs, in terms of: the number of Canadians forced by violence to depend on the State through reliance on welfare or imprisonment; the increased probability of violent criminality; the potential general decline in social order; and the demise of human rights, are beyond calculation.

Growing knowledge of social costs has contributed to a widespread realization that the scope of wife battering is larger than originally envisioned. We know now that, while concern with the physical brutality of wife battering cannot be reduced, violence against women in the family goes beyond hitting and other forms of physical violence. Wife battering includes psychological, sexual, verbal, and economic forms of violence that threaten the peace, security, and dignity of women across Canada and which limit their options and hopes. Society has also learned that wife battering, while most prevalent in legal and common-law marriages, often continues even after the union is dissolved. It occurs before marriage and even in early dating relationships. It is now realized that the needs of all battered women are not the same and that the needs of individual battered women change significantly during the course of a battering relationship.

Widespread Concern With Wife Battering Is A Sign Of Social Change

Society's expanding knowledge and growing concern with this issue has resulted in a realization that we are at a crossroads in terms of societal tolerance of violence and injustice, and in terms of efforts to combat violence against women and the suffering it produces. Wife battering has become an enduring and growing concern in society because, in our attempts to find solutions, we are clarifying our changing values and emerging responses to human suffering.

Society is at a turning point:

- in trying to give women the power and authority they warrant in society, without simply making them unwitting advocates of the existing power structure;
- in trying to understand how violence is built into the structure of the society and into the fabric of the family;
- in trying to forge protective, supportive, and preventive services which do not violate the individual's and the family's rights to privacy;
- in trying to create services to deal with human suffering which are not rooted in charity, but which will preserve the dignity and autonomy of individuals and emphasize their commonality with all people.

Increasingly, violence against women in the home is seen as both an indicator and a perpetuator of economic, social, and legislated inequality against women. Violence against women in the family is viewed as one of the negative ways that two prominent values in our society are realized: the values of aggressiveness and autonomy. The violence and isolation experienced in battering relationships are extreme manifestations of the aggressiveness and autonomy applauded in the public spheres and particularly in the paid work world. Violence against women in the family puts in question our adherence to these values, and raises hopes for new social options, based not in aggressiveness and autonomy, but in empathy and cooperation.

Increased knowledge of and concern with violence against women has resulted in new and expanded goals:

- the development of social, political, and economic policies to promote social justice;
- the encouragement of social responsibility through individual and collective action in order to reduce the potential for social injustice;
- the promotion of measures to encourage people, through their professional and non-professional working roles and through their friendships, communities, and families, to assist others who are being battered or who are in danger of being battered;
- the provision of information through various community agencies to all women and men on the risks and costs of violence in the home.

These goals are prominent in Canada, as evidenced in the descriptions of programs, attitudes, and hopes throughout this report. They are also shared by the international community. For example, the goals described above have been adopted by the Seventh United Nations Congress on the Prevention of Crime and the Treatment of Offenders.[1]

But no matter how self-evident and "right" these goals seem in principle, they are not easy to realize in practice. When these goals are compared with the actual progress made thus far in meeting the crisis needs of battered women and preventing violence against women in society, it is clear that much remains to be accomplished, especially in terms of programs.

Cautions For The Future

Two warning themes concerning service delivery have been traced throughout this report. First, the rhetoric of restraint has the potential to foster competition, ownership debates, and resistance to change. Second, although the philosophy of autonomy — a philosophy which emphasizes that the individual must be responsible for her/his actions — has helped to emphasize the batterer's responsibility for his violent actions and so has helped focus program responses to battering, it is also a philosophy which can restrict society's visions of potential service options. In addition, the philosophy of autonomy can be used to individ-ualize the problem of battering, divert attention from the social bases of battering, and place the primary responsibility for change on individual battered women, individual men who batter, and individual community workers. Furthermore, this philosophy can be used to replace creative, community-wide support for battered women with charity provided by agencies specializing in helping the "needy"; many women have described their experiences with this kind of help as demeaning.

It has been repeated throughout this report that these perspectives challenge progress toward greater social responsibility, cooperation, and service coordina-tion. First, they hinder efforts aimed at the reduction and eventual elimination of battering in our society. Second, they distract and discourage us from following the directions indicated by the wisdom and experience of battered women, shelter workers, and an increased knowledge of wife battering.

The ideological emphases on restraint and autonomy have resulted in six main policy and service-delivery trends which were identified in this study's discussions with service-providers and policy-makers across Canada. These trends threaten to subvert the goal of prevention of wife battering in Canadian society. A brief description of these trends follows.

- Battered wives generally have been portrayed and treated in program and policy initiatives as a homogeneous group. The special problems of aboriginal, immi-grant, young, disabled, or rural battered women are not sufficiently recognized, although they are mentioned almost universally. In addition, very little attention is paid to battered women who are **not** poor, even though these women also need services. This policy trend feeds into a syndrome which encourages the general public to distance itself from battered women and to assume that battered women are in some way "different", "abnormal", or "underprivileged" Canadians who don't merit a voice in determining their futures or in designing programs intended for their use.

- Just as battered women are assumed to be homogeneous, their experiences are also expected to be very similar from one woman to another and to stay consistent for individual women. The changing experiences and perceptions of individual women are too often dismissed, together with the woman's credibility, with the accusation that "she doesn't know what she wants". This assumption also has serious implications for the survival of programs to help battered women, since a program can be labelled "unsuccessful" because it does not respond to the entire range of the woman's changing needs.

- Not enough concrete support is offered to front-line service groups. The important role of front-line services is constantly lauded and, as mentioned earlier in this report, increased emphasis has been placed on community-based programs in policy statements and program philosophies. However, financial support for these programs is time-limited and often falls largely to the community. In wealthy communities, the need to raise funds from within the community can provide motivation, coordination, and result in successful programs. In poorer communities, it can mean that services will probably not emerge and, even if they do, that they will not be able to survive. The emphasis on community responsibility is also often translated in practice to mean that front-line services are not provided with needed resources and yet they are being asked to provide more and more services to a greater variety of Canadians.

- Practical inter-agency or inter-jurisdictional coordination is paid lip service, but too often is thwarted by competition and a concern with establishing control over service design as well as delivery. This trend is a spin-off of the trend to encourage community-based initiatives. Many policy documents and program blueprints stress the need for coordination, but then falter when the time comes to make specific recommendations for coordinating mechanisms, beyond the general recommendation that community or government coordinating committees will be formed.

- A very strong philosophical commitment to prevention is still not adequately or uniformly supported through financial commitments or actions. This problem is showing signs of beginning to reverse. For example, the federal government is increasingly shifting its sights toward prevention. However, there is a risk that prevention will remain more a philosophy than a reality if the collective wisdom and experiences of battered women and front-line workers is not taken seriously. There is also a risk that a philosophy of prevention will be used to pull back on essential government support for crisis services.

- The dangers of increased institutional control have not been seriously considered. Legislative and institutional alternatives can free women from violence, but they can also entrap if not used judiciously. It is undeniable that more aggressive arrest policies, once they are uniformly and routinely enforced, will provide women across Canada with more real choice. It is not clear, however, that using the criminal justice system to charge battered women with contempt of court if they refuse to testify against their partners is a positive step either in terms of the women's welfare or in terms of helping to reduce wife battering. The positive power of legislation and of many government-based programs cannot be denied. The continued participation of governments in preventing wife battering is essential. Nonetheless, the dangers of too much institutional control and the limits of appropriate government intervention should always be considered and tested against the wishes and perceptions of battered women, front-line workers, and other community members who may have less investment in building a "wife-battering empire".

This critique has not been introduced to detract from the very sincere efforts of policy-makers and service-providers to help battered women as well as their children and to reduce wife battering in our society. Nor has it been an attempt to dampen enthusiasm or to minimize accomplishments. It has been included only to sound a warning that, just as battering can take on a life of its own, so institutional hopes expressed through institutional structures can take on lives of their own, which can thwart the hopes of those trying to help battered women and dash the hopes of the battered women themselves.

The Final Word: Battered Women And Shelter Workers Speak Out

The words and insights of battered women and of the women working in shelters who have supported battered women over the years have echoed throughout this report. The wisdom they shared through this study can help sketch a blueprint for future programs to reduce wife battering in Canadian society.

These women remind us that all women are potentially battered women. They remind us that battered women are not weak, that they are not defined primarily by their victimization. Battered women remind us that the ability to live in a battering relationship requires strength. Programs designed for battered women should reinforce and utilize this strength, to help women redirect their strength so that they are not using it just to cope with the violence, but can begin using their strength to make rational decisions which will help end or reduce the violence.[2]

Based on this insight, the women quoted in this study remind us that battered women need support and encouragement. They do not need charity. They do not need labels which stigmatize and isolate them further. They need to know that they have the emotional support of the community and that the community will provide services to meet their emotional, health, financial, social, and legal needs.

The women in this report spoke as well of responsibility. They spoke of the need to share responsibility for individual action and social solutions among battered women, the batterers, the community, and society as a whole.

Women spoke of the need for ongoing community-based services and informal support, not just to deal with the crisis of violence, but to address the problem of wife battering at preventive and follow-up stages. This need can best be realized through the acknowledgement and development by community workers of their power in society, and through compassionate support by the neighbours, friends, and families of battered women. Women working on the front line spoke of the fact that community workers too often under-rate their own power, and so unwittingly increase their vulnerability to institutional programs which further undermine their power.

These principles do not provide all the solutions to wife battering, but they do provide an alternative vision of service delivery guided by society's goal to stop wife battering. Specific goals, based on these principles, have been recorded throughout this report; a comprehensive list of specific proposals for government action is given in Appendix A. Only a few will be highlighted here to give a composite picture of desired future programs, in short-, medium-, and long-term time frames.

Short-Term Goals

Women across Canada want existing transition houses to be given adequate support and, where necessary, new crisis shelters to be created to ensure that no battered woman is denied crisis shelter.

Funding should increasingly emphasize the expanded service-delivery role of shelters to include services for children and follow-up and preventive services rather than just their residential role.

The expertise of shelter workers and other women and men working with battered women and their children should be given adequate recognition through improved salaries, better working conditions, and through the general inclusion of these workers in advisory roles and policy-making bodies. Many women hope that community workers will facilitate their acceptance as experts in the field of wife battering by recognizing their own power and influence and by increasing this influence through information-sharing and coordinated action with other community workers across Canada.

Crisis alternatives for rural women should be expanded beyond safe housing, and an evaluation should be made of the adequacy of safe houses in terms of ensuring safety and support for battered women, especially in rural and isolated areas. These women need more crisis, preventive, and follow-up services which will allow them to prevent or escape the violence without being uprooted from their communities.

Women want all service-providers to revise their visions of appropriate options for women who must leave their partners, to include options appropriate for women with little education or work experience.

Battered women want their experiences and needs to be addressed in a more holistic way through service delivery. Programs should be developed which recognize and address the relationships between battering and various facilitating factors. An emphasis on "root causes", while important, may not always be the most direct way of meeting the needs of women. For example, we know that violence is likely to begin or to increase when a woman is pregnant. Information and counselling relating to wife battering should therefore be available routinely through pre-natal clinics and obstetricians. Similarly, while we know that alcohol doesn't "cause" wife battering, it is implicated in many violent incidents. Battered women want programs for their partners, their children, and themselves which recognize and address the link between alcohol or drug abuse and battering. There is a need for unified programs which address the needs of the women, the children, and the men simultaneously and which respect the hopes of some battered women to try to keep their families together. Programs which meet the special needs of aboriginal, immigrant, and teenaged women should be established.

Battered women and shelter workers also want some reassurance that programs being developed and already in place for battered women, for their children, and for batterers really do benefit battered women and their children. Shelter workers, as well as government representatives and other service-providers, want broad-based evaluations, particularly of safe-home networks and of counselling programs for batterers.

Medium-Term Goals

In the medium term, women across Canada want to shift the emphasis of program development so that preventive and follow-up services are stressed, while crisis services are maintained and augmented in accordance with women's crisis needs.

These services should be readily accessible in the community. To facilitate accessibility, some could be created as drop-in or store-front services. Others could be incorporated into ongoing community, recreational, or church programs for women, men, children, and families. Women emphasized the importance of out-reach programs, and stressed that outreach means reaching out to women, children, and men in the many facets of their lives. Outreach programs should be based on the recognition that wife battering affects these other facets of life and that wife battering may be manifested and experienced as a different kind of problem, like a child's poor grades at school, the withholding of sex by one partner, or insomnia, at least in the early stages of wife battering.

Women want alternatives for dealing with the batterer, including the possibility of removing the man from the family residence (rather than the woman and children).

Women want a broad-based reassessment of the child welfare system and of the child-care, residential, treatment, and educational programs for children currently available and needed for the future. They spoke of the need for sensitivity among pre-school, primary, and high school teachers to the problems of wife battering, of the need for educational programs about family relationships, of the need for group counselling for children who witness abuse, of the need for flexible child-care options including care in licensed centres, but also including support for more informal care options as well as subsidies for women caring for their own children in their homes.

Long-Term Goals

The long-term goals of battered women and shelter workers are to ensure the rights, dignity, and options of women and children in our society.

Battered women and their advocates want to promote the restructuring of Canada's legal, economic, health, and social institutions to establish and reinforce the equal value of women, children, and men in society. The long-term goal of battered women and their advocates is that new options — which will **not** be based on aggressiveness, competition, and autonomy — will be made possible through the support and reinforcement of our social institutions. Through these options, the value of unpaid work in the home, of child-rearing, of sharing responsibilities, can be acknowledged and rewarded together with paid work and career-based options.

Women want all children to be taught to deal with frustration and stress more creatively and less violently; parenting skills which do not depend on corporal punishment or psychological cruelty should be the norm. Together with learning that there are no "appropriate" or "allowable" victims, children should be taught skills to encourage better communication between men and women. Above all, women want their children to live and love without violence.

With these goals in mind, battered women and their advocates are prepared to work toward a future that does not include violence in the home, a future in which all Canadians have the right and the opportunity to achieve their potential free from the threat of violence.

Appendices

Proposals For Action

The author would like to make the following specific proposals for action in light of her analysis of the preceding study on battered women in Canada. It is well recognized that responsibility for action to reduce the suffering and incidence of wife battering does not rest solely with the federal government. Provincial/territorial and municipal governments, members of professional groups, front-line workers, and the general public must also take responsibility for action if we are to significantly reduce and ultimately prevent wife battering. However, in accordance with the mandate of the Canadian Advisory Council on the Status of Women (CACSW) to inform and advise the federal government, and in keeping with the focus of this report, the proposals which follow will target federal government responsibilities only.

Supporting Shelters For Battered Women And Their Children

I   In view of
- the very central role that shelter workers have played and continue to play in providing support and service to battered women and their children;
- the important contribution shelter workers have made in bringing wife battering to public attention and in expanding the understanding of Canadians concerned with wife battering;
- the transition houses' crucial service-delivery role, in addition to their sheltering role;
- the continuing problem of woefully inadequate funding faced by most transition houses;

The author proposes
1. that Health and Welfare Canada make available, immediately, to each of the shelters in Canada which serve battered women and their children, and which express a need for additional personnel, funds to pay the full-time salaries for at least three years, of the positions described below (individual houses would, of course, be consulted to determine that these positions in fact represent their most pressing personnel needs):
    (a)   a child-care coordinator, to design and coordinate an activity, counselling, and care program for the children of the women who stay in the shelters;
    (b)   an outreach worker, to facilitate the creation of: follow-up programs for women and their children after they leave the shelter, and outreach programs for women who do not need or want residential support from the shelter (these programs need not always be provided from the house, but funding should be given to the house to hire such a worker to ensure that full use is made of the expertise of house workers, to ensure that the women who stay at the house are given needed follow-up, and to help expedite contacts by the outreach worker with women who call the house for advice, information, or counselling, but do not wish to stay at the house);
    (c)   a public education coordinator, to enhance awareness and knowledge within the entire community, including other service-providers in the community with which battered women and their children have contact;
2. that Health and Welfare Canada, in order to facilitate the ability of existing staff in shelters to respond to the wide range of service needs of battered women and their children, immediately provide funds to support training programs for all shelter workers, where such training is needed and desired by the workers. Relevant training programs identified by workers through this study included

programs related to child development and dynamics, crisis counselling, follow-up services, and funding and legal issues. It is imperative that any training programs developed to deal with these and/or other training needs identified by individual houses be developed in close consultation with transition-house workers and transition-house associations.

II Because

- the per diem funding model is particularly tied to a **shelter** emphasis and a crisis-oriented model which does not recognize and support the wide range of services currently provided by transition-house workers;
- this funding model does not allow for the full development of other innovative services, particularly outreach, preventive, and follow-up programs, which are so necessary to reduce wife battering in our society;
- transition-house workers would need additional monies added to their annual budgets to be able to provide these needed services;
- although it is recognized that not all such services should be provided through transition houses, shelter workers do have an important role to play in the development of these services and, in some locations, are the appropriate providers of the service as well;
- the per diem model, which is essentially a welfare model, perpetuates the image of services for battered women as charity;
- this funding model creates recognized problems for many houses which are unable to keep the house in a good state of repair due to a lack of available funds;
- transition-house workers are poorly paid, and many houses reported that continuity in service delivery was made more difficult as a result of being forced by funding constraints to depend heavily or even completely, in some cases, on part-time and volunteer staff;
- the per diem funding model demands a time commitment and level of familiarity with bureaucratic procedure which is not consistent with the day-to-day operation of most front-line services;
- in order to address these basic problems created by the use of this funding model, which is clearly inappropriate for services as diverse and multi-purpose as transition houses;

The author proposes

1. that the Minister of Health and Welfare Canada meet first with other appropriate federal ministers and their advisors, including the Minister of Indian and Northern Affairs, and then with the provincial/territorial ministers responsible for the funding of social services, by October 1987, to discuss and plan the implementation of a sustaining funding model based on operating grants, with additional funds provided for special or experimental services, rather than on the current per diem model;
2. that, as part of these discussions, the low level of pay currently received by transition-house workers be given central attention and that an agreement be reached that transition-house workers, through a revised funding base, be paid more appropriate salaries, adjustable with the rate of inflation, in keeping with their expertise and the diverse roles they are required to play, and competitive with the salaries of other workers with similar demands and pressures (the appropriate contribution of municipal governments to any funding base agreed upon should be carefully considered in view of the very uneven ability and willingness of municipalities across Canada to contribute to cost-sharing of transition houses and other social services);
3. that representatives of transition houses and/or transition-house associations from all provinces/territories be invited to make submissions which would be

the basis for these discussions, and to participate in the discussions before any final decisions are reached. Workers in houses serving a large aboriginal population should be adequately represented in order that the particular funding problems reported by house workers when they provide shelter and other services to aboriginal women can be avoided in the design of a new funding base. The new funding base should be designed in such a way that funding discrepancies within and between provinces/territories can be minimized;

4. that a new funding model be announced by April 1988, for implementation across the country no later than September 1988.

III Because

- transition-house associations now exist in most provinces/territories;
- these associations facilitate information exchange among houses within their province or territory and also promote communication with houses in other jurisdictions;
- transition-house associations can save individual shelter workers considerable time by coordinating and rationalizing submissions to government and by coordinating and sharing public education tools;
- despite their important role, too many associations find their existence threatened by a chronic shortage of funds;

The author proposes

1. that Secretary of State Canada ensure that funding be provided for a minimum period of three years to existing associations to cover the costs of running transition-house association offices and their services;
2. that, in jurisdictions where no association currently exists, transition-house workers be consulted to determine if such an association would exist if funds were made available, and be given start-up funds to facilitate the creation of such an association;
3. that funds be provided by Secretary of State Canada to enable representatives of all the transition-house associations in Canada to meet at least once a year for the next five years;
4. that further funds be made available through Secretary of State Canada to facilitate networking among these associations throughout the year.

Strengthening Community Support

Because

- battered women, throughout this study, spoke of their hope and need to be given greater support and assistance by friends, extended family members, co-workers, members of their churches, and informal community groups not necessarily specifically mandated to provide an official service for battered women or their children;
- front-line workers and battered women feel that these support systems can be particularly useful in the early stages of battering, when the woman may feel something is wrong but may not yet define it as battering;
- informal support networks can also give strength to a woman once the violence has escalated, to help her make difficult decisions about her safety and her future;

The author proposes

1. that Health and Welfare Canada provide funding to promote the creation of more neighbourhood drop-in centres for women. These centres ideally would provide information on a variety of issues of concern to women, including — but not limited to — violence against women; could provide an informal, non-stigmatizing referral service and offer a place where women could meet friends

spontaneously to discuss problems, plans, or interests; and provide a meeting place for self-help and mutual aid groups;

2. that Secretary of State Canada sponsor a national conference followed by a series of local workshops on the role of self-help and mutual aid groups in supporting victims and survivors of violence in the family;

3. that the CACSW sponsor the production of a video on the ways informal support networks can help reduce the incidence and severity of wife battering;

4. that the National Clearinghouse on Family Violence produce, in consultation with representatives of provincial/territorial departments of education, a teacher's guide outlining the roles that families and friends can play in supporting and assisting battered women and their children;

5. that Health and Welfare Canada produce a similar pamphlet for public health nurses to help them stress in family skills workshops and in private home visits the positive role that families and friends can play in supporting and assisting battered women and their children;

6. that Secretary of State Canada sponsor a national conference on the expanded and positive role spiritual organizations could play in providing assistance and referrals to victims and survivors of wife battering;

7. that Employment and Immigration Canada and Labour Canada work with industries across Canada to encourage them to provide counselling groups for employees who are battering the women with whom they live, and general awareness sessions for all employees and managers to alert them to the significance of wife battering in human, social, and financial cost terms. Counselling groups and referrals should also be available through the work setting for victims of wife battering.

Evaluation

Although the author has no interest in diverting funds badly needed for direct service delivery, Canadians concerned with wife battering have expressed the need for more knowledge concerning the effectiveness of existing and developing service options in order to take decisive action and to make difficult decisions concerning the most-needed services with limited resources.

The author proposes

1. that Health and Welfare Canada, in conjunction with the Department of Justice and with Solicitor General Canada — and in consultation with transition-house workers and operators of services for men who batter — create and fund a coordinated, comprehensive evaluation of all existing Canadian programs for men who batter;

2. that particular emphasis be placed on the usefulness of these programs as an alternative sentencing tool for judges, and on the long-term effectiveness of these programs in reducing violence;

3. that the evaluation look at the reduction of violence among batterers who were ordered to attend the groups by the courts and, within this group, a comparison be made between those men whose attendance was ordered as a diversion from the criminal justice system and those whose attendance was ordered as part of the sentence;

4. that "success" in these evaluations be defined, not just in terms of completion of the course of group sessions, but in terms of long-term freedom from physical and persistent psychological violence, either in the relationship in which the man was involved when he entered the group or in subsequent relationships;

5. that Health and Welfare Canada undertake a comprehensive evaluation of safe-house networks (this evaluation is particularly important to assess the safety of such networks both for battered women and their children and for the

operators of safe homes and should also be used to determine whether safe houses are appropriate alternatives to transition houses in any situation, or whether safe houses are best used as emergency one-night stopovers until the battered woman and her children can be transported to a transition house or another more secure shelter);

6. that Health and Welfare Canada, in conjunction with CMHC, undertake an evaluation of second-stage housing alternatives, comparing, among other things, the benefits of designated second-stage residences housing several women and their children, with the benefits of subsidized single units with extra security, in both subsidized and non-subsidized complexes.

Promoting Coordination

In order to facilitate the development of community coordinating committees, where these do not currently exist, and to strengthen cooperation among service-providers, even where they do not deem a formal coordinating committee to be appropriate;

The author proposes

1. that Health and Welfare Canada provide funding for at least one year for a full-time worker based in a transition house or another front-line community agency, in as many communities as possible across Canada, to:
   (a) explore the availability of services used by, and of potential use to, battered women, their children, and battering men in that community;
   (b) produce a resource manual of such services to be distributed to all relevant service-providers;
   (c) identify problems of coordination across services experienced by different service-providers;
   (d) facilitate meetings among representatives of appropriate services to discuss how these problems could be overcome;
   (e) promote the creation of a community coordinating committee, where possible;

2. that all government departments continue to give priority to applications for pilot projects related to wife battering which include, as part of their aims, improved coordination in the community;

3. that the federal government examine its own funding policies, and where possible, facilitate discussions with appropriate provincial representatives concerning their funding policies to eliminate any practices which perpetuate funding inequities across services for battered women and their children or between services directed at the battered women and services directed at the batterer;

4. that recognition and support be given to the need for a wide diversity of services in the wife-battering area;

5. that Health and Welfare Canada and Solicitor General Canada, through their funding stipulations, encourage formal links between programs for men who batter and the transition houses in their location and, wherever possible, require that programs for men who batter offer, through their services, or in coordination with the transition house or with other local services, complementary and simultaneous counselling programs for the battered woman and her children;

6. that Health and Welfare Canada, through the National Clearinghouse on Family Violence, initiate an interdepartmental committee or series of meetings to explore the potential for greater information and statistical coordination across a variety of services;

7. that Health and Welfare Canada sponsor a meeting of provincial/territorial associations of transition houses and of provincial government representatives who are responsible for the issue of wife battering, or family violence generally,

to explore the possibility of developing a common information collection sheet which would facilitate the collection and sharing of data concerning wife battering across the country (this initiative should be coordinated with the work of the interdepartmental committee alluded to in the previous recommendation [number 6] so that transition-house statistics, as much as possible, could be compatible with data collection systems being developed or in existence in the criminal justice system, in hospitals, and in social service agencies);

8. that Health and Welfare Canada, Solicitor General Canada, and the Department of Justice all provide funding to encourage the creation of multi-agency resource centres, similar to the one in operation in London, Ontario, where women can receive advice, support, counselling, and referrals on a variety of different problems (these centres would be geared, not only to crisis assistance, but to reaching out to women in the very early stages of the violence; would also help stimulate the creation of self-help groups and other support groups for battered women and their children; and would coordinate transportation programs to transport battered women and their children to transition houses and to other needed services).

Helping Services, In Addition To Shelters, Address The Needs Of The Children Of Battered Women

Although many of the needs of children must be addressed through schools and services which fall under provincial/territorial jurisdiction, the federal government can play a facilitating role in promoting more responsible and creative programs to address the needs of the children who live in violent homes.

The author proposes

1. that the National Clearinghouse on Family Violence be given funds to identify all curriculum development initiatives completed, underway, or planned across Canada, to collect written material associated with these initiatives, to create a resource manual and/or information kit to encourage the sharing of such information by different school boards, and to sponsor a meeting of representatives from different school boards to discuss further action which could be taken by school personnel, including the provision of resource teachers to transition houses;

2. that, in recognition of the reported dearth of services for violent children, Health and Welfare Canada undertake a short study to assess the current availability of Canadians trained specifically to deal with very violent children and of the existence of college- and university-level courses designed to teach students skills in meeting the needs of these children;

3. that, following this study, Health and Welfare Canada meet with appropriate provincial/territorial government representatives to discuss the creation of a special family aid program for families with very violent children. While these workers could be called into transition houses to work on a one-to-one basis with violent children, their role would not be limited to either the child, or to the transition-house setting. These workers could be called upon by any agency or by private individuals to provide help to violent children or their families, and while their initial contact with the family would be through the child, they would be trained and mandated to work with all members of the family;

4. that, until such a global program is put in place, Health and Welfare Canada provide funds for pilot projects to implement and test this model, or other alternatives, for helping violent children;

5. that the Department of Justice prepare and distribute widely a brief statement for judges, outlining the prevalence and danger of allowing men who have

abused their children and who are separated or divorced from their wives to have access to their children, and exploring other ways to sensitize judges to this problem;

6. that Solicitor General Canada, the Department of Justice, and Health and Welfare Canada each provide funds for the development of protocols for professionals in the criminal justice, health, education, recreation, social service, and child welfare services to help workers in these areas identify and respond to children living in violent homes, regardless of whether the children are physically abused themselves;

7. that funds be made available through Health and Welfare Canada and through Solicitor General Canada for pilot projects to create community-based drop-in programs which could incorporate counselling for children and adolescents living in violent homes into a non-threatening, non-stigmatizing, recreational or educational environment;

8. that Health and Welfare Canada, and other federal government departments, through their policies and programs related to child care and parent support, ensure that, in addition to more widely available, high-quality care in licensed centres, more comprehensive support services be provided. These would include information programs about child care and development, counselling services, emergency care services, and homemaking services, and be available to parents of young children. Consideration would be given to providing remuneration for women caring for their children in their homes.

Improving The Criminal Justice Response

Although the author applauds ministers responsible for policing across Canada for encouraging the implementation of more aggressive charging policies in wife-assault cases, it is recognized that any major policy change necessarily results in a period of experimentation and uneven implementation when it is first instituted.

The author proposes

1. that the Solicitor General, in conjunction with the provincial ministers responsible for policing, undertake a rigorous, nation-wide evaluation of the implementation of the more aggressive police charging policies (now endorsed in every province and territory) in municipal and provincial police forces as well as in the RCMP, to determine how extensively these policies are being implemented, to assess the widespread social and financial costs/benefits of these policies, to determine how these policies have influenced the perceptions of battered women, batterers, and the general public to the police and toward the seriousness of wife battering, to uncover barriers to implementation identified by police officers, and to assess the cost/benefits of the policies for the battered women, the batterers, and their children;

2. that Solicitor General Canada, in conjunction with the provincial ministries responsible for policing, examine and evaluate operational guidelines for police use in cases of wife assault to determine if they could be made clearer and easier to implement; special attention should be paid to the guidelines concerning the rights of the police to remove the man from his home;

3. that Solicitor General Canada, in conjunction with the provincial departments responsible for policing, undertake an evaluation of all segments of police training programs dealing with wife assault;

4. that, on the basis of this evaluation, Solicitor General Canada and the relevant provincial departments ensure that this training is adequate in terms of the time allocated to the issue of wife battering and the expertise of the trainer, and further ensure that the training deals sensitively with the issue, and that it is offered to veteran officers as well as to recruits;

5. that the Department of Justice, in conjunction with provincial departments of justice, evaluate the effectiveness of training concerning wife battering currently available for Crown attorneys and other lawyers, and ensure that the training is adequate to promote the sensitive treatment of battered women and their children by lawyers dealing with these cases. As part of this evaluation, the relative effectiveness of Crown attorneys designated to deal solely or primarily with wife-assault cases, and Crown attorneys who deal with a wide range of cases, should be compared;

6. that, while it is recognized that the Department of Justice has no authority over judges, the Department of Justice, in view of the great need for increased sensitivity to the needs, concerns, and problems of battered women among judges (as reported by battered women and transition-house workers), explore ways to increase judges' awareness of current knowledge concerning wife battering and the reported inequities by judges toward battered women and their children;

7. that the Department of Justice restructure legal aid and criminal injuries compensation to make them more responsive to the needs of battered women;

8. that the Department of Justice and Solicitor General Canada make money available for pilot projects to increase the number of advocacy clinics where workers assist battered women in their dealings with the criminal justice system, accompany them to court, and through links with other services, also help women deal with social, health, and financial problems;

9. that the Department of Justice fund a study to determine the extent of the practice of charging women with contempt of court if they refuse to testify against their partners, to determine under which circumstances these charges are laid, and to determine whether this practice is more or less pronounced among Crown attorneys with significant training and experience in dealing with wife-assault cases;

10. that Solicitor General Canada sponsor a study to review the current guidelines, laws, and practices concerning police protection of battered women and their children, and to explore the potential for more effective protection beyond an identified crisis intervention while the woman still believes she is in danger.

Increasing The Sensitivity Of The Medical Community

The author proposes

1. that Health and Welfare Canada — in conjunction with provincial departments of health — develop and promote training programs for private physicians, nurses, hospital workers, and community health workers. Special emphasis should be placed on sensitizing private physicians to the problem;

2. that the National Clearinghouse on Family Violence continue to identify and collect all hospital protocols for dealing with wife battering currently developed in Canada and the United States;

3. that, following this collection process, a consultation for physicians be held to increase the awareness of available information and training tools, and if desired by consultation participants, a model protocol be developed and distributed to all hospitals across Canada, along with a training manual;

4. that Health and Welfare Canada sponsor a meeting of public health nurses to discover how public health nurses are dealing with wife battering, to identify any problems they experience, and to outline how Health and Welfare could help them overcome their problems, particularly in rural and isolated areas where public health nurses are often one of the only service-providers;

5. that Health and Welfare Canada sponsor a meeting of mental health professionals to discover how mental health professionals are dealing with wife battering, to identify any problems they experience, and to outline how Health and Welfare could help them overcome their problems.

Preventing Wife Battering

The author proposes
1. that the federal government support public education campaigns which reach out, not only to the general public, but also to a variety of professionals who work directly and indirectly with battered women and their children;
2. that, following consultation with transition-house workers and other front-line workers in the development of any such education campaign, services be increased to meet the growth in demand which would result from the campaign;
3. that the Prime Minister's Office, with Status of Women Canada, prepare an information kit for Members of Parliament concerning wife battering, to increase their sensitivity to the issue and to increase their receptivity to programs to assist battered women and their children; copies of this kit should also be made available to the Federation of Municipal Representatives;
4. that funds be made available by Health and Welfare Canada and by Solicitor General Canada for academic research into the causes and dynamics of violence in families and the use of violence by different family members in the same families;
5. that, in addition, more in-depth research into the links between wife battering and alcohol, pregnancy, and other precipitating factors be funded by these federal departments;
6. that Solicitor General Canada fund pilot projects expanding the types of programs for batterers to include residential counselling programs to which the batterer could be referred by either the police or the courts, in an effort to help prevent future violence in families where battering has occurred and to prevent the unnecessary victimization of women and children who are removed from their homes. These pilot projects would have to be undertaken together with a clarification of the rights of police officers to remove men from their homes;
7. that the federal government review all policies related to economic security to ensure that they expressly declare and support the value of women's and children's contributions to society.

Addressing The Special Needs Of Battered Women Who Are Doubly Isolated

The author proposes
1. that Health and Welfare Canada, in conjunction with provincial government departments, encourage, through funding, the creation of shelters and other support services which are designed to meet the special needs of aboriginal, immigrant, rural, disabled, teenaged, or older women who are also battered;
2. that special grants be awarded to existing and planned services enabling them to update their facilities to ensure access to these services by disabled women;
3. that special grants also be awarded to existing and planned services to allow them to hire translators as needed, including workers proficient in sign language, to help workers communicate with women who do not speak either of Canada's official languages;
4. that research be funded by Health and Welfare Canada, in conjunction with Indian and Northern Affairs Canada, to develop alternative service models for battered women in rural and isolated areas.

Questionnaire For Transition-House Workers

Thank you for agreeing to share your knowledge, experience, wisdom, and statistics with the Canadian Advisory Council on the Status of Women through this questionnaire. It is our hope that the information gathered will provide an invaluable tool to promote change which will benefit battered women, transition-house workers, and all women,across Canada.

The information gathered will be treated responsibly and in the strictest confidence. If you wish to remain anonymous, however, please simply fill in the province or territory in which your house is located in the space designated for house name and address below.

1. Name of House/Organization _____
2. Mailing Address _____
3. Contact Person _____
4. Telephone Number _____

Note: Where appropriate, for all the questions which follow, please give figures for the entire year of 1985, or for the fiscal year 1984/85, in keeping with your present method of information collection. However if your house has not been in operation for the full year, please give the figures for the months you have been in operation.

Can you please indicate below which time frame you will use?

calendar year 1985 _____
fiscal year 1984/85 _____
part of 1985 from: _____ 1985 to _____ 1985
                     month   month

A. Organization And History Of Your House

5. How long has your house been in operation? _____
6. Would you describe your house as: (please circle appropriate response)
   a. an interval or transition house only for battered women and their children
   b. a transition house for women in crisis
   c. an emergency or crisis shelter
   d. a safe house
   e. other — please specify _____
7. About what proportion of your calls are:
   a. requests for shelter from battered women _____ %
   b. requests for shelter for battered women but from friends, family, or service-providers _____ %
   c. calls from previous residents who don't want shelter _____ %
   d. crisis calls from other battered women who do not want to come to the house but want advice _____ %
   e. other crisis calls not concerning battered women _____ %
   f. other types of calls — please specify _____ %
   g. don't know _____ %
8. Does your house have a team leader or director? Yes No
9. Do the battered women who stay in your house assist in the day-to-day operation of the house? Yes No

10. Can you briefly describe the goals of your house in your dealings with battered women?

11. Are there any particular features of the organization or goals of your house which you feel contribute to the success of your program and which you feel might benefit other houses?

12. Have you made any major changes in the organization or goals of your house since you first opened? Yes No

    If yes, can you briefly describe what these changes are and why you made them?

B. Services Provided

13. What is the range of services you provide? Please indicate how often each service noted below is provided by circling the appropriate number as follows.

    1 = not provided
    2 = provided to less than 1/4 of our clients
    3 = provided to between 1/4 and 1/2 of our clients
    4 = provided to between half and 3/4 of our clients
    5 = provided to all or almost all of our clients

crisis counselling for resident women	1	2	3	4	5
crisis counselling for non-resident women	1	2	3	4	5
family counselling for women and children	1	2	3	4	5
counselling for resident children	1	2	3	4	5
counselling for non-resident children	1	2	3	4	5
activity program for the children	1	2	3	4	5
couple counselling	1	2	3	4	5
family counselling, including partner	1	2	3	4	5
parenting program	1	2	3	4	5
follow-up program	1	2	3	4	5
rape/sexual assault counselling	1	2	3	4	5
incest counselling	1	2	3	4	5
crisis line	1	2	3	4	5
public education	1	2	3	4	5
employment counselling	1	2	3	4	5
men's groups	1	2	3	4	5
alcohol program for women	1	2	3	4	5
alcohol program for men	1	2	3	4	5
drug program for women	1	2	3	4	5
drug program for men	1	2	3	4	5
accompaniment of women to home to get belongings	1	2	3	4	5
accompaniment of women to court	1	2	3	4	5
assistance dealing with social, financial, legal, health, housing services	1	2	3	4	5
protection	1	2	3	4	5
referral/information	1	2	3	4	5

    other — please specify _____
    don't know   _____
    would rather not answer_____

14. Are you open 24 hours, seven days a week? Yes No

15. Is any member of your staff proficient in sign language?
    Yes No Don't know

16. Is your house wheelchair-accessible? Yes No Don't know

17. What languages are the staff at your house able to speak?

18. Have language barriers between residents and staff ever posed a problem?
Yes   No   Don't know

19. Have you ever had to turn down a request for accommodation because you were not able to communicate with a woman in her language?
Yes   No   Don't know
If yes, what language did she speak?

20. Does your house have a policy to refuse women with:

active drug dependencies	Yes	No	Don't know
active alcohol dependencies	Yes	No	Don't know
severe visual impairment	Yes	No	Don't know
severe hearing impairment	Yes	No	Don't know
suicidal tendencies	Yes	No	Don't know
psychiatric problems	Yes	No	Don't know

other (please specify) _____
would rather not answer this question _____

21. Are there any other issues or problems related to service provision that you would like to raise?

22. Do you have any suggestions for recommendations you would like to see put forth in this area?

C.   Basic Statistics

Note: please use the time frame you indicated on page 1, i.e., fiscal year, calendar year, or period of months, for these questions.

23. What were the total number of approved, funded, or guaranteed beds available in your house?
If there was some variation in this number, can you please elaborate?

24. How many residents did you actually have the space to house?

25. What were the total number of residents accommodated?
How many of these were:
women on their own _____
women accompanied by children _____
children _____
men _____
don't know _____

26. Can you estimate or calculate the proportion of the children accommodated who were:

0-5 years _____ %
6-10 years _____ %
11-18 years _____ %
don't know _____

27. Do you have an upper age limit for boys?   Yes   No
If yes, what is that age limit?

28. Can you estimate or calculate the proportion of women who stayed with you and had:

no children _____ %
1 child _____ %
2 children _____ %
3 or more children _____ %
don't know _____

29. Now can you indicate the total number of residents accommodated by the major reason for admission?

physical abuse _____ #
emotional abuse with no physical abuse _____ #
sexual assault by spouse _____ #
physical and sexual assault by spouse/partner _____ #
abuse of children by father/step-father _____ #
abuse of children by women _____ #
physical or emotional abuse of women by their children ____ #
abuse of women by relatives other than their spouse or children _____ #
recent release of women with children from prison _____ #
transient women _____ #
housing crisis _____ #
others (please specify giving figures for each type of resident) _____ #
don't know _____

30. What is the official maximum length of stay for which per diems can be
received? _____
What is the actual maximum length of stay? _____
What is the average length of stay? _____

31. What was the number or % of requests for stay over 1985 which could not be accommodated for one of the following reasons:

lack of space _____ # or %
alcohol/drug problem _____ # or %
psychiatric disorder _____ # or %
not eligible for per diem _____ # or %
other _____ # or %
How many of these requests were for battered women? _____

32. On average, what proportion of your total beds were filled? _____ %

33. On average, what proportion of your funded beds were filled? _____ %

34. Are you able to accommodate women for whom no per diem can be
received? Yes No Don't know

If yes, can you estimate the number of women and children you
accommodated without receiving a per diem?
women _____ # children _____ #

D. Staffing

35. During 1985, or 1984/85, what was the average number of:

full-time staff _____
part-time staff _____
relief staff _____

36. What salary did you pay: (please indicate if hourly, daily, weekly or monthly
and if hourly, about how many hours worked per week)

your director/coordinator $ _____
your full-time staff $ _____
your part-time staff $ _____
your relief staff $ _____
your child care/counselling staff $ _____
other specialized staff
   (please specify position) $ _____

37. Do you consider your staff underpaid in terms of their:
    education   Yes No Don't know
    experience   Yes No Don't know

38. On average, how many volunteers worked in your house?
    How many hours did they each average per week?

39. Do you consider your house understaffed? Yes No

    If yes, how many additional staff do you feel you would need to adequately fulfil your operational goals?
    What specific positions, roles, or duties would you like these staff to fill?

40. Do you have an organized staff-training program? Yes No

    If yes, do you use a manual or other training materials which could be shared with other houses? Yes No

41. Do you use the same training program for paid staff and for volunteers?
    Yes No

42. Do you consider your training program adequate for:
    paid staff   Yes No
    volunteers   Yes No

43. Do you feel your staff would benefit from additional specific forms of training if time, funds and/or training resource people were available? Yes No

    If yes, can you elaborate on the training and types of resources needed to provide the training? _____

44. Can you pinpoint one or more major problem(s) which contribute to discontent or frustration among staff members?

45. Have these problems contributed to:
    staff leaving   Yes   How many? _____   No Don't know
    staff illness   Yes   No Don't know
    tension among staff members? Yes   No Don't know
    other problems (please specify) _____

46. Are there other issues or problems in the staffing area that you would like to raise?

47. Do you have any suggestions for recommendations you would like to see put forth in this area?

E. Funding

Note: While some of you may feel hesitant to reveal details on funding, we are asking for this information because it is our belief that to lobby effectively for change in this area we need a comprehensive knowledge of how different houses are funded across Canada. Please be assured that, like all the information in the questionnaire, this information will be kept strictly confidential. In addition, if you are unable or hesitant to give exact figures, approximations or "guesstimates" would be accepted gratefully. Please answer these questions in terms of the time frame indicated on page one. Thanks.

48. What was your annual operating budget? _____

49. Was this amount higher than your budget for the previous year?
    Yes No Would rather not answer
    If yes, by how much?

50. What proportion of your budget was provided by the:

    federal government _____ % Don't know
    provincial government _____ % Don't know
    municipal government _____ % Don't know
    United Way _____ % Don't know
    other community agencies (please specify) _____
    private donations by community members _____ % Don't know
    payment for room and board by battered women _____ % Don't know
    payment for room and board by other types of
      residents _____ % Don't know
    payment by residents for specific programs (please elaborate) _____
    other (please specify) _____

51. Is your house in favour of collecting money from women able to pay to cover expenses? Yes No Don't know Would rather not say

52. Did you receive any non-monetary support from community members or agencies, for example, free or discounted food from grocery stores, free or discounted transportation from taxi companies, etc.?
    Yes No Would rather not say

52a. If yes, please specify what services or goods you received and from what type of donor.

53. Please specify what types of funding federal, provincial, and municipal governments provided? (e.g., per diem funding, block funding demonstration grants, core funding, low-rate mortgages, Canada Works grants, etc.)

Federal	Provincial	Municipal
_____	_____	_____
_____	_____	_____
Don't know	Don't know	Don't know
Would rather not say	Would rather not say	Would rather not say

54. If you received per diem payments, what was the rate allocated for:
    women alone _____
    women with children _____
    children _____

55. Have these rates changed from last year?

    Yes
    No
    Don't know
    Would rather not say

    If yes, what was the rate last year for:

    women alone _____
    women with children _____
    children _____

56. Have there been other changes in per diem rates since your house opened?
    Yes No Don't know Would rather not say

    If yes, can you indicate how great a change there has been?

57. Have there been changes in "needs" tests for per diems since your house opened? Yes No
    If yes, please elaborate _____

58. Did you receive any funds specifically allocated for:

research	Yes	No	Don't know
publications	Yes	No	Don't know
conferences	Yes	No	Don't know
meetings with other agencies	Yes	No	Don't know
training	Yes	No	Don't know
salaries for specialized staff	Yes	No	Don't know

    (please specify) _____

59. Were you prevented by inadequate funds from providing certain types of services? Yes No Would rather not answer

    If yes, please elaborate _____

60. How much extra money would you have needed to provide these services? _____

61. Have you ever received "bail-out" funding because you were threatened with having to close your doors? Yes No

    If yes, when? _____ how much was provided? _____
    Did your need for a "bail-out" result in an increase in your per diem, core funding, or block funding? Yes No

    If yes, by how much?
    When did this increase take effect?

62. Have you recently been promised an increase in funding? Yes No

    If yes, how much of an increase has been promised? _____
    When is this increase to take effect? _____

63. Can you estimate about how much of your time is spent seeking and obtaining funding? _____
    Don't know Would rather not say

63a. Does this time spent prevent you from providing other services?
    Yes No Don't know Would rather not say
    If yes, which services?

63b. Can you indicate if paid or volunteer staff do the majority of your fundraising work.

paid staff	volunteer staff	about even
don't know	would rather not say	

64. Are there any other issues or problems in the area of funding that you would like to raise?

65. Do you have any suggestions for recommendations you would like to see put forth in this area?

F. Cooperation And Support Of Other Services

66. Can you please estimate the frequency of different sources of referral as follows:

   1 = never
   2 = less than 25% of the time
   3 = between 25% and 50% of the time
   4 = between 50% and 75% of the time
   5 = more than 75% of the time

police	1	2	3	4	5
lawyer	1	2	3	4	5
court	1	2	3	4	5
doctor	1	2	3	4	5
family/children's services	1	2	3	4	5
other shelters	1	2	3	4	5
self-referral	1	2	3	4	5
friend	1	2	3	4	5
religious/faith organizations	1	2	3	4	5
social services/welfare	1	2	3	4	5
family	1	2	3	4	5
domestic response team/family consultants	1	2	3	4	5
public health nurses	1	2	3	4	5
schools	1	2	3	4	5
other (please specify) _____	1	2	3	4	5
_____	1	2	3	4	5
_____	1	2	3	4	5

67. How would you describe your relationship with the following agencies?

   1 = Poor
   2 = Adequate
   3 = Good
   4 = Very Good
   5 = Excellent

police	1	2	3	4	5
lawyers/Crown attorneys	1	2	3	4	5
judges	1	2	3	4	5
other court officials	1	2	3	4	5
hospitals/doctors	1	2	3	4	5
family/children's services	1	2	3	4	5
other shelters/hostels	1	2	3	4	5
religious organizations	1	2	3	4	5
social services/welfare	1	2	3	4	5
domestic response team/family consultants	1	2	3	4	5
public health nurses	1	2	3	4	5
schools	1	2	3	4	5
United Way	1	2	3	4	5
men's counselling groups	1	2	3	4	5
others (please specify) _____	1	2	3	4	5
_____	1	2	3	4	5
_____	1	2	3	4	5

68. Since your house opened, have you experienced an improved or deteriorating relationship with: (please place an X under appropriate column)

	greatly improved	somewhat improved	deteriorating	about the same
police				
Crown attorneys/lawyers				
judges				
other court workers				
hospitals				
doctors				
public health nurses				
family/children's services				
other shelters				
faith organizations				
United Way				
men's counselling groups				
schools				
domestic response team/ family consultants				
other community groups (specify)				
any other groups (please specify)				

Please elaborate on any significant improvement or deterioration, and how these changes have affected your house.

69. Does your house participate in a multi-disciplinary community service advisory or planning group? Yes No

70. Do you have members of other community groups on your board? Yes No

71. Does your house participate on the boards of other community groups or agencies? Yes No

72. In your experience what are the five services most needed by battered women?

1. _____
2. _____
3. _____
4. _____
5. _____

73. Which of these services exist in your community?

74. For each of these services which exist in your community, can you indicate if battered women find them: very helpful, moderately helpful, not helpful. If possible, give reasons for their lack of success, where appropriate.

Service	How Helpful	Reasons for Success/ Lack of Success
_____	_____	_____
_____	_____	_____
_____	_____	_____

75. Are there any services/agencies using or attempting to use your house for a purpose which does not mesh with the goals of your house?   Yes   No
If yes, please elaborate.

76. Are there hospitals, clinics, and doctors in your community who are directly asking women whether they are being beaten?
Yes   No   Don't know
If yes, how widespread is this?

77. Is there a hospital protocol group in your community developing or implementing guidelines for dealing with wife battering?
(please circle appropriate response)
Yes, there is a hospital implementing guidelines
Yes, there is a hospital developing such guidelines
No
Don't know

78. Have the schools in your community asked members of your house to speak about wife battering:

to school board members	Yes No
to teachers	Yes No
to parent/teacher associations	Yes No
to students (specify grades)	Yes No
to other groups (please specify)	Yes No

79. Are any of the schools in your area incorporating information on wife battering in their curricula? Yes   No   Don't know
If yes, at what grade levels?
How many schools are doing this?
About how many teachers are using this information?
Is information on wife battering being included in the core curriculum?
Yes   No   Don't know

80. Are there other issues or problems in this area that you would like to raise?

81. Do you have any suggestions for recommendations you would like to put forward in this area?

G.   Terminology

82. There has been concern raised by some transition-house workers that the term "wife battering" tends to emphasize physical assault and so to de-emphasize the importance of emotional, verbal, financial, and sexual assault for many assaulted wives. Do you share this concern?
Yes   No

82a. If yes, can you suggest a more appropriate term?

H.   Housing: Crisis And Longer Term

83. Are you buying your house?   Yes   No   Would rather not answer

83a. If yes, who holds title to the house? (please check appropriate answer)
board of directors _____
municipality _____
region _____
other (please describe) _____

83b. Did CMHC arrange the mortgage?

    Yes
    No
    Don't know
    Would rather not say

83c. If your house is **rented**, would you, if a low-rate mortgage could be arranged through CMHC, prefer this option over renting?
    Yes No If no, why not?

84. What is the vacancy rate for apartments in your community/region? _____

85. Do women stay longer at your house than is absolutely necessary while waiting for housing to become available? Yes No Don't know

86. Would you estimate the average length of time it takes a woman to find other accommodation? _____ # weeks, months, etc.

87. Do you operate a second-stage housing program? Yes No

87a. If no, does some other group in your community/region operate such a program? Yes No

87b. If another group does operate such a program, do you cooperate with this group? Yes No

    If yes, in what ways? (please check all appropriate answers)
    referrals _____
    information-sharing _____
    resource-sharing _____
    other (please describe) _____

88. Some houses have reported that certain types of women do not want to go to a second-stage house even when it is in their community. Have you experienced this reaction? Yes No

88a. If yes, can you suggest the major reasons given and the types of women most likely to want another type of accommodation?

89. Are there any other housing alternatives available specifically for battered women in your community, for example, designated sections of some apartment blocks? Yes No Don't know

89a. If yes, can you describe this alternative and how many women and children can be housed?

89b. If yes, does this alternative appeal to those women who do not wish to live in a second stage-house? Yes No Don't know

90. Does your house at present operate a "safe home" program? Yes No

90a. If no, does some other group in your community/region operate such a program? Yes No

90b. If another group does operate such a program, do you cooperate with this group? Yes No

91. Are there other issues or problems in this area that you would like to raise?

92. Do you have any suggestions for recommendations you would like to see put forward in this area?

I. Legal Issues

93. Is there a provincial directive to police to lay charges in wife-battering situations? Yes No Don't know

93a. If yes, do the police in your area enforce this directive?
(please circle appropriate response)

all of the time
most of the time
some of the time
almost never
never
one force we deal with does, another doesn't

94. Is there a provincial directive to Crown attorneys to vigorously prosecute charges once laid? Yes No Don't know

94a. If yes, do the Crown attorneys in your area enforce this directive?
(please circle appropriate response)

all of the time
most of the time
some of the time
almost never
never
some do most of the time, others almost never

95. Is there a specific Crown attorney in your area designated to deal with wife-assault cases? Yes No Don't know

95a. If yes, in your opinion how effective has this designated Crown attorney been? (please circle appropriate response)

very effective   Why?
moderately effective   Why?
not very effective   Why?

96. Did the women who came to your house ever tell you they were concerned that the police might charge their husbands?
Yes No Don't know

96a. If yes, how common is this concern? (please circle appropriate response)

most women expressed the concern
about half of the women expressed this concern
about 1/4 of the women expressed this concern
almost none of the women expressed this concern

97. Can you estimate what proportion of women who stayed in your house did lay charges/informations against their husband themselves? _____ %
Don't know: no follow-up information available _____
Very few women who lay charges stay at our house _____

97a. Of these, about how many proceeded with the case to the end? _____ %
Don't know, no follow-up information available _____

97b. For those who did not proceed with the case to the end, what were the major reasons given?

97c. Of all those women who laid charges/informations themselves, can you estimate how many would have preferred the police to lay charges?
_____ # or % Don't know _____

98. Can you estimate what proportion of the women who stayed in your house reported that the police laid charges against their husbands? _____ %
Don't know: no statistics available _____
Very few women whose husbands are charged stayed in our house _____

98a. Of these women, how many asked to have the case dropped?
_____ % or # Don't know _____

98b. For those who asked to have the case dropped, what were the reasons given?

98c. In about how many cases did the courts comply with these requests to have the case dropped?_____ %
no follow-up data available _____

98d. In about how many cases did the courts stay the charges instead of dropping them? _____ %
no follow-up data available _____

99. When charges were not laid, can you estimate how many women wished the police had laid charges? _____ %

100. What were the major reasons police gave for not laying charges?
Don't know _____

101. Can you estimate what proportion of women who stayed at your house in 1985 were aware of the new charging policy? _____ %

101a. Of those who were aware, what proportion see it as:
a good policy _____ %
an ineffective policy _____ %
a bad policy _____ %
Why?

102. Do you feel that more women would want the police to lay charges if they knew that:

the partner would be sent to jail	Yes	No	Don't know
the woman and her children would be given 24-hour protection	Yes	No	Don't know
the man would be ordered to get special treatment	Yes	No	Don't know

103. Is your house in favour of the current more aggressive charging policies? (please circle appropriate answer)
Yes
No
Don't know
There are not more aggressive charging policies in our area

103a. If you answered "yes" or "no", can you indicate why or why not?

104. In your area about how many men were convicted of wife battering in 1985?
_____ # Don't know _____

105. In your location, when men are convicted of wife battering, about what proportion are sentenced to:
incarceration _____ % What is the average length?
fines _____ % How large is the average fine?
probation _____ % What is the average length?
court-ordered alcohol or drug treatment programs _____ %
family counselling _____ %
counselling for the batterer _____ %
other _____ %

106. Have there been any training programs or awareness seminars concerning wife assault, held in your area for:

judges	Yes	No	Don't know
justices of the peace	Yes	No	Don't know
Crown attorneys	Yes	No	Don't know
police officers	Yes	No	Don't know

106a. In your opinion, were these programs beneficial? Please elaborate.

107. What proportion of the women who stayed with you filed for divorce?
_____ % we don't see women at this stage _____

107a. Of those who did file for divorce, was physical cruelty included in the grounds? Yes No Don't know
If no, why not?

107b. Was mental cruelty included in the grounds? Yes No Don't know
If no, why not?

108. Is there a specific advocacy/support service in your location for women who are going to court? Yes No

109. Can you estimate what proportion of the women who stayed with you filed for custody? _____ %
don't know, no statistics available _____
don't know, we don't see women at this stage _____

109a. How many of these women were awarded custody?
_____ % Don't know _____

110. Can you estimate how many women applied for **ex parte** orders?
_____ % Don't know _____

111. Are there other issues or problems in the legal area that you would like to raise?

112. Are there related recommendations you would like put forth?

J. Children's Services

113. Does your house have a specific program for children? Yes No

113a. If yes, does your house provide:
(please circle all appropriate responses)
  a. counselling for resident children
  b. counselling for non-resident children
  c. a structured activity program for children
  d. a special play area for children within the house
  e. a special play area for children outside the house
  f. a worker responsible only for child care
  g. child-care counselling for the mothers
  h. daily outings for the children
  i. outings for the children two or three times a week
  j. accompaniment of children to school plus transportation when required
  k. medical care for the children
  l. other (please specify)

113b. How many staff are employed for this program?

113c. If you answered "no" to question 113, would you, if funds were available, like to develop a program specifically geared to the needs of chidren?
Yes No

114. What (other) services for children, if any, would you like to provide if you had sufficient resources?

115. Do you have a staff member who acts primarily as a children's program coordinator? Yes No

115a. If no, would you hire one if you had additional funds?

116. In your opinion, what are the five most-needed services for children in the community?

1. _____
2. _____
3. _____
4. _____
5. _____

117. Which of these services exist in your community?

118. Do you refer women to any of these services? Yes No
If no, why not?

K. The Relationship Between Child Abuse And Wife Battering

119. About what proportion of the battered women who stayed with you reported that their partner had abused their children:

physically _____ %
emotionally _____ %
sexually _____ %
don't know: no statistics kept _____
would rather not answer _____

120. On average, did these women report that this abuse occurred:
(please circle appropriate response)

daily
weekly
once or twice a month
occasionally
whenever the woman was beaten

121. About what proportion of all the partners had been abused as children?
_____ %
don't know: no statistics kept _____
would rather not answer _____

122. About what proportion of the partners who abused their children had been abused as children? _____ %
don't know, no statistics kept _____
would rather not answer _____

123. How many of the women who stayed with you have had their children taken away by the Child Welfare authorities? _____ %
don't know _____
would rather not answer _____

123a. Why were they taken away? Give the three most common reasons, if possible.

1. _____
2. _____
3. _____

123b. About what proportion of these women got their children back?
_____ % Don't know _____

124. How many women who were separated or divorced from their husbands, or living apart from their common-law partners, reported being ordered by the courts to allow their partners to visit their children when it was known that the partner had abused the children?
_____ % or # Don't know _____

125. In your estimation, what proportion of the battered women who came to your house had:

physically abused their children _____ %
emotionally abused or neglected their children _____ %
sexually abused their children _____ %

126. Did you report this abuse? Yes No Would rather not answer
Why or why not?

127. On average, did these women report that the abuse occurred:
(please circle appropriate response)

daily
weekly
once or twice a month
occasionally
whenever their partner assaulted or emotionally battered the woman

128. Did staff members witness any child abuse in the house?
Yes No Would rather not answer

128a. If yes, how many cases did they witness?

128b. If yes, how did your staff deal with this abuse?

129. Do staff members in your house report any problems working with women who batter their children? Yes No Would rather not answer

129a. If yes, how is your house dealing with these problems?

129b. Would you have a special training component dealing with this issue for your staff if you had the resources? Yes No

130. Were any of the children of the women who stayed at your house in 1985, known runaways? Yes No Don't know

130a. If yes, how many?

130b. If yes, in what age group did most of the runaways fall?

under 5 years
6-10 years
11-14 years
15+ years

131. About what proportion of the battered women who stayed with you reported being abused as children?

physically _____ %
emotionally _____ %
sexually _____ %
don't know _____
would rather not answer _____

132. About what proportion of battered women who abused their children reported being abused as children themselves?

physically _____ %
emotionally _____ %
sexually _____ %
don't know _____
would rather not answer _____

133. Can you estimate the number of battered women and their partners who abused their children, in each of the following age groups?

Age	Battered women	Batterers
17-25	_____ %	_____ %
26-35	_____ %	_____ %
36-55	_____ %	_____ %
56+	_____ %	_____ %
no figures available	_____	_____

134. Can you estimate the proportion of battered children which falls in each of the following age groups?

less than one year	_____ %
1-3 years	_____ %
4-5 years	_____ %
6-12 years	_____ %
13+ years	_____ %

135. How do the women who reported abusing their children feel their abusive behaviour could have been prevented?

136. Can you estimate the proportion of women who stayed with you who are abusing their children:

because of stress or situational conditions _____ %
because they experienced it as children and have come to see violence as a way of life _____ %

137. Are there any other issues relating to children's services and child abuse as they concern wife battering that you would like to raise?

138. Can you suggest any recommendations that you would like to see put forward relating to children's services and child abuse as they concern wife battering?

L.   Characteristics Of Women And Children Served

139. About what proportion of battered women who stayed in your house in 1985 and their batterers were in the following age groups?

Age	Woman	Partner
under 21	_____ %	_____ %
21-34	_____ %	_____ %
35-49	_____ %	_____ %
50+	_____ %	_____ %

140. About what proportion of the battered women you served are:

single	_____ %
separated	_____ %
divorced	_____ %
married	_____ %
living common-law	_____ %

141. Can you estimate what proportion of the women who stayed at your house had:

one or more pre-school children only _____ %
one or more child between 5 and 12 years old only _____ %
one or more pre-school child and
     one or more child(ren) 5-11 years old? _____ %

142. Now can you estimate how many children who accompany women to the house are:

under 2 years old _____
2-4 years old   _____
5-11 years   _____
12-15 years   _____
15+ years   _____

143. What proportion of battered women have lived with their partners:

less than one year _____ %
1-5 years   _____ %
6-10 years   _____ %
11+ years   _____ %

144. About what proportion of battered women who stayed at your house had left their current partners before? _____ %

144a. Of these, what proportion left mainly because of:

physical/emotional abuse of self _____ %
physical/emotional abuse of children _____ %
sexual abuse of self _____ %
sexual abuse of children _____ %
financial abuse _____ %
other major reasons — please specify _____ %

145. What proportion of the battered women who came to your house were working outside the home?

146. Of those women who worked outside the home, what proportion worked at jobs that were:

professional (e.g., lawyer, teacher, nurse) _____ %
white collar (e.g., clerk, secretary) _____ %
blue-collar skilled (e.g., cook, machine operator) _____ %
blue-collar unskilled (e.g., waitress) _____ %
other _____ %

147. What proportion of women who worked outside the home earned:

less than $7,000 a year _____ %
between $7,000 and $10,000 a year _____ %
between 10,000 and $20,000 a year _____ %
between $20,000 and $34,000 a year _____ %
over $34,000 a year _____ %

148. What proportion of women before leaving their partners had a family income of:

under $10,000 a year _____ %
between $10,000 and $20,000 a year _____ %
between $20,000 and $30,000 a year _____ %
between $30,000 and $45,000 a year _____ %
over $45,000 a year _____ %

149. What proportion of battered women who came to your house had completed:

grade school or less _____ %
some high school _____ %
a high school diploma _____ %
some college/technical school _____ %
college/technical school diploma or degree _____ %
university degree _____ %
graduate/professional degree _____ %

150. What proportion of the partners of women who stayed at your house worked:

regularly _____ %
irregularly _____ %
seasonally _____ %
were unemployed _____ %

151. Of the partners who were working, what proportion worked at jobs that were:

professional (e.g., doctor, accountant) _____ %
white collar (e.g., clerk) _____ %
blue-collar skilled (e.g., electrician, police) _____ %
blue-collar unskilled (e.g., construction worker) _____ %
other _____ %

152. What proportion of the partners were in the armed forces at the time of the battering? _____ %

153. What proportion of the partners had completed:

grade school or less _____ %
some high school _____ %
high school diploma _____ %
some college/technical school _____ %
college/technical school diploma or degree _____ %
university degree _____ %
graduate/professional degree _____ %

154. What proportion of women who came to you were:

Canadian citizens _____ %
sponsored immigrants _____ %
other _____ %

155. Of the sponsored immigrants, for how many had the sponsorship broken down? _____ %

156. Did any mail-order brides stay with you in 1985?
If yes, how many? _____

157. What proportion of the partners of the women who stayed with you were:

Canadian citizens _____ %
sponsored immigrants _____ %
other _____ %

158. What proportion of the battered women and their partners were:

	Women	Partners
white	_____ %	_____ %
black	_____ %	_____ %
treaty Indian	_____ %	_____ %
non-treaty Indian	_____ %	_____ %
Eurasian	_____ %	_____ %
other	_____ %	_____ %

159. What proportion of the partners had criminal records? _____ %

159a. Of these, what proportion had been:

convicted of assault against their wife? _____ %
convicted of assault against someone else? _____ %
convicted of other charges? _____ %

159b. Of those with criminal records, what proportion were on probation? _____ %

160. What proportion of the women who stayed with you reported a history of:

drug abuse   by themselves _____ %   by their partners _____ %
alcohol abuse   by themselves _____ %   by their partners _____ %

161. What proportion of the women who stayed with you in 1985 or 1984/85 had stayed at your house before:

only once _____ %
twice _____ %
three to five times _____ %
more than five times _____ %

162. What proportion of the women were:

local _____ %
from out of the city, town, village, or rural area _____ %
from out of the province _____ %

163. What proportion of the battered women were:

eligible for social assistance but not currently receiving it _____ %
receiving social assistance _____ %
not eligible for social assistance _____ %

164. Of those who were not eligible for social assistance, in your opinion how many would be able and willing to contribute money to their room and board? _____

164a. How many did contribute to their room and board? _____

165. Can you estimate what proportion of the women who stayed with you:

returned to their partners _____ %
went out on their own or with kids _____ %
went to live with another man _____ %
went to live with friends or relatives _____ %
don't know _____

165a. For those who returned to their partners, what were their major reasons for returning?

166. How many women reported that their partner threatened:

to kill them _____ %
to kill or harm their children _____ %
to kill or harm another relative or friend _____ %
to kill or harm their pet _____ %

167. How many women reported that their partners:
    regularly carried a weapon _____ %
    used a weapon or an object as a weapon during the assault _____ %
    threatened to use a weapon _____ %
    participated in the assault with other people _____ %

168. Of the women who contacted you in 1985 or 1984/85, do you know of any who have been killed? Yes No

    If yes, how many? _____ #

169. Can you give an estimate of the proportion of women who stayed with you and had been assaulted while pregnant? _____ %

169a. Of these women, in how many cases did the woman:
    miscarry _____ %
    become infertile as a result of the beatings _____ %
    give birth to a deformed or brain-damaged child _____ %
    have a premature delivery _____ %
    experience feeding difficulties _____ %
    don't know _____

M. The Relationship Between Pornography And Wife Battering

170. In your experience, is pornography related to an assaultive process?
    Yes No Don't know

171. Would you be willing to participate in a study to explore this relationship further? Yes No

172. Do you currently collect information on the relationship between pornography and wife battering? Yes No

172a. If yes, can you attach any relevant statistics for 1985 or 1984/85 to this completed questionnaire? Thanks.

Thank you for your invaluable help in completing this very lengthy questionnaire. The Canadian Advisory Council on the Status of Women and I will make every effort to ensure that your responses will be used to lobby for change which will reflect the realities, knowledge, and hopes of battered women and their closest advocates — transition-house workers.

Appendix C

Methodology

A lengthy written questionnaire (see Appendix B) was sent out to all known transition houses, associated safe-house networks, provincial/territorial associations of transition houses across the country, and second-stage shelters which could be identified. A concerted attempt was made to design the questionnaire so that it would reflect the concerns of transition-house workers and of the battered women who stayed at the transition houses.

Ideally, a report of this type would have grown primarily from personal conversations with battered women so that their hopes, thoughts, and experiences could be expressed in their own words. However, because of the private and dangerous nature of wife battering, there are special difficulties in research which uses personal interviews with battered women. Women who are being battered are not easy to identify, because many battered women choose to keep their battering secret. Many women could be placed in danger if the batterers discovered they were speaking to an interviewer about their experiences with battering. The lives of battered women trying to escape the violence are often in a state of flux so that contact is very difficult. Further, because wife battering is cyclical in nature, with tension-building phases, battering crises, and honeymoon stages, the woman's understanding of events surrounding the battering can be very volatile — changing radically from day to day. As a result, continued contact would be necessary to more accurately and sensitively capture the women's experiences. These and other obstacles escalate the potential human and financial costs of such an approach.

Accordingly, it was decided that, while some contact with battered women would be essential to ensure the credibility and depth of the report, most of the information would be gathered from service-providers who work directly with battered women, their children and/or the batterers.

While this decision produces some gaps in the information cited, since the data are derived primarily from one group of service-providers, it was a decision based on the following factors.

First, transition houses are still the major source of support and protection specifically for battered women in this country. Accordingly, the needs and perceptions of transition-house workers must be emphasized and responded to in policy and program support if the needs of battered women who use these services are to be met.

Second, many transition houses now keep fairly detailed statistics on the numbers and characteristics of the women who stay at the houses (such as age, occupation, number and ages of children, marital status, etc.) as well as on details of staffing, administration, and funding. While the data files themselves kept by shelters for battered women are confidential to protect the privacy and to ensure the safety of battered women, many of the statistics contained in them can be retrieved and shared without revealing the names or any identifying characteristics of specific women involved. The statistics gathered by the workers in different shelters are sufficiently similar to allow for their amalgamation into a general national picture.

Since no other national statistics of this scope and detail are currently available, these statistics are invaluable for giving us a partial picture of wife battering in Canada at a relatively modest cost.

Third, shelter workers spend considerable time talking directly to the women, and most houses attempt to express, through their programs and actions, the wishes and hopes of the women who come to them. Therefore, while it is acknowledged that no one can really "speak for" battered women or convey the depth of their anguish and the complexity of their experiences, shelter workers can represent some of the concerns of the many battered women who stay in crisis shelters better than anyone else other than the battered women. Through the statistics and comments of transition-house workers, it is hoped that some battered women can be given a national voice without jeopardizing their privacy and safety.

Based on these assumptions, the questionnaire was created following lengthy and repeated discussions with a selected group of transition-house workers and provincial association representatives. To ensure the policy relevance of the questionnaire from a national perspective, a number of federal government officials were also contacted to ascertain their concerns and to include questions which would gather information they considered important for the study.

To give the study even more richness, these written questionnaires were complemented by face-to-face interviews with many transition-house workers and representatives of the provincial/territorial associations of transition houses, selected police officers, Crown attorneys, court workers, provincial government officials, workers in second-stage houses, and counsellors of men who batter. To keep the cost of the project within reasonable bounds, the author travelled to 11 centres across the country and conducted personal interviews with as many workers as possible in each location. An assistant interviewed a variety of workers in several centres in Quebec. An attempt was made to schedule the trips at times which coincided with a meeting of the houses in that province or region to meet and interview the greatest possible number and variety of workers. Locations were also chosen where government officials, police, Crown attorneys, second-stage house workers, and counsellors of men who batter would be available. Since these locations were rarely in rural areas, the author and her assistant were not able to speak to as many workers from rural and isolated areas as they would have liked in order to adequately capture the unique facets and problems of wife battering and service provision in these regions. However, wherever possible, and with the untiring assistance of shelter workers in some provinces, day trips to houses in less accessible, outlying areas were made. Where that was not possible and where rural workers were not able to travel to meet either the author or her assistant, an attempt was made to conduct lengthy telephone interviews with rural workers.

An attempt was also made during the author's travels to speak directly to battered women. Time constraints made these conversations difficult, however, and contact was not initiated unless the author had several hours to devote to each woman. As an alternative, the author asked transition-house workers to request that women write letters to the author on a voluntary, and if preferred, an anonymous basis, describing their experiences, their hopes for the future, and their visions of the types of services they would find useful and supportive.

This request for letters from battered women was not as successful as had been hoped; only 22 women responded. This is not surprising, however, given the many strains battered women are under, the difficulty of encapsulating such emotional experiences in writing, and the fact that the author was a stranger and unable to give them any immediate, practical help in exchange for their time and revelations. Unfortunately, the low level of responses directly from battered women means that the author's assumptions and findings about the needs and desires of battered women necessarily have to be based on extrapolations from a few current interviews with battered women and on extensive "second-hand" reports from shelter workers. However, the author has used her memories of many informal conversations over the years with women who have been battered, the results of other studies based on reports by battered women, and letters sent to the author by battered women following the publication of *Wife Battering in Canada: The Vicious Circle*. These other sources have allowed the author to speak for a broader population of battered women than just those women who stay in transition houses, for it is well recognized throughout this study that women who stay in transition houses represent only a small portion of all battered women in Canada. Women who seek shelter in transition houses are generally women with young children and little access to financial resources. Not all, and probably not the majority of, battered women fit this description. Nonetheless, many of the long-term needs and particularly the hopes of battered women appear to be much the same, regardless of their financial circumstances, employment status, or age. It is only the means of fulfilling these needs and hopes which change with the individual and her circumstances.

Time Frame Used In This Report

Throughout the book, the author states that statistics reported refer to the calendar year 1985. This is not strictly true, since only 56% of the houses had statistics for the entire year 1985. Another 11% kept statistics for only part of 1985 because they had opened part-way through that year. The remaining 33% of the houses kept their statistics by fiscal year, that is, from March 1984 to March 1985, and therefore reported their statistics within that time frame.

While the time frames are not strictly comparable, adjustments to the figures have been made where possible; and the author has amalgamated figures for these different periods.

Response Received From Transition-House Workers

The responses from workers in the field were generally supportive and thorough. At the time of writing, there were 230 houses in Canada. One hundred and fifty-one houses returned their questionnaires. The overall response rate for the written questionnaire was therefore 66% — a gratifying response, given the length and complexity of the questionnaire. Variation in response rate among provinces seemed primarily to reflect inequities in funding levels which affected staff time available to complete the questionnaire. Because of this variation in response rate, however, no attempt was made in this report to compare figures for different provinces. Instead, the data for this study will be presented from a national perspective.

The overall response rate, in view of the limited time available to house workers and the detailed nature of the questionnaire, attests to the fact that transition-house workers have a great deal of information to share and want a national voice. It attests to their continued commitment to the needs of battered women. The response rate is also a tribute to workers representing the provincial/territorial associations of transition houses who provided such enthusiastic and constant support throughout the study.

Appendix D

Transition Houses And Shelters For Battered Women In Canada, And Provincial And Territorial Associations Of Transition Houses And Shelters

Transition Houses and Shelters

Northwest Territories

Emergency Family Centre*
Fort Smith, N.W.T.
(403) 872-2378

YWCA of Yellowknife (McAteer House)
Yellowknife, N.W.T.
(403) 920-2777
    873-4767

Yukon

Kaushee's Place
Whitehorse, Yukon
(403) 668-5733

British Columbia

Marguerite Dixon House
Burnaby, British Columbia
(604) 298-3454

Campbell River North
  Island Transition Society
Campbell River, British Columbia
(604) 286-3666

Chetwynd Women's Resource Centre*
Chetwynd, British Columbia
(604) 788-3793

Ann Davis Transition House
Chilliwack, British Columbia
(604) 792-3116
    792-0727 (after hours)

Cranbrook Safe Homes
Cranbrook, British Columbia
(604) 426-8407

Mizpah House
Dawson Creek, British Columbia
(604) 782-9176

Somenos House
Duncan, British Columbia
(604) 748-7273 (WAVA)

Meope Transition House
Fort St. John, British Columbia
(604) 785-5208

The ''Y'' Women's Emergency Shelter
Kamloops, British Columbia
(604) 374-6162

Central Okanagan Emergency Shelter
  Society
(Kelowna Women's Shelter)
Kelowna, British Columbia
(604) 763-1040

Ishtar Transition Housing Society
Langley, British Columbia
(604) 530-9442

Cythera House
Maple Ridge, British Columbia
(604) 467-9966

Mission Transition House
Mission, British Columbia
(604) 826-7800

Haven House
Nanaimo, British Columbia
(604) 754-7123

Nelson Emergency Shelter
  Programme
Nelson, British Columbia
(604) 352-3504

Emily Murphy House
North Vancouver, British Columbia
(604) 987-1773

Haven Homes
Parksville, British Columbia
(604) 248-2093

South Okanagan Women in Need
  Society
Penticton, British Columbia
(604) 493-7233

Port Alberni Transition House
Port Alberni, British Columbia
(604) 724-2223

Port Coquitlam Women's Transition
  House
Port Coquitlam, British Columbia
(604) 464-2020

Phoenix Transition House
Prince George, British Columbia
(604) 563-7305

Prince Rupert Transition House
Prince Rupert, British Columbia
(604) 627-8588

Amata Transition House
Quesnel, British Columbia
(604) 992-7321

Revelstoke Women's Shelter
  Society
Revelstoke, British Columbia
(604) 837-4362

Nova House
Richmond, British Columbia
(604) 270-4911

Shuswap Area Family Emergency
  (S.A.F.E.) Society
Salmon Arm, British Columbia
(604) 832-9616

Sunshine Coast Transition House
Sechelt, British Columbia
(604) 885-2944

Surrey Emergency Shelter*
Surrey, British Columbia
via Emergency Services
(604) 576-8636
        588-0188 (crisis line)

K'san House
Terrace, British Columbia
(604) 635-6447
        638-9982

W.I.N.S. Transition House
(Women in Need Society)
Trail, British Columbia
(604) 364-1718

Kate Booth House
Vancouver, British Columbia
(604) 872-7774

Munroe House (second-stage
  housing)
Vancouver, British Columbia
(604) 734-5722

Powell Place Sanctuary for Women*
Vancouver, British Columbia
via Emergency Services
(604) 668-3111

Vancouver Rape Relief and
  Women's Shelter
Vancouver, British Columbia
(604) 872-8212

For Vancouver area, see also
Burnaby, North Vancouver,
Richmond, and Surrey

Vernon Women's Transition House
Vernon, British Columbia
(604) 542-1122

Victoria Women's Transition House
Victoria, British Columbia
(604) 385-6611

Cariboo Women's Emergency Shelter
Williams Lake, British Columbia
(604) 398-6831

Alberta

Calgary Women's Emergency Shelter
Calgary, Alberta
(403) 245-5901
        245-4442

Calgary YWCA Residence
Calgary, Alberta
(403) 263-1550

Discovery House (second-stage
  housing)
Calgary, Alberta
(403) 290-0050

Sheriff King Home for Battered
  Women
Calgary, Alberta
(403) 266-0707

Camrose Women's Shelter
Camrose, Alberta
(403) 672-1035

W.I.N. Houses I and II
Edmonton, Alberta
(403) 479-0058

Unity House
Fort McMurray, Alberta
(403) 791-7505
        743-1190

Dr. Margaret Savage Women's
  Crisis Centre
Grand Centre, Alberta
(403) 594-5095

Odyssey House
Grande Prairie, Alberta
(403) 532-2672

Safe Home Network**
High Level, Alberta
(403) 926-3791

Yellowhead Emergency Shelter for
  Women Society
Hinton, Alberta
(403) 865-5133

Harbour House
Lethbridge, Alberta
(403) 320-1881

Lloydminster Interval Home
Lloydminster, Alberta
(403) 875-0966

Medicine Hat Women's Shelter
Society
Medicine Hat, Alberta
(403) 529-1091

Central Alberta Women's
Emergency Shelter
Red Deer, Alberta
(403) 346-5643

A Safe Place
Sherwood Park, Alberta
(403) 464-7233

St. Paul Crisis Association**
St. Paul, Alberta
(403) 645-5132

Wellspring Battered Women's
Support Service (Resource
Centre)**
Whitecourt, Alberta
(403) 778-6209

Saskatchewan

Moose Jaw Transition House
Moose Jaw, Saskatchewan
(306) 693-6511

Battlefords Interval House
North Battleford, Saskatchewan
(306) 445-2742

Pesim Waskayikan Interval House
Prince Albert, Saskatchewan
(306) 922-2100

Regina Native Women's Residence
Resource Centre
Regina, Saskatchewan
(306) 543-1212
545-2062

Regina Transition House
Regina, Saskatchewan
(306) 569-2292

Interval House Inc.
Saskatoon, Saskatchewan
(306) 244-0185

Shelwin House
Yorkton, Saskatchewan
(306) 783-7233

Manitoba

Westman Women's Shelter
Brandon, Manitoba
(204) 727-3644
727-4504
1-800-862-2727

Dauphin Crisis Centre***
Dauphin, Manitoba
(204) 638-8777

Portage Women's Shelter Inc.***
Portage La Prairie, Manitoba
(204) 239-5232

Selkirk Cooperative on Abuse
Against Women***
Selkirk, Manitoba
(204) 482-7882

Steinbach Family Crisis Centre
(Agape House)***
Steinbach, Manitoba
(204) 326-6062

Aurora House Crisis Shelter
The Pas, Manitoba
(204) 623-5497

North W.I.N. House
Thompson, Manitoba
(204) 677-2723
778-7273 (crisis line)

South Central Committee on
Family Violence Inc.***
Winkler, Manitoba
(204) 325-9956 (24-hour crisis
line — call collect)

Osborne House Crisis-Shelter for
Battered Women
Winnipeg, Manitoba
(204) 775-8197

Manitoba Committee on Wife
Abuse Crisis Line
Manitoba — 1-800-362-3344
Winnipeg — (204) 942-3052

Ontario

The residential services listed
consist of:
Transition Houses (T.H.)
Family Resource Centres (F.R.C.)
Multi-purpose Shelters (S)

People In Transition
(development stage)
Alliston, Ontario
(705) 435-9400

Atikokan Crisis Centre (T.H.)
Atikokan, Ontario
(807) 597-2868
597-6908

Yellow Brick House (T.H.)
Aurora, Ontario
(416) 727-1945
773-6481 (Oakridge)

Maggie's: A Resource Centre for
Women (S)
Bancroft, Ontario
(613) 332-3010

Women and Children Crisis
Centre (T.H.)
Barrie, Ontario
(705) 728-6300

Mississauga Family Resource
  Centre (F.R.C.)
Blind River, Ontario
(705) 356-7800

Muskoka Interval House (T.H.)
Bracebridge, Ontario
(705) 645-4461
1-800-461-1740

Brantford YM-YWCA (T.H.)
Brantford, Ontario
(519) 752-6568

Nova Vita Women's Shelter (T.H.)
Brantford, Ontario
(519) 752-4357

Leeds and Grenville Interval
  House (T.H.)
Brockville, Ontario
(613) 342-4724 (business
       342-8815 (crisis)

Family Crisis Shelter (T.H.)
Cambridge, Ontario
(519) 653-2422

Lanark County Interval House (T.H.)
Carleton Place, Ontario
(613) 257-5960

Chatham Kent Women's Centre Inc. (T.H.)
Chatham, Ontario
(519) 354-6360

Women in Crisis (T.H.)
Cobourg, Ontario
(416) 372-0746

Maison Baldwin House (T.H.)
Cornwall, Ontario
(613) 938-2958

North York Women's Shelter (T.H.)
Downsview, Ontario
(416) 635-9630

Hoshizaki House (T.H.)
Dryden, Ontario
(807) 223-3226

Avoca House (T.H.)
Eganville, Ontario
(613) 628-2522 (crisis)
       628-2154 (business)

Elliott Lake Women's Crisis
  Centre (T.H.)
Elliott Lake, Ontario
(705) 461-9868

Women's Habitat (T.H.)
Etobicoke, Ontario
(416) 252-5829

Three Oaks Foundation (T.H.)
Foxboro, Ontario
(613) 967-1857

Geraldton Family Resource
  Centre (F.R.C.)
Geraldton, Ontario
(807) 854-1529

Survival Through Friendship
  House (T.H.)
Goderich, Ontario
(519) 524-6245
1-800-265-5506

Women in Crisis/Marianne's
  Place (T.H.)
Guelph, Ontario
(519) 836-5710

Pavilion Transition House (T.H.)
Haileybury, Ontario
(705) 672-2128

Elizabeth Fry Society —
  Hamilton Branch (S)
Hamilton, Ontario
(416) 522-3343 (women only)

Good Shepherd Women's Centre —
  Martha House (S)
Hamilton, Ontario
(416) 523-8895

Hamilton Native Women's
  Centre (S)
Hamilton, Ontario
(416) 522-1501

Hope Haven Homes for Family
  Abuse (S)
Hamilton, Ontario
(416) 547-1815

Inasmuch House (T.H.)
Hamilton, Ontario
(416) 529-8149
       529-8140

Interval House for
  Hamilton-Wentworth (T.H.)
Hamilton, Ontario
(416) 547-8485 (business)
       547-8484 (crisis)

St. Simeon House for Women (S)
Hamilton, Ontario
(416) 522-0405

Maison Interlude House (T.H.)
Hawkesbury, Ontario
(613) 632-1131

Toll-free line for area code 613
1-800-267-4101

Habitat Interlude (F.R.C.)
Kapuskasing, Ontario
(705) 337-1122

Kenora Family Resource
Centre (F.R.C.)
Kenora, Ontario
(807) 468-5491

Women's Place
Kenora, Ontario
(807) 468-9095

The Women's House of Bruce
County (F.R.C.)
Kincardine, Ontario
(519) 396-9655 (crisis)
     396-9814 (business)
1-800-265-3026

Kingston Interval House (T.H.)
Kingston, Ontario
(613) 546-1777 (crisis)
     546-1833 (business)

Anselma House (T.H.)
Kitchener, Ontario
(519) 742-5894

Y.W.C.A. Residence (S)
Kitchener, Ontario
(519) 744-6507

Family Centre — Mission Service
of London (S)
London, Ontario
(519) 433-0641 (for families)

Rotholme Mission Services of
London (S)
London, Ontario
(519) 438-4651 (women only)

Sisters of St. Joseph — Residence
for Women in Need (S)
London, Ontario
(519) 679-9570

Women's Community House (T.H.)
London, Ontario
(519) 439-4543 (crisis)
     439-0755 (business)

Northshore Family Resource
Centre (F.R.C.)
Marathon, Ontario
(807) 229-2223
     229-1340

Canadian Mental Health Family
Resource Centre (F.R.C.)
Matheson (Black River), Ontario
(705) 273-2339

Mattawa Family Resource
Centre (F.R.C.)
Mattawa, Ontario
(705) 744-5567

Rosewood (Huronia Transition
House) (T.H.)
Midland, Ontario
(705) 526-4211

Halton Women's Place (T.H.)
Milton, Ontario
(416) 878-8555

Haven House (F.R.C.)
Manitoulin Island
Mindemoya, Ontario
(705) 377-5160

Interim Place (T.H.)
Mississauga, Ontario
(416) 271-1860
     271-1861

Moosonee Family Resource
Centre (F.R.C.)
Moosonee, Ontario
(705) 336-2456

Niagara Women in Crisis (T.H.)
Niagara Falls, Ontario
(416) 356-5800 (crisis)
     356-3933 (business)

Crisis Centre North Bay (S)
North Bay, Ontario
(705) 474-1031

Nipissing Transition House (T.H.)
North Bay, Ontario
(705) 476-2429

Ojibway Family Resource
Centre (F.R.C.)
North Bay, Ontario
(705) 472-3321

Hillside House Family Transition
Place — Dufferin (F.R.C.)
Orangeville, Ontario
(519) 941-1433 (crisis)
     941-5790 (business)

Auberge/Sedna Women's
Shelter (T.H.)
Oshawa, Ontario
(416) 728-7311
1-800-263-3725

Higgins House — Y.W.C.A.
(safe-home apartments)
Oshawa, Ontario
(416) 576-8880

Interval House of Ottawa-Carleton
(T.H.)
Ottawa, Ontario
(613) 234-5181

La Présence (T.H.)
Ottawa, Ontario
(613) 233-8297

Amity House (T.H.)
Ottawa, Ontario
(613) 234-7204

Women's Centre (Grey-Bruce Inc.) (T.H.)
Owen Sound, Ontario
(519) 371-1600
1-800-265-3722

Parry Sound Family Resource
  Centre (F.R.C.)
Parry Sound, Ontario
(705) 746-4800
1-800-461-1707

Bernadette McCann House for
  Women Inc. (T.H.)
Pembroke, Ontario
(613) 732-3131

Crossroads — 1 (T.H.)
Peterborough, Ontario
(705) 743-4135
1-800-461-7656

Crossroads — 2 (T.H.)
Peterborough, Ontario
(705) 743-8922

Ernestine's Women's Shelter (T.H.)
Rexdale, Ontario
(416) 746-3701

Women's Interval Home of Sarnia-
  Lambton (T.H.)
Sarnia, Ontario
(519) 336-5200
1-800-265-1412

Women in Crisis (Algoma) Inc. (T.H.)
Sault Ste Marie, Ontario
(705) 759-1230

Emily Stowe Shelter for
  Women (T.H.)
Scarborough, Ontario
(416) 264-4357

Haldimand-Norfolk Women's
  Shelter (S)
Simcoe, Ontario
(519) 426-8048
      426-8080
1-800-265-8076

Sioux Lookout Family Resource
  Centre (F.R.C.)
Sioux Lookout, Ontario
(807) 737-1438

Women's Place Inc. (T.H.)
St. Catharines, Ontario
(416) 684-8331
      684-4000

Women's Place (T.H.)
St. Thomas, Ontario
(519) 631-9800
      633-0155
1-800-265-4305

Optimism Place (T.H.)
Stratford, Ontario
(519) 271-5550

Sturgeon Falls Family Resource
  Centre (F.R.C.)
Sturgeon Falls, Ontario
(705) 753-1154
      753-1168

Genevra House (S)
Sudbury, Ontario
(705) 674-2210
1-800-461-0133

Beendigen Native Women's Crisis
  Home (S)
Thunder Bay, Ontario
(807) 622-5101

Community Residence (S)
Thunder Bay, Ontario
via Social Services Department
(807) 625-2430

Faye Peterson Transition
  House (T.H.)
Thunder Bay, Ontario
(807) 623-6600
1-800-465-6971

Anduhyaun Residence Inc. (S)
(native women's shelter)
Toronto, Ontario
(416) 920-1491
      920-1492

Evangeline Residence (S)
  (Salvation Army)
Toronto, Ontario
(416) 762-9636

Interval House (T.H.)
Toronto, Ontario
(416) 924-1491

Nellie's Hostel (S)
Toronto, Ontario
(416) 461-1084

Red Door (S)
Toronto, Ontario
(416) 469-4123

Stop 86 (S)
Toronto, Ontario
(416) 922-3271

Street Haven at the Crossroads (S)
Toronto, Ontario
(416) 967-6060 (women only)

Toronto Community Hostel (S)
Toronto, Ontario
(416) 925-4431

Walpole House (S)
Toronto, Ontario
(416) 923-5266

Women's Habitat of Etobicoke (T.H.)
Toronto, Ontario
(416) 252-5829

Women in Transition Inc. (T.H.)
Toronto, Ontario
(416) 967-5227

For Toronto area, see also
Etobicoke, Mississauga, and
Scarborough.

Chadwic Home (F.R.C.)
Wawa, Ontario
(705) 856-2848
1-800-461-2242

Women's Place (Welland and
    District) Inc. (T.H.)
Welland, Ontario
(416) 788-0113

Shirley Samaroo House (S)
Weston, Ontario
(416) 249-4364
(for immigrant women)

Naomi's Family Resource
    Centre (F.R.C.)
Winchester, Ontario
(613) 774-2138
       774-2105

Hiatus House (T.H.)
Windsor, Ontario
(519) 252-7781

Women's Emergency Centre
    Inc. (T.H.)
Woodstock, Ontario
(519) 539-4811
1-800-265-1938

Quebec

La Passerelle*
Alma, Quebec
(418) 668-4671

Maison Mikana
Amos, Quebec
(819) 732-9161

Maison des Femmes de la
    Côte-Nord
Baie-Comeau, Quebec
(418) 296-4799
       296-4733

Maison Fafard
Baie St-Paul, Quebec
(418) 435-2550
       435-3520

Le Clair de L'Une
Buckingham, Quebec
(819) 986-3359

Maison de Connivence
Cap-de-la-Madeleine, Quebec
(819) 379-1011

Auberge Camiclau
Chambly, Quebec
(514) 658-9780

Centre féminin du Saguenay
Chicoutimi, Quebec
(418) 549-4343

Horizon Pour Elle
Cowansville, Quebec
(514) 263-5046

Halte-Secours
Dolbeau, Quebec
(418) 276-3965

La Rose des Vents de Drummond
Drummondville, Quebec
(819) 472-5444

Centre des Femmes de Forestville
Forestville, Quebec
(418) 587-2533

Unies-Vers-Femmes
Gatineau, Quebec
(819) 568-4710

Pavillon Marguerite de Champlain
Greenfield Park, Quebec
(514) 672-8501

Centre Mechtilde
Hull, Quebec
(819) 777-2952

La Traverse
Joliette, Quebec
(514) 759-5882

La Chambrée
Jonquière, Quebec
(418) 547-7283

Le Parados
Lachine, Quebec
(514) 637-3529

La Citad'Elle de Lachute
Lachute, Quebec
(514) 562-7797

La Bouée Régionale du
    Lac-Mégantic
Lac-Mégantic, Quebec
(819) 583-1233

La Montée
La Malbaie, Quebec
(418) 665-4694

Le Toît de l'Amitié
La Tuque, Quebec
(819) 523-7829

Le Prélude
Laval, Quebec
(514) 682-3050

La Jonction Pour Elle
Lévis, Quebec
(418) 833-8002

Havre des Femmes
L'Islet-Sur-Mer, Quebec
(418) 247-7622

Carrefour Pour Elle Inc.
Longueuil, Quebec
(514) 651-5800

La Gigogne
Matane, Quebec
(418) 562-3377

Halte Femmes Haute-Gatineau
Maniwaki, Quebec
(819) 449-2513

La Passe-R-Elle des Hautes
  Laurentides
Mont-Laurier, Quebec
(819) 623-1523

Assistance aux Femmes
Montreal, Quebec
(514) 270-8291

Auberge Transition
Montreal, Quebec
(514) 481-0496

Escale pour Elle
Montreal, Quebec
(5l4) 351-3374

Inter-Val
Montreal, Quebec
(514) 933-8488

La Dauphinelle
Montreal, Quebec
(514) 598-7779

Le Chaînon*
Montreal, Quebec
(514) 845-0151

Maison d'Hébergement d'Anjou
Montreal, Quebec
(514) 353-5908

Maison Marguerite*
Montreal, Quebec
(514) 932-2250

Multi-Femmes
Montreal, Quebec
(514) 523-1095

Secours aux femmes (shelter for
  immigrant women)
Montreal, Quebec
(514) 271-8445

Maison d'Hébergement de Pabos
Pabos, Quebec
(418) 689-6288

Refuge pour femmes de l'Ouest de
  l'Île
Pierrefonds, Quebec
(514) 620-4845

La Maison la Montée
Pointe au Pic, Quebec
(418) 665-3981

Centre Femmes (Y.W.C.A.)
Quebec, Quebec
(418) 683-2548

Expansion-Femmes de Québec
Quebec, Quebec
(418) 653-1343

La Maison d'Accueil Kinsmen
Quebec, Quebec
(418) 688-9024

Maison des Femmes de Québec
Quebec, Quebec
(418) 692-4315

Maison de Lauberivière*
Quebec, Quebec
(418) 694-9316

La Débrouille
Rimouski, Quebec
(418) 724-5067

Le Centre-Femmes du
  Grand-Portage
Rivière-du-Loup, Quebec
(418) 867-2254

L'Auberge de l'Amitié Roberval
Roberval, Quebec
(418) 275-4574

Alternatives pour Elles
Rouyn, Quebec
(819) 797-1754

West Island Women's Shelter
Roxboro, Quebec
(514) 620-4845

La Séjournelle
Shawinigan, Quebec
(819) 537-8348

L'Escale de l'Estrie Inc.
Sherbrooke, Quebec
(819) 569-3611

La Source
Sorel, Quebec
(514) 743-2821

Maison Havre l'Éclaircie
St-Georges de Beauce, Quebec
(418) 227-1025

La Clé sur la Porte
St-Hyacinthe, Quebec
(514) 774-1843

Le Coup d'Elle
St-Jean-sur-Richelieu, Quebec
(514) 346-1645

Maison d'Ariane
Saint-Jérôme, Quebec
(514) 432-9355

L'Ombre Elle
Ste-Agathe des Monts, Quebec
(819) 326-1321

Maison Hélène Lacroix*
Ste-Foy, Quebec
(418) 527-4682

Maison d'Accueil le Mitan Inc.
Ste-Thérèse de Blainville, Quebec
(514) 435-3651

La Gîtée
Thetford Mines, Quebec
(418) 335-5551

Résidence de l'avenue A
Trois-Rivières, Quebec
(819) 376-8311

Le Nid
Val d'Or, Quebec
(819) 825-3865

L'Accueil
Valleyfield, Quebec
(514) 371-4618

Maison du Réconfort
Verdun, Quebec
(514) 768-8648

L'Entre-temps
Victoriaville, Quebec
(819) 758-6066

Centre Amical de la Baie*
Ville de la Baie, Quebec
(418) 544-4626
      544-7490

Centre des femmes*
Ville-Marie, Quebec
(819) 622-0111

New Brunswick

Foyer d'Accueil Vallée Lourdes*
Bathurst, New Brunswick
(506) 548-2350

Maison Notre-Dame
Campbellton, New Brunswick
(506) 753-4703

Centre de Dépannage*
Edmundston, New Brunswick
(506) 735-6859
      735-3971

Women in Transition Inc.
Fredericton, New Brunswick
(506) 455-1498

Cross Roads for Women
Moncton, New Brunswick
(506) 853-0811

Donna Anderson Apartments
   (second-stage housing)
Saint John, New Brunswick
(506) 632-9289

Hestia House Inc.
Saint John, New Brunswick
(506) 634-7570

Fundy Region Transition House
St. Stephen, New Brunswick
(506) 466-4485

Accueil Sainte-Famille*
Tracadie, New Brunswick
(506) 395-2212

Prince Edward Island

Anderson House
Charlottetown, P.E.I.
(902) 892-0960

Nova Scotia

Naomi Society*
Antigonish, Nova Scotia
(902) 863-3807

Bryony House
Halifax, Nova Scotia
(902) 423-7183

Chrysalis House
Kentville, Nova Scotia
(902) 582-7877

Tearmann House
New Glasgow, Nova Scotia
(902) 752-1633

Sydney Transition House
Sydney, Nova Scotia
(902) 539-2945

Juniper House
Yarmouth, Nova Scotia
(902) 742-8689

Newfoundland and Labrador

Transition House
Corner Brook, Newfoundland
(709) 634-4198

Libra House
Goose Bay, Labrador
(709) 896-8251

Labrador West Family Crisis
   Shelter*
Labrador City, Labrador
(709) 944-7962

Haven of Hope*
St. John's, Newfoundland
(709) 726-3714
      726-3715

Presentation House*
St. John's, Newfoundland
(709) 754-1714

Transition House
St. John's, Newfoundland
(709) 753-1461

*   Emergency shelters provide accommodation to women in crisis; however, they do not necessarily offer the same services as transition houses. Please note that some may exclude children and some may also provide accommodation to men.

**   Short-term refuges

***   Manitoba has developed a model that includes a crisis office and a safe-house network. Some communities also maintain a "satellite" home that is open to battered women.

Provincial and Territorial Associations

Alberta

Alberta Council of Women's Shelters
c/o Edmonton Women's Shelter Ltd.
Room 4
11602 — 40th Street
Edmonton, Alberta
T5W 2K6
(403) 471-6709

British Columbia and Yukon

B.C./Yukon Society of Transition Houses
P.O. Box 33904
Station D
Vancouver, British Columbia
V6J 4L7
(604) 879-4937

Manitoba

Manitoba Committee on Wife Abuse
400 — 777 Portage Avenue
Winnipeg, Manitoba
R3G 3L1
(204) 774-1794

New Brunswick

New Brunswick Association of
Transition House Workers
P.O. Box 1143
Fredericton, New Brunswick
E3B 5C2
(506) 454-1498

Ontario

Ontario Association of Interval
and Transition Houses
229 College Street, #202
Toronto, Ontario
M5T 1R4
(416) 977-6619

Prince Edward Island

Transition House Association
P.O. Box 964
Charlottetown, P.E.I.   C1A 7M4
(902) 892-3790

Quebec

Regroupement provincial des maisons
d'hébergement et de transition pour
femmes victimes de violence
306A, Carré St. Louis
Montreal, Quebec   H2X 1A5
(514) 842-0607

Saskatchewan

Provincial Association of
Transition Houses
c/o 1700 College Avenue
Regina, Saskatchewan   S4P 1B9

Newfoundland and Labrador

Transition House Association for
Labrador/Newfoundland
c/o St. John's Transition House
P.O. Box 6208
St. John's, Newfoundland
A1C 6J9
(709) 753-1461

At present, the Northwest Territories and Nova Scotia do not have associations.

The information in this appendix is taken from *Transition Houses and Shelters For Battered Women in Canada/Maisons d'hébergement et de transition pour femmes victimes de violence au Canada*, published by the National Clearinghouse on Family Violence, Health and Welfare Canada, Ottawa, January 1987.

Notes

Notes

Introduction: After the Laughter

1. Canada, House of Commons, *Debates*, May 12, 1982, p. 17734.

2. This information was provided by the Working Group for the Federal/Provincial Task Force on Justice for Victims of Crime, Ottawa.

3. Canada, House of Commons, Standing Committee on Health, Welfare and Social Affairs, *Wife Battering: Report on Violence in the Family* (Ottawa: Queen's Printer, May 1982), p. 10.

4. Figure for the total number of shelters in Canada in 1987 provided by the National Clearinghouse on Family Violence, Health and Welfare Canada, January 21, 1987.

5. For example, at the Seventh United Nations Congress on the Prevention of Crime and the Treatment of Offenders held in Milan, Italy, August 25-September 6, 1985, a draft resolution on domestic violence — prepared by several countries, including Canada — was adopted. This resolution urged all member states to ensure a sustained effort for dealing with the problem of wife battering. It also suggested that the Eighth Congress consider domestic violence as a separate item and invited all member states to adopt specific measures making criminal and civil justice systems more sensitive in their responses to domestic violence.

6. The term "partner" has been used throughout this study to refer to men who batter the women with whom they live. Although it is not a perfect term, since "partner" conveys the idea of one who shares their life with another person on the basis of equality, it is preferable to the other possibilities (spouse, husband) which are tied to legal marital status.

7. The number of transition houses across Canada was provided by the National Clearinghouse on Family Violence in July 1986. This number tallies with the total number of houses (and houses just about to open) included in the mailing lists provided by the provincial/territorial associations of transition houses to the author of this study, in February 1986.

8. It is impossible to give a more accurate figure because the number of women who were turned away from the houses and who also requested shelter specifically because they were battered is unknown.

9. This percentage is based on Intake Data Summary figures for 1985 reported by the London Battered Women's Advocacy Clinic Inc., to the Ontario Women's Directorate and to the Department of Community and Social Services.

Shattered Hopes: The Meaning of Wife Battering for Victims and Survivors

1. Deborah Sinclair, *Understanding Wife Assault: A Training Manual for Counsellors and Advocates* (Toronto: Ontario Ministry of Community and Social Services, Family Violence Program, 1985), p. 65.

2. Ibid., p. 65.

3. Linda MacLeod, *Wife Battering in Canada: The Vicious Circle* (Ottawa: Canadian Advisory Council on the Status of Women, 1980), p. 7.

4. Canada, House of Commons, Standing Committee on Health, Welfare and Social Affairs, *Wife Battering: Report on Violence in the Family* (Ottawa: Queen's Printer, May 1982), p. 7.

5. Sinclair, *Understanding Wife Assault*, p. 17.

6. Ibid., p. 15.

7. Alberta, Social Services and Community Health, *Breaking the Pattern: How Alberta Communities Can Help Assaulted Women and Their Families* (Edmonton: November 1985), p. 14.

8. Quebec, Ministère des Affaires sociales, *A Policy Respecting Assistance for Abused Women* (Quebec: 1985), p. 7.

9. Gerry Léger, *Victims of Crime: Discussion Paper on Topic III*, prepared for Solicitor General Canada, for the Seventh United Nations Congress on the Prevention of Crime and the Treatment of Offenders, Milan, Italy, August 25-September 6, 1985, p. 4.

10. Murray A. Straus and Richard J. Gelles, "Societal Change and Change in Family Violence from 1975 to 1985 as Revealed by Two National Surveys", *Journal of Marriage and the Family*, vol. 48 (August 1986), p. 9.

11. For example, see: Murray A. Straus and Richard J. Gelles, "Reader's Column", *Crime Victims Digest* (January 1986), p. 4.

What Do We Know About the Battered Women and the Batterers in Canada?

1. Linda MacLeod, *Wife Battering in Canada: The Vicious Circle* (Ottawa: Canadian Advisory Council on the Status of Women, 1980), p. 13.

2. Jean Giles-Sims, *Wife Battering: A Systems Theory Approach* (New York: Guilford Press, 1983), p. 138.

3. Finding reported by Desmond Ellis at the John Howard Society of Canada Conference, *Violence in Canadian Society*, Ottawa, June 1986.

4. National Council of Welfare, 1986 *Poverty Lines* (Ottawa: Supply and Services Canada, 1986) p. 10.

5. Ibid., p. 10.

6. Intake figures for 1985 reported by London Battered Women's Advocacy Clinic Inc., to the Ontario Women's Directorate and to the Department of Community and Social Services.

7. William A. Stacey and Anson Shupe, *The Family Secret: Domestic Violence in America* (Boston: Beacon Press, 1983), p. 120.

8. Carol LaPrairie, "Family Violence in Rural, Northern Communities: A Proposal for Research and Program Development", prepared for the Research Division, Programs Branch, Solicitor General Canada, Ottawa, 1983, p. 3.

9. Audrey McLaughlin, "An Analysis of Victims/Victim-Witness Needs in Yukon", prepared for Department of Justice Canada and the Department of Justice, Government of Yukon (March 1983), p. iii.

10. Judith Muir, A *Handbook on Planning and Managing Police-based Victim Assistance Programmes*, vol. 1 (Ottawa: Solicitor General Canada, January 1985), p. C-18.

11. McLaughlin, "An Analysis of Victims/Victim-Witness Needs", p. 33.

12. Ibid., p. iii.

13. Sharon Wilde-Stevens, "Preliminary Report: Crisis Line Statistics", prepared for the Manitoba Committee on Wife Abuse, Winnipeg (October 7, 1985), p. 3.

14. McLaughlin, "An Analysis of Victims/Victim-Witness Needs", p. iii.

15. Canada, Statistics Canada, *Population: Age, Sex and Marital Status* (Ottawa: Supply and Services Canada, 1982), 1981 Census of Canada, catalogue no. 92-901, table 7, p. 7-1.

16. LaPrairie, "Family Violence in Rural, Northern Communities", p. 12.

17. Ibid., p. 7.

18. Ibid., p. 11.

19. Canadian Council on Social Development, "Native Crime Victims Research", prepared for the Department of Justice, Ottawa (August 1984), p. 4.

20. McLaughlin, "An Analysis of Victims/Victim-Witness Needs", p. 44.

21. Bob Duncan, *Amerindian Police Program Evaluation: Executive Summary* (Ottawa: Indian and Northern Affairs Canada, Evaluation Branch, September 1983), p. 8.

22. Wendy Burton, "Native Women in Transition", *B.C./Yukon Society of Transition Houses News Letter*, vol. 2, no. 1 (March 1986), p. 7.

23. Canada, House of Commons, *Debates*, May 16, 1986, p. 13351.

24. For example, a psychological profile of batterers is included in Alberta, Social Services and Community Health, *Breaking the Pattern: How Alberta Communities Can Help Assaulted Women and Their Families* (Edmonton: November 1985), p. 17.

25. Ibid., p. 17.

The Social Costs of Wife Battering

1. D. Dorothy Ayers-Counts' study reported in *The Ottawa Citizen*, April 8, 1986.

2. Lee H. Bowker, *Beating Wife Beating* (Lexington, Mass.: Lexington Books, D.C. Heath and Company, 1983), pp. 44-45.

3. Peter Jaffe, David A. Wolfe, S.K. Wilson, and L. Zak, "Critical Issues in the Assessment of Children's Adjustment to Witnessing Family Violence", *Canada's Mental Health*, vol. 33, no. 4 (December 1985), pp. 15-19.

4. Lenore E. Walker, *The Battered Women Syndrome* (New York: Springer Publishing Company, 1984), p. 10.

5. Donald G. Fischer, *Family Relationship Variables and Programs Influencing Juvenile Delinquency*, Programs Branch User Report No. 1985-06 (Ottawa: Solicitor General Canada, 1985), p. 41.

6. Alberta, Social Services and Community Health, Office for the Prevention of Family Violence, *Alberta's Special Report on Family Violence: Ideas for Action* (Edmonton: August 1985), p. 3.

7. John L. Evans, "Costs of Crime: Introduction", *Impact*, no. 2 (1984), pp. 1-3.

8. Bruce R. Levens and Donald G. Dutton, "Domestic Crisis Intervention: Citizens' Requests for Service and the Vancouver Police Department Response", *Canadian Police College Journal*, monograph # 1 (summer 1977), pp. 29-50.

Through Women's Eyes: Our Growing Understanding of Wife Battering

1. Jeffrey A. Fagan, Douglas K. Stewart, and Karen V. Hansen, "Violent Men or Violent Husbands?: Background Factors and Situational Correlates", in *The Dark Side of Families: Current Family Violence Research*, ed. David Finkelhor, Richard J. Gelles, Gerald T. Hotaling, and Murray A. Straus (Beverley Hills, California: Sage Publications, Inc., 1983), p. 49.

2. For example, such findings are cited in Maria Roy, *The Abusive Partner: An Analysis of Domestic Battering* (New York: Van Nostrand Reinhold Company, 1982), pp. 86-88.

3. Lenore E. Walker, "The Battered Woman Syndrome Study", in *The Dark Side*, p. 40.

4. Keith M. Farrington, "Stress and Family Violence", in *The Social Causes of Husband-Wife Violence*, ed. Murray A. Straus and Gerald T. Hotaling (Minneapolis, Minnesota: University of Minnesota Press, 1980), pp. 94-113.

5. Helga Jacobson, Co-ordinator, *A Study of Protection for Battered Women* (Vancouver: Women's Research Centre, 1982), p. 5.

6. Lee H. Bowker, *Beating Wife Beating* (Lexington, Mass.: Lexington Books, D.C. Heath and Company, 1983), p. 8.

7. Straus and Hotaling, *The Social Causes*, p. 19.

8. Marion Boyd, ed., *Handbook for Advocates and Counsellors of Battered Women* (London, Ontario: London Battered Women's Advocacy Clinic Inc., 1985), pp. 12-13.

9. Anne Ganley, "Causes and Characteristics of Battering Men", in *Wife Assault Information Kit* (Victoria: Ministry of the Attorney General, April 1986), pp. 68-69.

10. Research supporting this hypothesis is summarized in Straus and Hotaling, *The Social Causes*, pp. 14-15.

11. Ibid., , p. 15.

12. Ganley, "Causes and Characteristics", p. 70.

13. Roy, *The Abusive Partner*, p. 96.

14. This case was briefly summarized in the *Toronto Star*, Saturday, July 19, 1986, p. A2. Brian Vallee has also written a book, *Life with Billy*, recounting Jane Hurshman's story.

15. Susan Schechter, *Women and Male Violence: The Visions and Struggles of the Battered Women's Movement* (Boston: South End Press, 1982), p. 20.

16. Michael D. Smith, *Woman Abuse: The Case for Surveys by Telephone*, The LaMarsh Research Programme Reports on Violence and Conflict Resolution, Report #12 (Toronto: York University, November 1985), p. 29.

17. London Battered Women's Advocacy Clinic Inc., untitled paper presented to the Ontario Women's Directorate and to the Ontario Department of Community and Social Services.

18. Walker, "The Battered Woman Syndrome Study", p. 8.

19. Alberta, Social Services and Community Health, *Breaking the Pattern: How Alberta Communities Can Help Assaulted Women and Their Families* (Edmonton: November 1985), p. 17.

Programs for Children

1. Mary Kendall Scanlon, *Children in Domestic Violence: Final Report*, prepared for WIN House (Edmonton: Edmonton Women's Shelter, October 1985), p. 20.

2. William A. Stacey and Anson Shupe, *The Family Secret: Domestic Violence in America* (Boston: Beacon Press, 1983), p. 71.

3. This cycle was first identified in a published form by Lenore E. Walker, in *The Battered Woman* (New York: Harper and Row, 1979).

4. Louise Armstrong, *The Home Front: Notes from the Family War Zone* (Washington, D.C.: McGraw-Hill Book Company, 1983), p. 64.

5. Scanlon, *Children in Domestic Violence*, p. 49.

6. Ibid., p. 48.

7. Pat J. Kincaid, *The Omitted Reality: Husband-Wife Violence in Ontario and Policy Implications for Education* (Concord, Ontario: Belsten Publishing Ltd., 1982), p. 152.

Criminal Justice Initiatives: The Law as a Symbol of Change

1. One recent document that summarizes these principles is: Quebec, Ministère de la Justice and Ministère du Solliciteur général, *Action Policy on Conjugal Violence* (Quebec: 1986), p. 34.

2. Canadian Advisory Council on the Status of Women, *Council Recommendations* (Ottawa: March 1986), Wife Battering recommendation, January 1980, listed under Battered Women (F1.1).

3. United Nations, *Report of the World Conference to Review and Appraise the Achievements of the United Nations Decade for Women: Equality, Development and Peace*, Nairobi, Kenya, July 15-26, 1985 (New York: 1985), A/Conf. 116/28, p. 254.

4. L.G. Lerman, *Prosecution of Spouse Assault: Innovations in Criminal Justice Responses* (Washington, D.C.: Centre for Women Policy Studies, 1981), p. 39.

5. London Battered Women's Advocacy Clinic Inc., *Final Report* (London, Ontario: March 1985), p. 48.

6. Pamela Smith, *Breaking the Silence: Descriptive Report of Follow-up Study of Abused Women Using a Shelter* (Regina: University of Regina, 1984), p. 80.

7. Ibid., p. 126.

8. Ibid., pp. 126-127.

9. Ibid., p. 128.

10. Quebec, *Action Policy*, p. 10 and p. 11.

11. Peter Jaffe and Carole Anne Burris, *An Integrated Response to Wife Assault: A Community Model*, Programs Branch User Report No. 1984-27 (Ottawa: Solicitor General Canada, 1984).

12. Smith, *Breaking the Silence*, p. 80.

13. For example, the Canadian Federal-Provincial Task Force on Justice for Victims of Crime recommended that ''All current court orders which prevent a man from seeing or harassing his spouse should be enforced by all police forces'' (Canadian Federal-Provincial Task Force on Justice for Victims of Crime, *Report* (Ottawa: Supply and Services Canada, 1983), recommendation 39, p. 117). In addition, the Federal-Provincial Working Group on Justice for Victims of Crime, in their follow-up report, stressed that police enforcement of court orders was still not uniform and identified existing attempts to increase uniformity; see: Canadian Federal-Provincial Working Group on Justice for Victims of Crime, *Justice for Victims of Crime: Implementation Report* (Ottawa: 1985), p. 355.

14. The CACSW has made four sets of recommendations endorsing the principle of a unified family court system. See: Canadian Advisory Council on the Status of Women, *Council Recommendations* (Ottawa: March 1986), Jurisdiction of Family Courts recommendation, April 1974, and Establishment of Family Courts recommendation, June 1974, both listed under Family Court (C5.1); and Integrated Family Court recommendation, October 1974, and Proposals of the Law Reform Commission, January 1975, both listed under Family Court (C5.2).
The role of the criminal justice process regarding wife battering is discussed in an upcoming CACSW publication on women and the criminal law.

15. S. Riopelle-Ouellet, *Evaluation of the Hiatus House Complainant Support Program*, Crime Victims Working Paper No. 13 (Ottawa: Department of Justice Canada, March 1984), p. i.

16. Judith Muir and Denise LeClaire, *A Police Response to Domestic Assaults*, Programs Branch User Report No. 1984-11 (Ottawa: Solicitor General Canada, 1984), p. iv.

17. British Columbia Wife Assault Policy and Implementation Team, ''B.C. Wife Assault Policy Monitoring and Evaluation Report'', prepared for the Executive Committee, Ministry of the Attorney General, Victoria (March 3, 1986), p. 2.

18. In September 1986, the CACSW made the following recommendation concerning the proposed Canadian Judicial Education Centre:
    The CACSW recommends to the federal Minister of Justice
    1. the establishment and necessary funding for a Canadian Judicial Education Centre to provide equitable and comprehensive training programs for the judiciary with special emphasis on equality guarantees under the Charter of Rights and Freedoms and under relevant provincial legislation as they affect women;
    2. that the training program be mandatory at an introductory level and that continuing education be provided on a voluntary basis.
    Canadian Advisory Council on the Status of Women, *Council Recommendations* (Ottawa: March 1986), Canadian Judicial Education Centre recommendation, September 1986, listed under Canadian Charter of Rights and Freedoms (D1.5).

19. Melanie Lautt, *An Exploratory Assessment of the Needs of Victims/Witnesses in the City of Saskatoon: The Perceptions of Formal Agents* (Ottawa: Department of Justice Canada, Research and Statistics Section, Policy Planning and Development Branch, 1982), p. 136.

20. Quebec, *Action Policy*, p. 24.

21. London Battered Women's Advocacy Clinic Inc., *Final Report*, pp. 50-51.

22. This is a paraphrase of a sentence in London Battered Women's Advocacy Clinic Inc., *Final Report*, p. 51.

23. Reported in *The Gleaner*, Fredericton, New Brunswick, May 16, 1986.

24. Susan Schechter, *Women and Male Violence: The Visions and Struggles of the Battered Women's Movement* (Boston: South End Press, 1982), p. 182.

25. Statement made by Inspector John Robinson at the conference *Violence in Canadian Society*, sponsored by the John Howard Society of Canada, Ottawa, June 1986.

26. Lenore E. Walker, *The Battered Women Syndrome* (New York: Springer Publishing Company, 1984), p. 143.

27. Schechter, *Women and Male Violence*, p. 182.

Programs for Batterers

1. For a fuller discussion of this issue, see: Dale Trimble, "Confronting Responsibility: Men Who Batter Their Wives", in *Mutual Aid Groups and the Life Cycle*, ed. Alex Gitterman and Lawrence Shulman (Illinois: F.E. Peacock Publishers, Inc., 1986), p. 235.

2. Ibid., p. 233.

3. Maria Roy, *The Abusive Partner: An Analysis of Domestic Battering* (New York: Van Nostrand Reinhold Company, 1982), p. 172.

4. Ibid., p. 229.

5. Reported in *The Gazette*, Montreal, January 9, 1986, p. D-14.

6. James Browning, *Stopping the Violence: Canadian Programmes for Assaultive Men* (Ottawa: National Clearinghouse on Family Violence, Health and Welfare Canada, 1984), p. 12.

7. Colin Meredith and Ellie Conway, *The Study for the Planning of Victim Assistance Services on P.E.I.: Summary Report for the P.E.I. Committee on Victim Assistance*, Programs Branch User Report No. 1984-34 (Ottawa: Solicitor General Canada, 1984), p. 25.

8. Andy Wachtel and Bruce Levens, *Vancouver Therapy Groups for Assaultive Males — A Program Development Review*, Programs Branch User Report No. 1984-75 (Ottawa: Solicitor General Canada, 1984), p. 42.

9. Ibid., p. 43.

10. Edward E. Gondolf, *Men Who Batter: An Integrated Approach to Stopping Wife Abuse* (Holmes Beach, Florida: Learning Publications, Inc. 1985), p. 6.

11. Browning, *Stopping the Violence*, p. 18.

12. Gondolf, *Men Who Batter*, p. 7.

13. Susan Schechter, *Women and Male Violence: The Visions and Struggles of the Battered Women's Movement* (Boston: South End Press, 1982), p. 176.

14. Jan Barnsley, *Feminist Action, Institutional Reaction: Responses to Wife Assault* (Vancouver: Women's Resource Centre, May 1985).

15. Browning, *Stopping the Violence*, p. 18.

16. Gondolf, *Men Who Batter*, p. 86.

Community Support

1. This typology of programs was taken from: Alberta, Social Services and Community Health, Office for the Prevention of Family Violence, *Alberta's Special Report on Family Violence: Ideas for Action* (Edmonton: August 1985), p. 5.

2. Report on a study by Paula Caplan, entitled *The Myth of Women's Masochism*, cited in the *Toronto Star*, November 15, 1986.

3. Linda MacLeod, *Wife Battering in Canada: The Vicious Circle* (Ottawa: Canadian Advisory Council on the Status of Women, 1980), p. 35.

4. Pauline M. Adams, *Report on Victim's Legal Information Needs Survey* (Ottawa: Department of Justice Canada, Research and Statistics Section, Policy Programs and Research Branch, December 1984), p. 19

5. Lee H. Bowker, *Beating Wife Beating* (Lexington, Mass.: Lexington Books, D.C. Heath and Company, 1983), p. 17.

6. Wm. K. Steubing, *Victims and Witnesses: Experiences, Needs and Community/Criminal Justice Response* (Ottawa: Department of Justice Canada, Research and Statistics Section, Planning and Development Branch, March 1984), p. 18.

Conclusion: Prevention Through Caring, Continuity, and Support

1. Gerry Léger, *Victims of Crime: Discussion Paper on Topic III*, prepared for Solicitor General Canada, for the Seventh United Nations Congress on the Prevention of Crime and the Treatment of Offenders, Milan, Italy, August 25-September 6, 1985, p. 8.

2. For an elaboration of this point, see: Lee H. Bowker, *Beating Wife Beating* (Lexington, Mass.: Lexington Books, D. C. Heath and Company, 1983), p. 123.

Bibliography

Bibliography

Adams, Pauline M. *Report on Victim's Legal Information Needs Survey*. Ottawa: Department of Justice Canada, Research and Statistics Section, Policy Planning and Development Branch, December 1984.

Alberta. Social Services and Community Health, Office for the Prevention of Family Violence. *Alberta's Special Report on Family Violence: Ideas for Action*. Edmonton: August 1985.

Alberta. Social Services and Community Health. *Breaking the Pattern: How Alberta Communities Can Help Assaulted Women and Their Families*. Edmonton: November 1985.

ARA Consultants. "Program Evaluation Report on the Community Mediation Service: Kitchener/Waterloo". Prepared for the Research Division, Programs Branch, Solicitor General Canada, Ottawa, July 1983.

Armstrong, Louise. *The Home Front: Notes from the Family War Zone*. Washington, D.C.: McGraw-Hill Book Company, 1983.

Australia. Women's Policy Co-Ordination Unit, Department of Premier and Cabinet. *Criminal Assault in the Home: Social and Legal Responses to Domestic Violence — Discussion Paper*. Victoria, Australia: July 1985.

Barnsley, Jan. *Feminist Action, Institutional Reaction: Responses to Wife Assault*. Vancouver: Women's Research Centre, May 1985.

Bowker, Lee H. *Beating Wife Beating*. Lexington, Mass.: Lexington Books, D. C. Heath and Company, 1983.

Boyd, Marion, ed. *Handbook for Advocates and Counsellors of Battered Women*. London, Ontario: London Battered Women's Advocacy Clinic Inc., 1985.

British Columbia Wife Assault Policy and Implementation Team. "B.C. Wife Assault Policy Monitoring and Evaluation Report". Prepared for the Executive Committee, Ministry of the Attorney General, Victoria, March 3, 1986.

British Columbia. Women's Programs, Ministry of Labour, and Ministry of the Attorney General, in cooperation with the Justice Institute of British Columbia. *Information Relating to Wife Assault in British Columbia*. Victoria: January 1985.

Browning, James. *Stopping the Violence: Canadian Programmes for Assaultive Men*. Ottawa: National Clearinghouse on Family Violence, Health and Welfare Canada, 1984.

Canada. Solicitor General Canada, Programs Branch, Research and Statistics Group. *Canadian Urban Victimization Survey, Bulletin 4: Female Victims of Crime*. Ottawa: 1985.

Canada. Status of Women Canada. *Federal/Provincial/Territorial Report on Wife Battering to the Meeting of Ministers Responsible for the Status of Women, Niagara-on-the-Lake, May 28-30, 1984*. Ottawa: 1984.

Canada. Status of Women Canada. *Final Report of the Federal/Provincial/Territorial Working Group on Wife Battering*. Prepared for the Ministers Responsible for the Status of Women. Ottawa: June 1986.

Canadian Advisory Council on the Status of Women. *Council Recommendations*. Ottawa: March 1986.

Canadian Federal-Provincial Task Force on Justice for Victims of Crime. *Canadian Federal-Provincial Task Force on Justice for Victims of Crime: Report*. Ottawa: Supply and Services Canada, 1983.

Cini, Maltaise E. *Causes of Wife Assault: An Overview*. Ottawa: Department of Justice Canada, Research and Statistics Section, Policy Planning and Development Branch, December 1984.

Connors, Jane. *Violence Against Women: A Comparative Compendium of Legal Provisions*. Prepared for the Meeting of Commonwealth Ministers Responsible for Women's Affairs, Kenyatta Conference Centre, Nairobi, Kenya, July 13, 1985.

Dobash, R.E. and R.D. Dobash. "Patterns of Violence in Scotland". In *International Perspectives on Family Violence*. Ed. Richard J. Gelles and C.P. Cornell. Lexington, Mass.: D.C. Heath and Company, 1983.

Dutton, Donald G. *The Criminal Justice System Response to Wife Assault*. Programs Branch User Report No. 1984-26. Ottawa: Solicitor General Canada, 1984.

Dutton, Donald G. and Bruce R. Levens. *Crisis Intervention Training for Police*. Programs Branch User Report No. 1985-02. Ottawa: Solicitor General Canada, 1985.

Finkelhor, David; Richard J. Gelles; Gerald T. Hotaling; and Murray A. Straus, eds. *The Dark Side of Families: Current Family Violence Research*. Beverly Hills, California: Sage Publications, Inc., 1983.

Giberson, M. Bette, Coordinator. "The Plight of the Victims of Family Violence in New Brunswick". Women in Transition House Incorporated, New Brunswick, July 1985.

Giles-Sims, Jean. "A Longitudinal Study of Battered Children of Battered Wives". *Family Relations*, vol. 34, no. 2, April 1985, pp. 205-210.

——————— *Wife Battering: A Systems Theory Approach*. New York: Guilford Press, 1983.

Gondolf, Edward E. *Men Who Batter: An Integrated Approach to Stopping Wife Abuse*. Holmes Beach, Florida: Learning Publications, Inc., 1985.

Green, Holly Wagner. *Turning Fear to Hope*. Camden, N.Y.: Thomas Nelson Publishers, 1984.

Hodgins, S. and G. Larouche. *Marital Violence: antecedents and consequences*, Ottawa: Solicitor General Canada, 1980.

Hofeller, Kathleen. *Battered Women, Shattered Lives*. Palo Alto, California: R and E Research Associates, Incorporated, 1983.

Jaffe, Peter. *The Effectiveness of the Family Consultant Service with the London Police Force: The Prevention of Family Strife*. Ottawa: Solicitor General Canada, March 1981.

Jaffe, Peter and Carole Anne Burris. *An Integrated Response to Wife Assault: A Community Model*. Programs Branch User Report No. 1984-27. Ottawa: Solicitor General Canada, 1984.

Jaffe, Peter and David A. Wolfe. "Children of Battering Women: The Relation Between Child Behaviour, Family Violence and Maternal Stress". Canada, 1984.

Jaffe, Peter; David A. Wolfe; S. K. Wilson; and L. Zak. "Critical Issues in the Assessment of Children's Adjustment to Witnessing Family Violence". *Canada's Mental Health*, vol. 33, no. 4, December 1985, pp. 15-19.

Kincaid, Pat J. *The Omitted Reality: Husband-Wife Violence in Ontario and Policy Implications for Education*. Concord, Ontario: Belsten Publishing Ltd., 1982.

LaPrairie, Carol. "Family Violence in Rural, Northern Communities: A Proposal for Research and Program Development". Prepared for the Research Division, Programs Branch, Solicitor General Canada, Ottawa, 1983.

Lefkowitz, Monroe M.; Leonard D. Eron; Leopold G. Walder; and L. Rowell Huesmann. *Growing Up to be Violent: A Longitudinal Study of the Development of Aggression*. New York: Pergamon Press, Inc., 1977.

Léger, Gerry. *Criminal Charges as a Means of Assisting Victims of Wife Assault*. Programs Branch User Report No. 1984-85. Ottawa: Solicitor General Canada, 1984.

Léger, Gerry. *Victims of Crime: Discussion Paper on Topic III*. Prepared for Solicitor General Canada, for the Seventh United Nations Congress on the Prevention of Crime and the Treatment of Offenders. Milan, Italy, August 25-September 6, 1985.

Lerette, Peter. *Study of the Restigouche Family Crisis Interveners Program*. Programs Branch User Report No. 1984-76. Ottawa: Solicitor General Canada, 1984.

Levens, Bruce R. with Donald G. Dutton. *The Social Service Role of Police: Domestic Crisis Intervention*. Ottawa: Solicitor General Canada, Research Division, 1980.

London Battered Women's Advocacy Clinic Inc. *Final Report*. London, Ontario: March 1985.

MacLeod, Linda. *Wife Battering in Canada: The Vicious Circle*. Ottawa: Canadian Advisory Council on the Status of Women, 1980.

McKay, Tom. "Introduction to the Calgary Police Crisis Team Manual, 1985". Calgary, 1985.

McLaughlin, Audrey. *Kaushee's Place: Yukon Women's Transition Home*. Final report of a three-year demonstration project jointly sponsored by National Welfare Grants, Health and Welfare Canada; Department of Indian and Northern Affairs (Yukon Region); and Department of Health and Human Resources, Government of Yukon. Whitehorse: Yukon Women's Transition Home, March 31, 1983.

Meredith, Colin. *Overview and Annotated Bibliography of the Needs of Crime Victims*. Programs Branch User Report No. 1984-18. Ottawa: Solicitor General Canada, 1984.

Meredith, Colin and Ellie Conway. *The Study for the Planning of Victim Assistance Services on P.E.I.: Summary Report for the P.E.I. Committee on Victim Assistance*. Programs Branch User Report No. 1984-34. Ottawa: Solicitor General Canada, 1984.

Morgan, Steven M. *Conjugal Terrorism: A Psychological and Community Treatment Model of Wife Abuse.* California: R and E Research Associates, 1982.

Muir, Judith. *Crime Victims' Needs in Calgary.* Programs Branch User Report No. 1984-9. Ottawa: Solicitor General Canada, 1984.

_____ *A Handbook on Planning and Managing Police-based Victim Assistance Programmes.* Vol. I. Ottawa: Solicitor General Canada, January 1985.

Muir, Judith and Denise LeClaire. *A Police Response to Domestic Assaults.* Programs Branch User Report No. 1984-11. Ottawa: Solicitor General Canada, 1984.

NiCarthy, Ginny; Karen Merriam; and Sandra Coffman. *Talking It Out: A Guide to Groups for Abused Women.* Seattle, Washington: Seal Press, 1984.

Norquay, Geoff and Richard Weiler. *Services to Victims and Witnesses of Crime in Canada.* Ottawa: Solicitor General Canada, Research Division, 1981. Updated for Department of Justice Canada, 1984.

Olson, Esther Lee. *No Place to Hide.* Wheaton, Illinois: Tyndle House Publishers, Inc., 1984.

Ontario. Standing Committee on Social Development. *First Report on Family Violence: Wife Battering.* Toronto: Legislative Assembly, November 1982.

Pagelow, Mildred Daley. *Family Violence.* Westport, Connecticut: Praeger Publishers Division of Greenwood Press, Inc., 1984.

Prince Edward Island Committee on Victims of Crime. "Second Report of the P.E.I. Committee on Victims of Crime". Presented to the Honourable George R. McMahon, Q.C., Minister of Justice, Charlottetown, February 1986.

Quebec. Ministère des Affaires sociales. *A Policy Respecting Assistance for Abused Women.* Quebec: 1985.

Quebec. Ministère de la Justice et Ministère du Solliciteur général. *Action Policy on Conjugal Violence.* Quebec: 1986.

Roberts, Albert R. with Beverly J. Roberts. *Sheltering Battered Women: A National Study and Service Guide.* New York: Springer Publishing Company, 1981.

Roy, Maria. *The Abusive Partner: An Analysis of Domestic Battering.* New York: Van Nostrand Reinhold Company, 1982.

Roy, Maria, ed. *Battered Women: A Psychosociological Study of Domestic Violence.* New York: Van Nostrand Reinhold Company, 1977.

Scanlon, Mary Kendall. *Children in Domestic Violence: Final Report.* Prepared for WIN House. Edmonton: Edmonton Women's Shelter, October 1985.

Schechter, Susan. *Women and Male Violence: The Visions and Struggles of the Battered Women's Movement.* Boston: South End Press, 1982.

Schudson, C.B. "Criminal Justice System as Family: Trying the Impossible for Battered Women". In *Domestic Violence, 1978.* Washington: United States Congress House Committee on Education and Labour, 1978.

Scutt, Jocelynne. *Even in the Best of Homes: Violence in the Family.* Sydney, Australia: Penguin Books, Australia Ltd., 1983.

Sherman, Lawrence W. and Richard A. Berk. "The Minneapolis Domestic Violence Experiment". In *Information Relating to Wife Assault in B.C.* Victoria: B.C. Ministry of Labour, Women's Program, January 1985.

Sinclair, Deborah. *Understanding Wife Assault: A Training Manual for Counsellors and Advocates.* Toronto: Ontario Ministry of Community and Social Services, Family Violence Program, 1985.

Smith, Michael D. "Effects of Question Format on the Reporting of Woman Abuse: A Telephone Survey Experiment". York University, Toronto, 1986.

_____ *Woman Abuse: The Case for Surveys by Telephone.* The LaMarsh Research Programme Reports on Violence and Conflict Resolution, Report #12. Toronto: York University, November 1985.

Sonkin, Daniel Jay and Michael Durphy. *Learning to Live Without Violence: A Handbook for Men.* San Francisco: Volcano Press, 1982.

Stacey, William A. and Anson Shupe. *The Family Secret: Domestic Violence in America.* Boston: Beacon Press, 1983.

Star, Barbara. *Helping the Abuser: Intervening Effectively in Family Violence.* New York: Family Service Association of America, 1983.

Straus, Murray A. and Gerald T. Hotaling, eds. *The Social Causes of Husband-Wife Violence.* Minneapolis, Minnesota: University of Minnesota Press, 1980.

Straus, Murray A. and Richard J. Gelles. "Reader's Column". *Crime Victims Digest.* January 1986.

_____ "Societal Change and Change in Family Violence from 1975 to 1985 as Revealed by Two National Surveys". *Journal of Marriage and the Family,* vol. 48, August 1986.

Straus, Murray A.; Richard J. Gelles; and S.K. Steinmetz. *Behind Closed Doors: Violence in the American Family.* Garden City: Anchor Press, Doubleday, 1980.

Taub, Nadine. "Adult Domestic Violence: The Law's Response". *Victimology,* vol. 8, no. 1-2, 1983.

United Nations. Economic and Social Council Committee on Crime Prevention and Control. *Women and the Criminal Justice System.* A written statement submitted by the International Alliance of Women, Vienna, Austria, March 21-30, 1984. New York: 1984, E/AC.57/1984/NGO.6.

United Nations Committee II. "Victims of Crime". Draft report presented at the Seventh United Nations Congress on the Prevention of Crime and the Treatment of Offenders. Milan, Italy: August 25-September 6, 1985.

United States. Attorney General. *Attorney General's Task Force on Family Violence.* Washington, D.C.: September 1984.

Walker, Lenore E. *The Battered Woman.* New York: Harper and Row, 1979.

_____ *The Battered Women Syndrome.* New York: Springer Publishing Company, 1984.

Waller, Irvin. "United Nations Declaration on Justice, Protection and Assistance for Crime Victims: A Magna Carta for Victims". Final report prepared for Solicitor General Canada, Ottawa, August 1984.

Waller, Irvin and Dick Weiler. *Crime Prevention through Social Development: A Discussion Paper for Social Policy Makers and Practitioners.* Ottawa: Canadian Council on Social Development and Canadian Criminal Justice Association, November 1985.

Wilde-Stevens, Sharon. "Preliminary Report: Crisis Line Statistics". Prepared for the Manitoba Committee on Wife Abuse, Winnipeg, October 7, 1985.

Wilson, Elizabeth. *Women and the Welfare State.* London: Tavistock Publications, 1977.

Women's Information Switchboard/Adelaide Women's Community Health Centre. "Aspects of Violence in the Immigrant Family". Adelaide, Australia, August 1981.

The Canadian Advisory Council on the Status of Women was established as an independent advisory body in 1973 in response to a recommendation by the Royal Commission on the Status of Women. Its mandate, "to bring before the government and the public matters of interest and concern to women" and "to advise the Minister on such matters relating to the status of women as the Minister may refer to the Council for its consideration or as the Council may deem appropriate", is wide and may be interpreted to cover all Council activities on behalf of Canadian women.

The Council is an autonomous agency that reports to Parliament through the Minister Responsible for the Status of Women. This allows the Council to maintain a voice within Parliament and at the same time maintain the right to publish without ministerial consent.

The following were members of the Canadian Advisory Council on the Status of Women at the time of publication (1987):

Sylvia Gold
President
Ottawa, Ontario

Patricia Cooper
Vice-President
Calgary, Alberta

Clarisse Codère
Vice-President
Montreal, Quebec

Monique Bernard
Mont St-Hilaire, Que.

Myriam B. Bernstein
Montreal, Quebec

Erminie Joy Cohen
Saint John, N.B.

Shanon Louise Cooper
Mayo, Yukon

Jo-Ann Cugnet
North Battleford, Sask.

Héleyne D'Aigle
Edmundston, N.B.

Edith Daly
Montague, P.E.I.

Lawrie Montague Edinboro
Chatham, Ontario

Marthe Gill
Pointe Bleue, Quebec

Alison Hinchey
New Waterford, N.S.

Darlene Julianne Hincks
Regina, Saskatchewan

Veronica Mae Johnson
Dollard des Ormeaux, Que.

Monica Matte
Montreal, Quebec

Robert McGavin
Toronto, Ontario

Linda Oliver
Halifax, Nova Scotia

Jane Pepino
Toronto, Ontario

Marie Daurice Perron
Hodgson, Manitoba

Cécile Rémillard-Beaudry
Winnipeg, Manitoba

Agnes Richard
Gander, Newfoundland

Margaret Strongitharm
Nanaimo, B.C.

Margaret Taylor
Belleville, Ontario

Ann Tweddle
Edmonton, Alberta

Eva Voisey
Whale Cove, N.W.T.